RAY ELIOT

The Spirit and Legend of Mr. Illini

Doug Cartland

SAGAMORE PUBLISHING
Champaign, IL

Production Manager: Susan M. McKinney
Dustjacket and photo insert design: Michelle R. Dressen
Proofreader: Phyllis L. Bannon

ISBN: 1-57167-015-7
Library of Congress Catalog Card Number: 95-69133

Printed in the United States.

To Mom, Ray Eliot's only child—
you carried his spirit to the next generation.

To Cathy, my beautiful and long-suffering wife,
and to the best children in the world, Timothy, Benjamin, and
Susannah—you allowed me to dream. May I return the favor.

———————————————————

CONTENTS

Acknowledgments vii

Foreword ix

Introduction... xiii

1	Grampa Ray 1
2	Annie's Song.. 7
3	Maine 13
4	Maggie 21
5	Illinois 27
6	Blueboys 39
7	Minnesota 51
8	The Vanishing 69
9	Ohio 85
10	Whiz Backs 91
11	Thorns.. 107
12	Roses 125
13	Orator 141
14	USC 153
15	Desserts 167
16	Michigan State 181
17	The Racket 195
18	Tribute to Desire 209
19	The Final Drive: Master of the Two-minute Offense 223
20	Sketches 231
21	His Own: A Word to Us *From Ray Eliot's Speeches* 249

ACKNOWLEDGMENTS

During this project there have been so many who have helped me immeasurably. I hope I got them all:

To Cathy Cartland, who is my wife, but also my editor. This project could not have been completed without your expertise.

To Dad, for the conversations, insights and suggestions. To my brother Jack and my sister-in-law Jill for giving me a research base in the East. To my sisters Mary, Jeni, and Susan, for reading the manuscript and sharing your memories and encouragement.

To Mr. Bob Hope for taking time out of an incredible schedule to give me input.

Thanks to the Greater Boston Area Chamber of Commerce and the fine people at Brighton High School, especially Principal Juliette Johnson, Registrar John Henry, and Mr. Tom Boyle—Brighton H.S. class of 1921.

A big thank you to Bonnie Dwyer, Librarian and Archivist, Donald W. McDade Director of Publications, and Evelyn Foss, my grandfather's special friend at Kent's Hill Preparatory School in Maine.

To his boys from Illinois College in Jacksonville: Ira Clark, John Doyle, Sam Pinson, Mike Zupsich, and Sam Mangieri for the memorable "roundtable" discussion. Thank you to Mr. Bob Merris, Vice President for Development and Alumni Relations at the College for organizing my get-together with these men.

And a special thank you to Mr. Charles Bellatti, former Sports Information Director at the University of Illinois and Jacksonville native, who took part in that discussion and checked my manuscript for accuracy.

To my grandfather's Fighting Illini who shared their insights with me, especially, Alex and Lou Agase, Eddie Bray, Mike Kasap, Pete Palmer, Chuck Boerio, Bill Butkovich, J.C. Caroline, Art Dufelmeier, Dike Eddleman, Sam Rebecca and Roger Wolf. To Mrs. Geraldine Young, Buddy's wife, for the memories she had of Mr. Illini. And I can't thank Mr. Ray Nitschke enough for writing such an appropriate and touching foreword.

Thanks to friends like Fritzi and Denny Frary for a wonderful day-long chat. To Julia "Totsie" Drury and Barbara Sandklev for the tour around Staten Island and a look at my grandmother's roots. Also thank you to Larry Stewart, Lou Boudreau, Margaret Selin, Shaw Terwilliger, Ben Cracken Jr., and Mr. and Mrs. Bob Wright—all friends of the former Illinois coach for helping me sketch this great man.

For his assistance I thank Loren Tate, Executive Sports Editor of the Champaign *News-Gazette*.

To Mr. Ron Guenther, University of Illinois Athletic Director, for his support and encouragement in the project.

To Mr. Tom Porter, Director of Marketing and Public Relations at the University of Illinois, and his staff for their timely and constant help. Thanks to Illinois Sports Information Director Mike Pearson and his staff, especially Office Manager Janice Revell.

Thank you also to Manoosh Houanessian, Senior Receptionist at the Pasadena Tournament of Roses for all of her gracious help.

A tip of the hat to Sharon Sumpter, an Archives Associate at The University of Notre Dame.

I appreciate Linda Young's work *Hail to the Orange and the Blue—100 Years of Illinois Football Tradition*. It made wonderful reference material.

Thanks to Cara Eddy for her transcription work.

To my bosses at WMCW 1600 AM Radio in Harvard, Illinois, Mianne and Dave Nelson, for understanding how important this project was to me and giving me the flexibility to get it done.

To the wonderful people of the greatest hometown in America—Harvard, Illinois—who provide an environment for success and always seem to offer encouragement at the right time.

Thank you to everyone who would not let me settle for the ordinary. I hope I have not.

FOREWORD

Not everyone knows that I was a quarterback when I came out of Proviso High School in Maywood, Illinois in 1954 to attend the University of Illinois and play football for Coach Ray Eliot. I had always wanted to be a quarterback. I wanted to control the game, I could pass the ball pretty well, and was a pretty good athlete. I was the number-one freshman quarterback at Illinois, too.

But just before my sophomore season, Coach Eliot brought me into his office and said, "Ray, I've got something to tell you and you may not like it. We need you to play fullback on offense and linebacker on defense (we went both ways in those days) rather than quarterback and free safety."

I think he felt I had the tough makeup to handle those positions, and we had about four veteran quarterbacks at the time. Even so, I was disappointed, so he said gently, "Let me put it to you this way, Ray: would you rather be the third-string quarterback or the first-string fullback?"

I lifted my head for a moment and answered, "Well, Coach, I'd rather be the first-string quarterback."

He said, "Ray, I'm sorry to tell you, but you are not going to be a quarterback."

I remember sitting there crying in his office because I sure wanted to play quarterback, but as I look at it now, it was probably the greatest thing that ever happened to me. The rest— as they say— is history.

The first time I met Ray Eliot was at our high school football banquet my senior year. He was the guest speaker and I was sitting up at the podium. I remember watching the crowd as he spoke softer, then louder, then faster, then slower, and then faster again. He had the crowd mesmerized. I was looking down at the audience and he had everyone at the edge of his seat and in the palm of his hand. Whatever he said, they just couldn't wait for the next word to come out of him. He talked about character and about winning, about the importance of education and about what it took to be a good person. He believed that football wasn't everything—that there was more to life. It was inspiring and I was deeply impressed.

I could have gone anywhere in the country to play football. I had even been offered a $3,000 signing bonus to play professional baseball—that was good money then. But from that night, I knew I was going to Illinois. He hit me right where I lived. He talked about things that I wanted to hear and I felt like he cared about his student athletes. I was proven right.

My dad had died when I was only three, my mom during high school, and when I went to Illinois, Coach Eliot became aware of my background. He knew that I needed special attention and he gave it to me. I'm sure it made a difference that he had lost his dad at a very young age also.

Coach Eliot would sit me down and ask me how school was going and how I was getting along. He kept me close to his office—he even made arrangements for me to live right across the street. He kept good tabs on me, knowing I needed all the help I could get. I think I was kind of a unique project for him. He knew I liked him and I knew he cared for me, so there was a real bond there.

I looked up to him not only as a football coach, but a good, decent person—a father figure. He always talked to me as a father talks to a son. He would tell me to have fun, but to be careful. He knew I was a little wild and belligerent and at times felt sorry for myself.

Ray Eliot always took care of me. He made me feel very comfortable, because I knew he was someone I could trust and that he would tell me right from wrong. He wanted me and others like me to have a better life. Ray Eliot was there when I needed him.

In his career, Coach Eliot won his share of championships, but we didn't win any in the years I was at Illinois. As a matter of fact, our records were pretty average. But—and I don't know if people understand the impact of this—we beat the team ranked number one in the country three years in a row from 1955-57. We upset Michigan State in 1955, Michigan in 1956, and Minnesota in 1957. They were all ranked number one when we beat them. I don't think there has been another college team in the history of the game that has beaten a team ranked number one three years in a row. I'm telling you, when Ray Eliot wanted to win a game, he won that game!

Some years later, on "Ray Nitschke Day" in Green Bay, I asked him to come up to speak. He addressed the banquet the night before and the crowd at Lambeau Field the next day in his typically stirring manner. He had a gift. I have never heard a greater motivational speaker than Ray Eliot. I've listened to a lot of guys—I mean a lot of guys— I've been through them all, but no one has had as inspiring a message. Whether in a locker room, banquet hall, or part of a huge crowd at Lambeau, if you weren't fired up listening to one of his speeches, then you were dead.

I was blessed to have played for Andy Puplis at Proviso, Ray Eliot at Illinois, and Vince Lombardi with the Green Bay Packers. At every level I had the best coaches that any athlete could ever have. My only disappointment is that Ray Eliot has never received the appropriate recognition for his successes on the gridiron and his tremendous contributions to the game of football and to young men and women everywhere. It is a tragic omission that he has never been inducted into the National College Football Hall of Fame. This must be corrected.

I hope you enjoy this account of his life written by his grandson. I am pleased that the story of this truly great man is finally being told. I tell you—Ray Eliot was for real! I am so proud that he touched my life.

—Ray Nitschke

INTRODUCTION

It had been a rough game—a dog fight really—and the Fighting Illini had come up short.

"We played as well as we knew how but still lost," said 1956 Illini MVP David Walker. "After the game, in my extreme fatigue and depression, I wanted nothing more than to find the nearest hole and forget the world existed. As I sat alone in my remorse, I felt a gentle hand on my shoulder. As I raised my head I was astonished to see this man, Coach Ray Eliot, on his hands and knees, unlacing my shoes and assuring me that everything would be all right."

No scene could be concocted that would better sum up Ray Eliot. Humility, empathy, example, leadership, service, love for his boys, football and life all portrayed in one snapshot of compassion.

"The Ray Eliot I will always remember," continued Walker, "is a kind man, an extremely human and personal man and a man deeply devoted to young men."

His devotion to young men, and resolute, old-fashioned loyalty to the University of Illinois, set Eliot apart and made his affectionate title "Mr. Illini" a natural.

"He literally gave his life to the University," says Eliot's friend and radio partner Larry Stewart. "When there was a crisis, he was the one to turn to. He was the glue that held the athletic association together. He had that ability to make you love your university."

Eliot fully embodied the meaning of the Fighting Illini spirit he helped define.

"The spirit of the Fighting Illini is something special," he'd preach. "It's special because it symbolizes dignity, courage, game intelligence or smartness, sportsmanship and the inspiration to never permit the word 'can't' to come into your life—the never-say-die attitude. Sir, it has these very precious meanings."

In the summer of 1979, he spoke before the Illinois General Assembly in Springfield and bellowed, "The symbol of the Fighting Illini is one of a warrior. Not an animal like a Wolverine or Gopher, not a bird like a Hawk or a Cardinal and certainly not a Buckeye..."

Chuck Studley, a former Fighting Illini great—one of Ray Eliot's boys—once wrote a letter to the coach that said in part, "Books have been written about and statues erected to some of the great men of years gone by. These symbols are trite and without meaning when compared with the love and respect your players and fellow coaches have for you."

Thanks a lot, Chuck—I didn't need the reminder.

Because the depth of the feelings that Ray Eliot garnered was immeasurable, this book risks being trite also and, for that reason, was a frightening task. His life, his spirit, his quality were more enormous than any paper and ink can hold.

In reading this account of Eliot's life, one might think, "This guy's too good to be true." Believe me, in the three years it took to write it, I often had the thought myself. But, be assured, what is set forth in these pages is an unabashed, honest portrayal of one of the most distinguished gentlemen that college football has had in its ranks. Keeping in mind that time romances all stories to some degree, the book you are about to read is straightforward.

Ray Eliot, head coach of the Fighting Illini football fortunes for 18 years, ambassador of the game all his life and teacher of what he called "young America" forever, was a great and a humble man, one of unparalleled honesty and integrity. He was one of the great coaches of his day; a brilliant innovator, strategist, psychologist and motivator. And he was a winner.

His most important successes were on the gridiron of men's hearts, though. He changed the course of lives forever. His love of life was contagious, his words of wisdom piercing, and his inspiration riveting. One of the most powerful orators of the twentieth century, Mr. Illini was a passionately caring individual. He was loved by virtually everyone who knew him, and virtually everyone who met him was enthralled.

Rather than write "about" Ray Eliot's life, I attempted in this book to show his life to the reader. Better to see his life presented as an example, I thought, than be subjected to a mere sermon. I wanted it to be a creative account of a great man who happened to love sports and used it for the basis of his life's work—educating "young America."

Eliot was once called "Champaign-Urbana's most beloved citizen." But his life transcends Champaign-Urbana, and his story transcends Illinois and football. It is for anyone, anywhere and in any walk of life. He brought pride to Illinois; he brought pride to the human race.

I cannot tell his story as he would, because he would not tell it. He was too modest for that. I can only hope that I tell his story in a way that will somehow benefit others. That would be Ray Eliot's greatest joy and, if he were to write a book, his only motivation.

"The boy is more important than the game."

—Ray Eliot

1

Grampa Ray

*"More people will miss Ray Eliot
than any other person that ever
served the University of Illinois."*

—Harold "Red" Grange
February, 1980

December's winter roared in with a cold wallop in 1979, as we kibitzed at Katsinas' Restaurant in Champaign. Family and friends, including my grandfather Ray Eliot and me, were sitting around a table enjoying warm drinks and conversation.

I don't remember how the subject came up, but the discussion turned to war—no war in particular, just war. I suppose I made some implication of my feelings as we chatted, because at one point my grandfather looked across the table at me and asked whether or not I would go and fight if the United States went to war. I did not want to answer because we had had this discussion before, and I knew where it would lead. This did not seem to be the time or place for it. I put off his question with a shrug, implying that I didn't really want to get into it.

For all of his 74 years, Grampa Ray had been a man of strong passion, sometimes relentless, and he pressed me. I again evaded the question.

"C'mon," he egged me on, "would you go or not?"

I felt that I was being baited and that he would not accept a non-answer for an answer.

"No, I wouldn't," I said, firmly but quietly.

"See?" he scoffed as he leaned to a friend next to him. "He'll enjoy all of the benefits of living in this country but will not fight to protect it." His friend wanted to stay out of it also, sensing the perilous direction of this conversation.

I was angry at being pushed, and made my argument that I didn't know how we could say "I love my neighbor" and in the next instant "go and blow his face off."

Most everyone at the table was uncomfortable now. On the heels of my statement, Grampa Ray was told he had a phone call, and left the table. I took the opportunity to leave, too, as I had an appointment. I chose not to say good-bye to him and ill feelings lingered. I would never have occasion to speak to my grandfather again.

Larry Stewart, the longtime radio voice of the Fighting Illini, called me one Sunday afternoon just two months later to inform me of my Grampa Ray's death. Grampa Ray had acted as color commentator with Stewart for years on the radio and they had become very close.

Stewart told me that Grampa Ray had finished playing his customary winter game of gin rummy at the Urbana Country Club, and he was taking a shower. As he finished and stepped out of the stall, he was struck suddenly with a massive heart attack. The paramedics soon arrived and tried to revive him, but to no avail.

After I finished speaking to Stewart, I stood silent and momentarily stunned in the kitchen of my Urbana apartment. I thought of Gram—she and Grampa Ray had just celebrated their 50th wedding anniversary the summer before. I thought of my mother (my grandparents' only child) and the closeness she had with him. I quickly drove to my grandparents' home in Champaign.

I was the first of our immediate family to arrive. I remember pulling up in the back of the house that I had grown so attached to over the years. My family's many visits had given me ample opportunities to build wonderful memories. The old red brick home always brought good feelings to me, but the feelings this time were much different.

I stepped out of the car, not noticing the tree that my brother and I used to climb as kids. I briskly walked toward the house, unaware of the back patio where my brother and sisters and I used to scare away the starlings in the trees, banging the tops of garbage cans, with Grampa Ray leading the charge.

I was oblivious to the piece of sod by the corner of the patio, given to my grandfather by the University of Illinois. It was from the 50-yard line of Zuppke Field, where he used to stand commanding his troops in their many gridiron battles. The University tore out the sod when they laid what my grandfather called "that godawful astro turf."

Walking through the door and up the familiar three steps to the kitchen, I strode into the living room. To my surprise several people were there already. There was Loren Tate, sports editor of the Champaign *News-Gazette*, taking notes in the cream-colored recliner that I had sat in often, watching football games and shows like Lawrence Welk and Ed Sullivan with my Gram and Grampa Ray. A few others were also sitting about.

Straight across the room was Gram, sitting in her chair, situated around the corner of the fireplace, barely in sight of the TV. I had always felt that she really didn't watch TV but was just glad for the companionship of its noise. I would have to be her companionship today.

"Doug, Doug he's gone, Ray is gone!" she cried as I entered the room. I knelt in front of her and held her hand. I hesitated, not knowing what to say.

"Grampa Ray is with the Lord," I said, wanting in some way to comfort her.

"Did you hear that?" she exclaimed to everyone in the room. "Doug said that Ray is with the Lord. That's right, that's right, he's with the Lord." I was a little embarrassed but felt good that I had apparently said the right thing.

Soon I was talking on the phone with my mother, assuring her that everything was okay at my end. Mom soon made her way down from Des Plaines, Illinois, and the rest of the family followed.

I loved my grandfather. He was my hero growing up. There was nothing I wanted more than to be just like him. I wanted to be a coach. I wanted to move people the way he did. I wanted to be lifted on the shoulders of my players after a Rose Bowl victory like he was. He was proud of what I wanted, but did not encourage or discourage me in it.

Ours was a collision of generations. He grew up in a time when authority was generally not questioned, I in a time when people, it seemed, lived to question authority. Surely, neither generation was all right nor all wrong.

I had begun to veer from the traditional "get your education and get on with your life" path. I left college without finishing. Grampa Ray implored me to get my diploma.

He said, "Just get your education and then do whatever you want. Just have that education to fall back on." I said that God would provide for me. He asked if God didn't help those who helped themselves. I said only if Ben Franklin wrote the Bible.

He wanted to thrust upon me some common sense, but more than that, a spirit to live my life by. He saw my excuses beyond the rights or wrongs of our arguments. War was certainly not the issue with us (I have since modified my views)—making something of my life was.

To him I was lazy, wasting my opportunities as fast as I could get them. I thought he was trying to mold me into a robot, going on with its life without ever questioning or doing what it really wants.

"And who's to say," I would argue, "that everyone has to achieve success in the same way?"

Grampa Ray helped get me into the University of Illinois, and I left after a year and a half. My heart was in the end but not in the means to the end. When I wanted to go back, he obliged, only to see me quit again. I saw it as searching, he saw it as irresponsible. We were both right.

All the while I loved him and it hurt me to know that he was not happy with me. It bothered me so much that the second time I quit school, in the fall of 1979, I did not have the courage to face him. I just did it. Nothing was ever spoken of it between us.

I remember writing him a letter when I first went to college in 1976. I thanked him for helping me into the University and insisted that I would make good on his kindness to me. He told me later that it was the best letter that he had ever gotten in his life.

He loved me too...

I helped my mother choose the casket—it was blue, of course. He was buried with an orange and blue tie on—fitting for "Mr. Illini."

When I entered the funeral parlor for the first time and saw Grampa Ray, I expected him to get up and smile and say something like "Hey Doug, how's the boy?!"

"Could he really be dead," I thought, "this man so full of life and vigor?"

There were many flowers in the large room. There were flowers from Bob Hope, former President Richard Nixon, Illinois Governor Jim Thompson and many great coaches he had coached against, including Ara Parseghian, Woody Hayes, and Duffy Daugherty. I recall standing with my mother in the reception line, greeting person after person who were in one sense sad and in another glad talking about the man who had meant so much to them personally.

And they came, from former players to administrators to friends to the young high school boy who had heard but one of his speeches, and was so moved that he had to come thank the man one more time.

I don't remember how Father Ed Duncan eulogized my grandfather. I do remember standing in front of the pallbearers before his body was taken to the church.

"There has been a lot of talk about Grampa Ray being Mr. Illini," I began. "Well, there is another side to what he was all about."

As I spoke, I remember looking at the attentive faces of legends such as Lou Boudreau and Buddy Young, feeling almost overwhelmed that such a group was listening to me. I chalked it up to their respect for my grandfather.

"His absolute first priority on this earth was his family," I went on. "I couldn't count how many times he told me that he would do anything for anyone in his family. And I couldn't count the times that he told me to love and take care of my family always. I've heard a lot of former ball players of his say that they would run through a brick wall for Grampa Ray; well, I know also that he would run through a brick wall for anyone of his family."

I believed what I was saying with all my heart. He had proven himself again and again. As I spoke, I thought of my relationship with him—how it had been as I grew up and how it ended. And I thought of the man he was.

"I'd like to pray," I bowed my head. "Father, we thank you first that you allowed Grampa Ray to have a very full and happy life. You gave him the opportunity to do what he liked best and that was to care for people. We thank you for the effect that he had on the lives of his friends, players, and associates. We thank you also for the great effect that he had on his family..."

I then led everyone in the Lord's Prayer.

Many people attended his funeral. Some I recognized, most I did not. There were the big smiles and handshakes from the Agase brothers, Alex and Lou, and there was the long procession, my grandfather's last ride, through the campus streets. I remember seeing people stop along the sidewalks to watch. Half of them seemed to know who it was that went by and half stopped out of curiosity, wondering who was being honored so.

I read the Bible passages at the grave site. He was put to rest in the cemetery east of Memorial Stadium, just about on the 50-yard line and a stone's toss from the burial sites of Bob Zuppke and George Huff.

In the evening we went back to that old red brick house and watched the reports of his funeral on the TV news. Sportscaster Dan Roan was joking about how my Grandfather would walk into the press box during a basketball game and wonder aloud what that round ball was they were using.

Another channel played a tribute. With the Varsity Men's Glee Club singing "Hail To the Orange," we heard part of Father Duncan's eulogy and then saw ourselves coming out of the church door following the casket. Grampa Ray was placed in the back of the hearse and the procession began as the strains continued.

For the first time, my eyes filled with tears.

2

Annie's Song

"It's the heart afraid of breaking,
that never learns to dance.
It's the dream afraid of waking,
that never takes a chance.
It's the one who won't be taken,
who cannot seem to give.
And it's the soul afraid of dying,
that never learns to live . . . "

—"The Rose"
Amanda McBroom

Kickoff came on June 13, 1905. The game of life began for Ray Eliot Nusspickle at his Manhattan home, born the only child of Adolph and Anna in their first year of marriage. Nusspickle was a German name that young Ray bore until he made Eliot his last name some years later.

Anna, affectionately called "Annie" by her husband, was 24 years old when little Ray was born. Of Dutch descent, she had been raised as Anna Bulgin in Twillingate, Newfoundland.

Annie was a homemaker, while Adolph, nine years her senior, earned a living as a Manhattan butcher. Their home on West 99th Street contained the practical furnishings of a lower-middle income family. Outgoing and fun-loving was he, and quiet and respectable was she, but they loved each other deeply. With Ray added to the mix, they were a very happy and close family.

How devastating it must have been, then, when Adolph was lost in 1911. History evidences no protracted illness, so he probably died suddenly on that September day. In any event, he was 39 years old, and he left behind a terribly saddened 30-year-old widow, untrained in any profession, and a six-year-old son.

After a modest funeral, Annie buried Adolph in a simple grave at St. Michael's Cemetery in Queens on September 13. Suddenly faced with the responsibility of providing for her only child, she was distraught.

But it just so happened that in the time of her greatest need, Brighton, a little borough of Boston, was booming. Brighton was annexed to the city of Boston in 1874 and grew rapidly in the years that followed. As the industrial revolution swept the Northeast, Brighton became home to many of the commuters who found work downtown. Between 1894 and 1930, Brighton grew from 15,000 residents to 60,000, quadrupling in less than 40 years (it has 65,000 residents today).

Indeed, where jobs are people go, and where people go houses are built, and when houses are built someone has to clean them. This Annie Nusspickle could do, so shortly after the death of her husband, she packed up young Ray and their belongings and headed to Brighton. She soon found work cleaning the homes of the well-to-do, including that of Adolph Zukor, the great motion picture producer and president of Paramount Pictures.

Annie and Ray moved into a house of their own at 15 Langley Road in Brighton. Taller than it was wide, the Nusspickle home was a typical city dwelling, built on the side of a hill in close quarters to the houses next door. It was practical, a short walk from a business district and just a mile from the three-story red brick high school where Ray would begin to etch his name in the athletic history of America.

"We were invited over to one of my mother's client's homes for Thanksgiving dinner," Ray laughed as he told the story to friends many years later. "I was maybe eight or nine years old. It was a fancy place, so before we went Mom spent time coaching me on proper dinner manners. She told me how to sit and how to eat, what to say and all. She was so worried that I would say or do something inappropriate. Of course, the first thing that happened when we sat down for dinner was that she knocked over her cup of coffee with her elbow."

Annie, who never remarried, may not have been adept with that cup of coffee, but she certainly was proficient at bringing up a little boy on her own and instilling in him the characteristics that would make for his greatness.

She was large-boned, about 5'5" or 5'6", with brown hair, blue eyes, and wonderfully soft skin. Described as "pleasant and kind" by those who knew her, Annie was honest and fair as a woman and a mother. Although she displayed a British-like reserve and was somewhat quiet, she had a delightful sense of humor and knew how to enjoy people.

Annie believed that "cleanliness is next to godliness," thus she was immaculate of house and person. Though not wealthy, she wore classy dresses and hats and always looked her best when she went out. Even a trip to the corner grocer would be a reason to dress just so. But this woman who would present herself at her best in public was also at her best sitting on the floor of her Manhattan apartment in a patched housecoat, playing "Go Fish" with cards fashioned by her only grandchild out of cut-up Cornflakes boxes.

After rearing Ray in Brighton and seeing him settled in the Midwest, Annie moved back to Manhattan in the 1930s. She had with her what she thought were enough savings to enable her to live out her life independently, no longer needing to work. She outlived her resources, however, and Ray and his wife Margaret would financially support her the last ten years of her life. They even tried to talk Annie into moving to Champaign to live with them, but this she refused, saying that she did not want to impose, and that she wanted to keep her own life intact. Though these may have been honest enough reasons, inwardly Manhattan was home—where she had met and married the man she loved, and where her only child was born—and she didn't want to leave.

Although intensely proud of Ray, Annie was not able to attend a lot of football games in which he coached (it is said that she used to take clippings about her son from the Eastern papers, however, and tape them all over her walls at home). When she could make it, family members recall how she would stand beaming outside the stadium after the game. When Ray would appear, win or lose, she would forget anyone was watching and give him a great big motherly hug and kiss. He didn't mind. In more than one speech many years down the road, Ray thought of Annie when he described mothers as "God's most precious gift to man."

Fenway Park was just a trolley ride from the Nusspickle's Brighton home. Indeed, young Ray took advantage of this at every opportunity. He frequently sat in that cozy stadium in the shadow of the "green monster" to watch the Red Sox play.

But Ray was not satisfied to be a spectator. He loved to play and had ambitions of his own. Ray wanted to play baseball at Brighton High School, and he also wanted to participate in football. His gridiron ambitions would have to clear one major hurdle, however. That hurdle was his mother.

Now Annie had no problem with her boy playing the more gentlemanly game of baseball, but this football thing was another matter. As most mothers, she was concerned that her son would get hurt. On this, Ray, ever the salesman, went to work.

One day Ray took all of his equipment home, both baseball and football. He put on his football shoulder pads (such as they were in those days), leather helmet and pants with his catcher's mask, shinguards, and chest protector from baseball. He walked in before his mother wearing the combination of gear.

"See mom," he said artfully, "I can't possibly get hurt." Annie, either not knowing the sports that well or, more likely, winking at her son's ambition, gave him her blessing. She could not have known what ramifications her decision would have.

In the short term, Brighton High benefited. In 1920 as a sophomore, Ray was the starting tackle when the football eleven won its first Boston District High School League championship in 17 years. Brighton went unbeaten and was tied only by East Boston High School; Ray was elected all-district for his football prowess.

Ray was an all-district catcher on the Bengal's baseball team, too, and Brighton won a conference championship while he was there. In addition to all that, he ran track and played hockey. In baseball and hockey he was elected captain.

In the long run, Annie's decision was the key that eventually unleashed a force in college football and the public arena that would benefit unnumbered lives.

Of course, Ray did not understand the importance of his mother's permission either. Sports may have been Ray's first love, but his original choice of a profession was auto mechanics. This was not all that surprising considering Brighton High School. When Brighton High was established in 1841, public high school as an institution was only 20 years old, and Brighton was one of only 25 such schools in the entire United States. In the 1920s high schools still did not function as the college preparatory schools they are today. Their mission was to provide a higher level of practical training that was, most commonly, a final educational experience for young men entering the job force.

Ray attended a high school that had a renowned automotive department. Many students went from school to the mechanics profession without considering much else.

Of course, burdening Ray's young shoulders was his single mother and, in his mind, the need to start a profession quickly to help support her. He had already gone to work as soon as he was able, first as a delivery boy for a grocery store and then in a bakery. Fiercely loyal, he could not easily ask his mother to support him for further education. Thus, upon graduation in 1923, Ray took a job with a Buick garage in Brighton. It didn't take long, though, before the auto mechanics business got old. He worked for a summer, then decided he had to move on.

"I worked with 25 or 30 men in the same shop," he said later. "I considered how many there were of them and that there was only one supervisor. Everyone wanted that supervisor's job, and I realized that I was never going to get it. The numbers were not favorable."

Interestingly, Eliot never did show an enthusiasm for mechanical things later in life. If something broke, he called someone else to fix it.

Something else was calling Ray Eliot Nusspickle. Something else was strumming the harp strings of his heart. There was a different blue print, a higher call . . . Indeed, it was dentistry.

3

Maine

Luther Sampson, then twenty-eight years old, a carpenter by trade, left his home in Marshfield, Massachusetts on a trip of exploration. Intending to locate on the Hudson River, Sampson traveled west. He had not proceeded far, however, when he felt a strange urge to go in the opposite direction. He dismounted in a forest, hitched his horse, and turned aside into the grove to seek Divine direction in prayer.

Sampson determined then that when he reached the next fork in the road, if his mind was still inclined eastward, he would let his horse choose the way. He remounted, by and by reached a fork and gave his horse the reins. Sampson soon found himself heading toward the rising, instead of the setting sun.

He continued his travel east until he reached the locality now known as Kent's Hill in the town of Readsfield in the south-central portion of the Province of Maine. Here he procured a parcel of 250 acres and returned home.

The year was 1798.

Twenty-two years later, in a small, white, one-room cottage on that land, Sampson helped organize what became known as Kent's Hill College Preparatory School.

—*The History of Kent's Hill*
E.R. French

Forks in the road are handled differently by different people. Some leave hold of the reins and trust Divine guidance. Robert Frost looked for footprints and then took the road with fewer.

When Ray Nusspickle realized that being an auto mechanic was not for him, he took the fork in the road from Massachusetts to Maine as Luther Sampson had done 125 years before. Nusspickle, certainly a believer in Divine guidance, yet trusting that, "God helps those who help themselves," took firm hold of his reins and his life, and at 18 years old, headed to Kent's Hill.

Perhaps the reins were just a mite unsteady, though, when, sitting with his mother, he had to explain his aspirations to move on from Brighton.

Annie was protective and loving. To dote over her only son was her greatest joy. Now he would be in another state without much money and with minimal opportunities to visit. He whom she had nurtured alone, whom she had cherished more than life itself, the only manly presence left in her world, would be gone. He was grown now, she knew, but the letting go did not come easily. Still, because she loved him, she relinquished him to his future.

Kent's Hill was not one of the more expensive prep schools but, of course, money was still necessary in order to attend. Ray had saved from his summer as a mechanic; Annie had saved, too. Ray would help further by working summers at Camp Kinewapha, a vacation spot for wealthy girls in Maine, and by playing semipro baseball for Wilton, a town about 22 miles northwest of The Hill.

Because Brighton High School's primary purpose was not to prepare its students for college, Nusspickle had to attend Kent's Hill for three years in order to complete the requirements needed for higher education. He had no idea where he would eventually want to go to college, and what he wanted to do as a profession was even more an elastic question.

Nusspickle at one point considered the ministry very seriously. Anyone who heard his speeches later in life would not be surprised by this. His orations always had a high moral bent, stressing honesty, integrity, kindness and sometimes the Bible itself. As a matter of fact, as he struggled in other classes (Nusspickle was no better than an average student through most of his schooling) he would always pull B's in his Bible classes. He also had a natural care and compassion for others, but the call of the ministry was never clear.

Finally, under the encouragement of his mother, the 18 year old enrolled at Kent's Hill in predentistry. Annie thought it a good, solid profession from which to make a living.

Nusspickle's athletic career at Kent's Hill was highly successful and, at times, even inspiring. As good as he was, he might have been even better if his eyesight had not deteriorated to the point of him needing glasses. This made it tough enough to play baseball, but even more difficult to play football (while Nusspickle was at The Hill, he also won letters in track and basketball).

The boy from Brighton eschewed the gridiron in his first year at Kent's Hill. He did play baseball, though, and was looked upon as an experienced player who could bring immediate help.

He was the starting catcher and batted third from the outset of the 1924 season. The Hilltoppers won their first three games that year and went on to a solid 12-4 finish. In the game that meant most, however, they lost to the hated Hebron Big Green 2-1. Hebron was a nearby prep school and the major rival of Kent's Hill.

Also winning their first three games in a row the following autumn were the Kent's Hill gridders. It was no small help to the squad that, when the annual call was issued on the second day of school for those that would like to go out for football, this time among the 35 candidates reporting was the sophomore from Massachusetts, Ray Eliot Nusspickle.

Nusspickle, who had spent most of his time on the line at Brighton High School, found himself at fullback for the Hill, and promptly scored four touchdowns in their second game against the University of Maine Freshmen. The Hilltoppers won 37-0 as Nusspickle also showed himself a force on defense, "tackling hard and knocking down passes," said the school yearbook, *The Kent's Hill Breeze*.

Nusspickle also scored the next week as The Hill beat the Colby Freshmen 14-0, but the bubble burst in the following game when Hebron beat the Hilltoppers 3-0.

With Nusspickle running well in their only drive for a touchdown, Kent's Hill got back on the winning track the next week by shutting out Bates Second Team 7-0. The Hilltoppers went on to post a 4-2-1 record, although their goal line was crossed in only one game, that a 27-0 loss to Coburn Classical.

It was back to baseball the next spring, but only two lettermen returned. One was the newly elected captain Nusspickle behind the plate. Keyed by the heavy hitting of their bespectacled catcher and leader, the Kent's Hill nine rolled to an 8-3 record, but were beaten once again by the Hebron Big Green 7-3. This time, however, the Hilltoppers had a chance for revenge.

On June 6, 1925 Hebron travelled to Kent's Hill with an opportunity to become the undisputed prep school champion of the state of Maine. A win by The Hill would force a tie for the championship between these two bitter enemies. The large crowd sat on pins and needles as the two nines battled back and forth. With their stable captain showing the way, Kent's Hill thrilled the faithful with an 8-5 win over Hebron for a share of the state championship.

"The faculty, school and team appreciate Captain Ray Nusspickle," reported The 1924-25 Kent's Hill Breeze. "Ray has been an excellent leader and sportsman. He has set a good example to his teammates throughout the year by his hard work and good spirit. Without a doubt he is the best catcher in the state as far as prep schools are concerned and his steady work behind the bat has inserted a world of confidence into his team. Another good thing, Ray will be back next year."

He would be back the next year, on the baseball diamond and the gridiron. But then, it might have been a year to stay off the football field. Struggling through a rash of injuries, Kent's Hill's gridders finished 0-5-1 in Nusspickle's final season—a season in which he was elected captain. They even had a game cancelled because of bad weather in that unlucky year. The one chance to redeem an otherwise dismal season would be a win over Hebron in their annual clash.

Students and faculty worked as hard as the football team for this October fight. A piano was brought down to the dinner room and songs were practiced before each meal. Meetings were also held in the chapel, where cheers were perfected.

With the sun shining brightly on that autumn day, the alumni returned to The Hill, hearts brimming with the hope that the Hilltoppers would stun their old rivals in what *The Breeze* called "the objective game of the year."

Though Hebron was heavily favored, Kent's Hill hung on heroically. There was no score at the half, but in the third quarter the Big Green drove down to the Hilltopper one-foot line and had a first down. Kent's Hill dug in, and on four tries Hebron could not break the plane of the goal line.

As the game ground on, however, the number of Big Green substitutes wore down the boys from The Hill, and Hebron scored twice. The Hilltoppers' only points came on a safety after a blocked punt. Hebron vanquished its neighbors 14-2.

Despite the loss, the failures of that season were "forgotten by the students after viewing the remarkable exhibition of fight and gameness shown against Hebron," said *The Breeze*. "In this game every man was a star, but Hank Horne and Ray Nusspickle shone above the rest."

And Nusspickle's star was not ready to fall yet, not with another baseball season to go. The winter of 1925-26 went longer than usual, so the captain and his nine got a late start in the spring. The team went out to shovel off the field on April 15th, the first scheduled day of practice, only to find six inches of ice beneath the several inches of snow.

Without much opportunity to get into baseball shape, the Hilltoppers played their first game at Waterville on April 28th and won 12-7. They finished the season 8-3 as they did the year before, except this time on a down note.

Kent's Hill hooked up with Hebron with a chance to tie for the state prep school championship for the second year in a row. During the regular season the Big Green had beaten the boys from The Hill 3-1 after scoring two runs in the seventh on Hilltopper errors. Everyone expected another close game in the playoff, but Hebron, playing on its own field, rolled over Kent's Hill by the score of 9-4 for the championship. The Big Green had exacted its revenge for the year before.

Now Annie Nusspickle had brought up a well-rounded young man and Ray had interests outside of athletics. Aside from his studies and sports activities, Nusspickle was president of his junior and senior classes, president of the K.H. Club his junior year and vice-president his senior year, a member of the glee club his sophomore and junior years, and president of the Calliopean Society his senior year.

The Calliopeans were a literary society with an emphasis on public speaking and debate. In addition, the preamble to the Calliopean constitution stated that they were "to be courteous in speech and action, and maintain and practice a due regard for the opinions of others." All members had opportunities to test their speaking skills and they would give each other feedback and discuss at length styles of debate and public presentations.

For example, on February 13, 1926, Nusspickle's senior year, at the joint meeting of the Calliopeans and the Eromatheans (the rival literary society on campus), Nusspickle, as president of the society, was put forward to debate. The resolution was that the proposed child labor amendment to the federal constitution, which would set standards for the protection of children, should be ratified by the state of Maine. Nusspickle argued effectively in the affirmative.

Of course, it was public speaking as much as coaching that made Ray Eliot Nusspickle famous later. The Calliopeans, no doubt, first watered and cultivated the seed in his heart.

Naturally, all work and no play would have made Ray a dull boy. Dull he was not.

One of the jokes on campus was that Nusspickle was quite interested in the raising of chickens and that he used to go to the nearby town of North Leeds to get further instructions. Actually, in North Leeds was Evelyn Foss, a fellow student and his main romantic interest while he was at Kent's Hill. He was not limited in his dating, but during his senior year, Evelyn and he got fairly serious.

"We used to have a wonderful time," Evelyn Foss Coolidge says now, 65 years later. "We had such fun and he was such a gentleman."

When they graduated, Nusspickle was voted most popular boy and Foss was voted most popular girl in their class. It is safe to say that they were the most popular couple in school. After graduation, though, they went their separate ways and no long distance relationship developed.

The school yearbook also chronicles that Nusspickle had a notorious reputation for "jollying the profs." In other words, he was not just the life of parties, but also of the classroom.

Nusspickle, indeed, was ever the center of attention in class, at dances, at casual gatherings and in more devious exploits. Once he and his buddies tried to lead a cow up into the gold-domed belfry of the administration building. The cow was only part way up the stairs when the headmaster came running over from his quarters to find out what a cow was doing in Bierce Hall! As he stormed through the front door, Nusspickle and his fellow conspirators snuck out a back window and were never found out.

Nusspickle's nickname at The Hill was "Toots" but no one seems to know why or where he got the name. He did, though, accept it in fun, as he did when he was voted the graduate with the largest feet.

"We are sure Ray . . . will not lose his balance," joked *The Breeze*.

But *The Breeze* had other things to say about Nusspickle in his last days at Kent's Hill.

"Ray is one of the kind that Kent's Hill is proud of," it said. "He is willing to work, and work with a smile. He has had many honors given to him and has earned every one of them. He is another in which modesty is a predominating characteristic."

Annie was not able to make it to Maine for her son's graduation, the trip would be too much. But the school's principal, Mr. T.W. Watkins wrote her a letter. In it, he told her how sorry he was that she could not attend.

"Raymond has made a good record in his studies and a record far above the average as a man of clean character and good purposes," he wrote in the letter dated June 25, 1926. "We know that with hard work and attention to business he will be successful. I am glad that you have loaned him to us for so long."

Success was to be his, but at this point he still thought it would be in dentistry. The next year he enrolled at Tufts College, a dental school in Massachusetts, and, on the side, played a little professional hockey for the Boston Shamrocks. But he couldn't do the microscope work needed at dental school because of his poor eyesight. He explained with a chuckle, however, that "when I considered spending a lifetime looking into people's mouths I changed my mind." Whatever the real reason, he did not continue long at Tufts.

Where had the fork in the road finally brought him? When he said "no" to dentistry had he finally found his real life's ambition? At some point in the time he had spent at Kent's Hill, during his short tryst at Tufts, in the midst of all of the competition on the athletic field, between all of the activities, honors and achievements, and somewhere amongst the fun, the romance and the tom-foolery, somewhere down at the very bottom of him, coaching had caught his heart, and Red Grange his imagination.

4

Maggie

"When the golden sun is sinking,
And your mind from troubles free,
While of others you are thinking,
Will you sometimes think of me?"

—Maggie to Ray, 1928

She was a beautiful, regal woman, 5-foot-11 inches tall, slender with blonde hair and blue eyes. Educated and sophisticated, she had attended a business school, worked as an executive secretary in New York and as a school teacher on Staten Island. Her looks and her brains made it easy for her to get a job as a legal secretary in 1926 Boston and to gain entrance to Portia Law School there.

Margaret Mary Crowley was drawn to Massachusetts by the desire to be close to her younger sister, Jean, and Jean's husband Sam, who had moved to Boston a couple of years earlier. In addition, Margaret had grown up with a deep love of and commitment to the law, and a dream of someday becoming an attorney. Not long after Margaret's move, however, Jean became very ill and moved back to Staten Island to be tended by her mother. Soon Margaret quit law school and returned to help care for her sister. But shortly thereafter, Jean, Margaret's very closest sister and dearest friend, died.

While living on Staten Island and sorting out her future during the summer of 1928, Margaret, now 29 years old, traveled back to Boston to visit Frances Costello, a woman she had met while doing business in Boston, and with whom she had stayed when she first moved there. One weekend night during Margaret's stay, Frances invited some friends over. Included in the gathering was a 23-year-old, enthusiastic rogue from Brighton named Ray Nusspickle.

Margaret had never met this young man with the strange last name, but they chatted amiably enough. They talked of their families, of life, and got a chuckle out of little coincidences like their birthdays being in the same month. At one point during the evening a game of Post Office was proposed, and soon it was Nusspickle's turn to go out of the room and call on somebody to join him. He called Margaret and promptly proposed marriage to her. She laughed at first, assuming he must be joking, but realized in a moment that he was not. Stunned, this lawyer want-to-be stumbled for words. After all, they had just met, she was six years older than he and, of course, there was Jack.

Margaret would say with a grin later that "Ray swept me off my feet," but, though she didn't say no, she did have to think about it—and for good reason. Jack was a Boston newspaperman introduced to Margaret by his sister Mary. By the time she had met this Nusspickle character, Margaret had been seeing Jack for almost five years. Things had cooled a bit between them, though, with her move back to Staten Island and her inability to get the man to tie the knot. Jack had been very nonchalant about their relationship, confident that she would always be there when he was ready to marry. This frustrated Margaret to no end, and she and Jack were on the outs.

So Nusspickle's bold offensive was timely, and he was not going to be put off by her speechlessness. Nusspickle began to sell her on the idea in much the same way he did his mother on football ten years before. What added earnestness to Nusspickle's plea was that he would be leaving that autumn for his freshman year at the University of Illinois, and he did not know when he would see her again. In the end, he needn't have worried. Though Margaret did not say yes that night, after six months and exactly three dates, she succumbed.

When the engagement was final, Margaret wired Jack the news. Desperately heartbroken and kicking himself for an opportunity lost, Jack went out on a two-day drunk and married a woman he had never met. Whether that marriage lasted is not known, but the ghost of this lost opportunity was not exorcised until almost 20 years later, when Margaret and Jack were finally able to sit down and hash through all of the pain and misunderstandings. They would never be married, but they were reconciled.

Ray and Margaret would be wed, no matter that they seemed so different. Had they been a battery, Ray would have been the positive and Margaret the negative. Ray was outgoing, energetic, boisterous, and the center of attention. Maggie (as Ray called her) had her share of fun, but she was more serious, studied, somewhat quiet and impatient. He was ever trusting and a bit naive, she was matured by her life in business. He was impetuous, she was slow. He acted, while she thought.

Their upbringings were almost as different as their personalities, too. Ray Nusspickle came from a small family in which he was the only child, Maggie Crowley was the fourth child of eight. While Ray grew up on the poorer side of middle class in the heart of Manhattan, Maggie's upbringing was more comfortable. Her parents, John and Elizabeth (Jennie) Crowley, were born in New York City. John's father had been a blacksmith with a thriving business that included shoeing all of the horses of the New York City Police Department. John, having graduated when he was 16 years old from City College of New York, eventually made a very good living at the post office, and he and his bride moved to rural Staten Island.

John and Jennie built a house on the corner of Hendricks and Westervelt Avenues, an upper-class neighborhood comprised mainly of lawyers and doctors. The only way to reach Staten Island was by boat and that kept it rural, which was just the way residents liked it. Entertainment on a weekend evening was to take the short jaunt up Toad Hill and watch the giant, ocean-going ships come in. Nobody but the most amorous teenagers complained.

Maggie attended Curtis High School, a large, gray, gaunt-looking building about a two-block walk from her home. It was here that she dared dream a dream foreign to most women at the dawn of the 1900s. Always independent and strong-willed, Maggie wanted to be a career woman, and set out to do just that. In 1928 though, at a time when her life seemed unfocused, Ray Nusspickle stepped into the picture.

When he told her that he wanted to be a football coach, her first reaction was, "What? Any imbecile can coach football!"

Still—by mutual consent—she pursued her law degree no longer, choosing instead to go to Illinois and support Ray in his dream. Her mind did change about football, however. Admitting that all she knew about it when they first met was that "it was a chance to get dressed up," she later stated, "Football is a tough, scientific game and the best character builder I know."

Ray, of course, made sacrifices too. Reared an Episcopalian, he was marrying a woman who was a loyal Roman Catholic. Maggie wanted to be married at St. Peter's Catholic Church, where she had been baptized as an infant and attended church faithfully as she grew. Established on Staten Island in 1839, St. Peter's is a large and majestic house of worship with a huge A-shaped roof, multiple steeples and a rich tradition in the Crowley family. For Ray to be married in a Catholic Church, he needed to undergo the rite of "First Communion." This he did without hesitation under the tutelage of the Very Reverend Charles Cassidy, who later officiated their wedding. They would be a Roman Catholic family.

A morning of moderate temperatures, bathed in sunshine, greeted the wedding celebrants on June 27, 1929. With Ray away at school in Champaign, Illinois, Maggie had to do the bulk of the planning. Things went off without a hitch for everyone, that is, except the best man. Running terribly late, Maggie's cousin James Drury, Jr. (the father of the future television "Virginian"), had to change into his tuxedo on the ferry as he crossed to Staten Island. Doing double-time to the church, he made it the moment before the 9:30 a.m. ceremony was to begin.

The wedding was average in size, but grand nonetheless. Ironically, Mary, sister to Maggie's old flame Jack, was one of the bridesmaids. Less than a year after they had met at a friend's home in a silly little game of Post Office, Ray and Maggie walked the aisle of St. Peter's as man and wife, and nothing but death would separate them.

After the service, everyone made the short trip to Maggie's brother's house on Hylan Avenue for the reception. Jack Crowley's home had a large yard on which a tent had been pitched for the occasion. The Atlantic Ocean lapped a beach just across the street and down the hill. The party, catered elegantly, began with breakfast. A five-piece orchestra provided the backdrop and the dancing music all afternoon, evening and into the wee hours of the next morning. Ray, as always, was the life of the party, and he and the others kept themselves revived by heading down to the ocean and taking a dip. It is said that the band stayed alert by free access to the bar.

 Though the day after the wedding was dull and rainy, it was not so in Ray and Maggie's hearts. They spent what Ray called a "glorious day" of fun and silliness at a friend's house.

"The four of us played bridge," he wrote in their honeymoon log. "And the girls received a very severe beating from the boys."

His attitude contradicted, however, the cartoon that Maggie must have taped to the opening page of the log: "A man is like an automobile," it said. "Once a woman learns how to run one— she soon gets a license!"

Later they laughed together as they went past the site of the reception and drove up Toad Hill on Staten Island to see the sights.

June 29th was the 35th wedding anniversary of Maggie's parents, and in the morning everyone, including the newlyweds, brought them gifts and flowers. They all had breakfast together, then, for Ray and Maggie, it was off to New York to catch the *S.S. Minnekahda* for a trip across the Atlantic and a honeymoon in Paris. As many as 26 family members and friends came to see them off.

"Another beautiful, sunshiny day," Ray described their second day after a lovely first night. "Blue sky, flecked with fleecy white clouds. I lit a match on deck and the gentle breeze did not blow it out."

Ray got a kick out of how they were treated as quite the distinguished couple. He loved the meals and that they were given the center table in the dining room.

Ray and Maggie spent their days on board playing shuffleboard ("I am a good player . . . Margaret not so good."), bridge ("Beat Margaret as usual, then she showed a remarkable streak of luck and finally beat me . . . She is elated."), and making new friends. In the evenings they dined elegantly, watched "Hoot" Gibson movies and other entertainment, sipped champagne, enjoyed the swings and danced late into the night.

The fun caught up with them after several days, however. "Seems to me this is going to be a funny night before the Fourth," Ray wrote on July 3rd.

It was a late night of partying and dancing, and the next morning they didn't hear the breakfast bell and rose late. Ray did have time and energy enough to critique a Fourth of July speaker later that day, though. "Didn't like his attitude," he wrote.

The first land sighted at 11:30 the evening of July 7th was Scilly Island, and they passed the Edingstone Lighthouse an hour later. Next morning they landed at Plymouth at 7:30, and, with 150 other passengers, boarded *The Tender*, a smaller vessel that took them to France. The happy couple spent two splendid weeks there, then made the return trip home.

It was almost easier for Ray and Maggie to get from New York to France than it was for them to relocate to Illinois, where they would make their home while Ray finished his schooling. First, they needed a vehicle, and Jim Drury offered his old Model T Ford. It was a two-seater that had seen better days, but Ray and Maggie paid their cousin $25 for it. With hard tires that made the ride more like a rodeo, a missing passenger side window and rain pouring down for much of the trip, they made their way to the land of Zuppke and Grange. And so it was that the future first couple of the Fighting Illini arrived at their kingdom in a bouncing "Tin-Lizzy," with Ray's Illinois athletic jacket strapped over the opening of the passenger-side window to keep his new bride from getting wet.

5

Illinois

We're poor little lambs who've lost our way.
Baa-baa-baa.
We're little black sheep who've gone astray.
Baa-baa-baa.

Gentleman songsters off on a spree,
Doomed from here to eternity.
Lord have mercy on such as we.
Baa-baa-baa.

—"The Wiffenpoof Song"
(Minnigrode, Pomeroy,
Galloway, Valle, Hart)

Red Grange had brought much to Illinois. The greatest running back anywhere in the first half of the 20th century helped launch the most successful decade in Fighting Illini football history. Swift and smart, the "Galloping Ghost" turned an entire nation's eyes to Champaign, Illinois. His five touchdowns (four in the first 12 minutes) against the powerful Michigan Wolverines in the 1924 Memorial Stadium inaugural game rates as one of the great legends in sports history. Michigan had shut out its previous three opponents and would shut out its next three, but that Saturday afternoon the Illini, behind Grange, blew out the Wolverines 39-14. Grange brought excitement, success and prestige to Illinois. Who would have known that his legend would also bring the man who would someday become head coach of the Fighting Illini gridders for 18 years, restore the greatness of Illinois football, later uphold the University's reputation in dark times, and so encompass the spirit of the place that he would be forever known as "Mr. Illini?"

Ray Eliot Nusspickle would peruse the pages of the Sunday *Boston Globe* and be mesmerized by "The Ghost" and his exploits. Illinois had not meant much to him before, just another university, just another team. Champaign-Urbana was a long way from home, and schools like Princeton, Yale, and Army naturally had more of his attention. But the fire of football coaching was growing in him now, and the spirit of Grange fanned the flame. As a mist of smoke is drawn through a fireplace chimney, so Nusspickle's heart was drawn west to Illinois.

At the same time Nusspickle was being awakened by "the Ghost," he ran across some brochures with information about the coaching school at Illinois. Practically speaking, Nusspickle realized he couldn't make a better choice. If coaching was his thing, why not learn from the best? The University of Illinois had one of the elite physical education schools in the country, and Bob Zuppke, later elected to the National College Football Hall of Fame, was one of the most successful coaches of his day, capturing national championships in 1914, 19, 23 and 27. Head coach at Illinois for 29 years through 1941, Zuppke had an earned reputation for being one of football's most innovative pioneers. He was a man of principle, though, whose philosophy of life went well beyond the perimeter and strategies of the football field. These principles were revealed often by Zuppke in his famous short, penetrating and insightful quips.

He was funny, for example, when he described an All-American football player as "a swift runner, (who has) weak opposition and a poet in the pressbox—especially the latter." He also said, "Footballs are made to bounce crooked, and as long as they do that you've always got a fighting chance." When he talked about the alumni, he said they were loyal "when the team wins all of its games."

But he was very serious when he said, "Victory in football is 40 percent ability and 60 percent spirit," or, "Don't lose hope; it may be the worst fumble you ever make." And he was pointed when he stated that "The main idea of competition before everything else should be to earn your opponent's respect whether you win or lose."

Zuppke mentored the likes of Grange and the late George Halas, granddaddy of the National Football League, who attended Illinois and played for Zup in the late teens. Zuppke's impact on football on every level cannot be minimized, and if there is a problem in the sport today, it is possibly because the game has forgotten the principles that men like Zuppke built into its foundation.

"Wrongly conducted, football is a school of bad manners, vulgarity, subterfuge, evasion and brutality," Zup was quoted in the book *Zuppke of Illinois* written by Grange in 1937 to celebrate his former coach's 25th year at the home of the Fighting Illini. "Rightly conducted, it promotes honor, courage, self-control, and self-abnegation, harmony and courtesy in youth. The teams of two fine schools playing clean, fair football can set an example in sportsmanship to 80,000 people.

"Rightly conducted, football enriches the emotional life of the players and spectators," he continued. "To tens of thousands of boys and youths whose names never break into newsprint nationally, it presents an opportunity to compete, to excel, to harmonize and to develop latent power. Football constitutes an effective alternate to our increasing artificial environment. I sincerely believe what I have just said and hope you will always find me in the front rank of those who are forever fighting to keep football a game—a game played to win—but a game!"

In his desire to keep football "a game," Zuppke disdained recruiting and scholarships. He saw the pitfalls years before college football as a whole would feel their detriment. Why young men should be paid through a scholarship to play football he never knew, and the graft that had already become a part of the recruiting process sickened him.

His attitude toward the process would be his downfall on the field, his program becoming less and less successful in the 1930s as he lost out in the war for "blue-chip" high school talent. Zup, however, stood firm to his principles. It was this unwavering tenacity of spirit that almost got him fired in 1938, but that also caused his Illini players and friends to love and respect the man known to them as "The Little Dutchman."

Indeed, no player believed in Zup more than the 23-year-old, half-blind freshman from the East Coast, who showed up on the U. of I. gridiron in the fall of 1928. Ray Eliot Nusspickle had left his mother and his (as of then unannounced) wife-to-be Maggie, stuck out his thumb and hitched rides all the way from Brighton, Massachusetts, to Champaign-Urbana, Illinois. He landed in Champaign with $6.83 in his pocket, a shirt on his back and two more in a canvas-covered cardboard suitcase.

The first order of business for the newcomer was to find a place to live. Nusspickle needed to locate shelter with cheap rent, so he settled on the attic of a house on Fourth and Green Streets. In the winter time it was cold because the little attic had no heat.

"No heat, period," he would say later. "When I wanted to study, I'd go downstairs into one of the other rooms."

As a matter of fact, Maggie had displayed her deft sense of humor by sending an electric hair grower for her already balding fiance. Nusspickle, however, put it on his head just to warm himself up. He could not stand up straight in the makeshift apartment, either, because of the angle of the roof.

"My bed was under the eaves and every morning I'd bump my head when I got up," he said. "I was convinced if I didn't die of frostbite I'd surely have a fatal concussion."

But up on one of those angled eaves, directly above his bed, he tacked a little piece of tattered paper which contained a simple statement upon which he would stake his entire life. "If you think you can do it, you can," it said.

There were no scholarships given out for athletics at Illinois then and Nusspickle scrambled to secure finances. He was told by the Dean of Men that he didn't have enough money to enroll, so he pawned his watch to get the fee.

Next he set out to find work. He purchased a local paper and wandered up and down the streets of this unfamiliar town. He checked out place after place for employment and even stopped people on the street, asking them if they knew where he could get a job.

After awhile he came upon a department store in the middle of campus, only a couple of blocks from his new home. But when he asked for a job, he was turned down. He went back to that store six more times to ask for work and was denied. Finally, on his eighth visit, after a week of wandering from place to place and being rejected all over town, the owner, exasperated, asked him if he had ever cooked before because he needed a short order cook for his fountain. Ray the salesman was on stage again.

"Sure," he stated beaming. "Back in Boston I spent quite a bit of time at Fenway Park as a short-order cook."

Well, his story was half true. He had spent a lot of time at Fenway, but he had never cooked a thing in his life.

Nusspickle was apparently convincing enough because the man hired him. Back in the kitchen, Nuss, as he was sometimes called by friends and teammates, told the regular cooks, "I can't boil water, but I need this job and need it badly. Don't give me away. Just show me what to do and I'll learn." Actually, Eliot later became a fairly accomplished cook, and his "Filet of Sole a la Eliot" and stuffed turkey caught on big with friends and family. He found cooking a relaxing escape during those rough football campaigns.

Nusspickle went through his freshman year getting up at 5:30 in the morning to stoke the furnace at his boarding house. Then he worked the breakfast shift at the fountain, went to classes from 8 until 3 in the afternoon, had football or baseball practice from 3 until 6, was back to the fountain until 10:30, and then went to his studies.

His sophomore year he moved into a supervisory role for Frank Robeson at Robeson's Roof Garden. Later he worked as a janitor for the University. The University hired him at 35 cents per hour in his junior year, and he labored with a fellow student named Shaw Terwilliger. Friends couldn't imagine a couple of co-workers with stranger names than Nusspickle and Terwilliger, so they dubbed them the "Cats and Jammer" twins after the comic page characters.

During his senior year, Nusspickle was taken on board by Ben Cracken, who managed the upkeep of all of the athletic grounds for the University. Cracken had supervised the building of Memorial Stadium in the early 1920s for Athletic Director George Huff. One day Nusspickle went to Cracken and told him that one of his in-laws had passed away in New York and asked for seven to ten days off to go to the funeral. Cracken said yes without hesitation, but queried how he was going to get there. Nusspickle told him that he would go east the same way he came west, with his thumb. Well, Cracken, a big, tough, yet thoughtful man, would have none of that. He purchased train tickets for Nusspickle and surprised him with them the next day. Nusspickle was dumbfounded. He told Cracken that nobody had ever done anything that kind for him before.

Nusspickle went on his trip and when he came back, asked Cracken to take two dollars out of every paycheck until he had paid back those tickets in full. Cracken never wanted to be paid back, but the young man insisted.

Nusspickle became very close to the Cracken family and later, when he became an assistant at Illinois and after Ben Cracken passed away, he came to their home on a regular basis to do work around the house for Ben's widow and son.

"I was 13 years old at the time," says Ben Cracken Jr. today, "and I tried to tell him that I was old enough and I could do that work. But he told me 'No,' that they were his chores. He wouldn't think of taking a penny for it either."

The tenacity Nusspickle showed in paying back Cracken's kindness, he also displayed on the football field. As it was at Kent's Hill, though, his success had to come despite his poor eyesight. Bob Zuppke always said that Nusspickle would be an All-American "if he could just see across the line of scrimmage."

"He was so nearsighted," wrote David Condon in the Chicago Tribune *Grafic* Magazine in 1951, "he could spend a summer at a bathing beach and see only water!"

Says Larry Stewart: "Talk about nearsighted! It was our first trip together (as broadcast partners in 1960). We, of course, had our hotel room together and I turned in early, having the bed closest to the door. Ray stayed up with some folks a while longer. Well, he comes into the room and takes his glasses off and then he stumbles over my bed and falls on top of me. I weighed about 135 pounds and he weighed about 235—I thought I was dead. After that we made a pact: whenever we went on the road and we were in the room together with split beds, I took the bed furthest away from the front door. That pact lasted for 20 years."

Former *Chicago American* Sports Editor Leo Fischer told the story of when he first met Eliot at school. A member of the Illini staff grabbed Fisher and said, "Come over here. We got a guy who wears glasses and catches for the baseball team and plays tackle for the football team. He's either a brave guy or he's nuts."

Really, he was desperate. His freshman coach took him aside and tried to convince him that, because of his eyes, he shouldn't be playing football.

"But I would have frozen to death that winter if I hadn't won that freshman sweater," Nusspickle laughed once.

Indeed, his toughness was never questioned. Upon his accepting a coaching position later at Illinois College, the *Jacksonville Daily Journal* reported that through all of Nusspickle's athletic career, which included four years of high school, three of prep and four at Illinois, he never missed a practice session. The *Journal* was ready to put that in "Ripley's Believe It or Not," but those that knew him were not surprised. When Nuss's resolve was tested, even as a fledgling 190-pound rookie, he was up for the challenge.

"It was my opening scrimmage as a freshman," he related once. "I lined up against one of the toughest men I ever knew, the late Butch Nowak. I was an eager beaver kid from the East and I was going to show Nowak. But Butch showed me from the start. Nowak glared at me and drew an imaginary line across the grass, dragging his right foot through the turf. He stared me down, spat some chewing tobacco on the ground and said, 'Kid, you come across that line and you're going back without any teeth.'

"Well," Ray finished the story, "I don't remember much else, but I do still have my teeth."

As for his eyes, Nusspickle tried everything, even having a special helmet developed so he could wear his glasses while he played. It was a normal leather helmet with ear covers, but a leather Batman-like mask came down over the forehead to the nose with two openings for the eyes. The sides of the mask extended to the ear covers. In the eye holes was an unbreakable glass that would protect the glass of his spectacles. Of course, with the mask Nusspickle's peripheral vision was limited and if rain, mud or dust latched itself to the glass, his eyesight would be worse than it was without glasses. As with all players at times too, his helmet would get knocked cockeyed on his head, moving the eyeholes. And seeing through two panes of glass sometimes gave him that Coke-bottle effect. Nonetheless, this device at least kept him on the field and helped him earn varsity letters as an offensive lineman in 1930 and 31. He didn't like the facemask when it was developed in the 1950s because he felt it took away from the toughness of the game and feared the helmet would soon become an aggressive weapon. It did. But he may have been the very first player in the history of organized football to wear one.

Though his eyes were a great handicap and "might have discouraged a man of lesser determination," reported Champaign-Urbana's *Evening Courier*, "Nusspickle was named by the (conference champion) Ohio St. Buckeyes as the toughest man they had played against that season (1931)."

When Nusspickle arrived on the scene, the Illini were fresh from winning the Western Conference (Big 10) championship themselves and their fourth and final national championship under Zuppke. They followed that unbeaten 1927 season by going 7-1 and winning another conference championship in Nusspickle's freshman year, 1928. The year 1929 brought a 6-1-1 record and a second place finish behind Purdue. From there it was downhill, as the Illini went 3-5-0 in 1930 and 2-6-1 in Nusspickle's final year, 1931.

On the baseball diamond Nusspickle was one of the first college catchers in the country to wear glasses. His sophomore year, he was the backup, but soon won the starting job—and a varsity letter—primarily because of a hot bat. Maybe it was marriage that agreed with him so much (he and Maggie had walked the aisle the summer before), but whatever the reason, he rolled through the last half of the season and ended up hitting over .350. The Illini finished second in the conference that year and won the championship the next, though Nusspickle's role was reduced as his bat cooled and a kid named Paul Chervinko emerged as a force behind the plate. He finished his career a backup as the Illini were once again second in the Western Conference race in 1932.

But his baseball career did not end without trial, either. Once, an inside fastball shattered his glasses, leaving splinters of glass in his eyes. What could have been a tragedy, however, ended up just another bump in the road as doctors were able to remove the splinters without further damage to his vision.

Nusspickle had not chosen Illinois in hopes of becoming a professional athlete; his eyesight would never permit it. But as bad as his physical eyes may have been, the eyesight of his heart was 20/20. All through his schooling at Champaign, his soul was set on leading and serving young America as an athletic coach.

He entered the U of I in the Physical Education School and despite the rigors of a job, practice, and the new responsibilities of marriage, he pulled the best grades of his life. He didn't fail a course and most of his marks were above average. The physical education curriculum gave the future leader a well-rounded knowledge of each sport, coaching and coaching techniques, as well as some expertise in physiology, anatomy and injuries.

Aside from the P.E. curriculum, Nusspickle had opportunities to delve into other areas that interested him. He took, for instance, a course called "Principles of Effective Speaking" his sophomore year. The story goes that at one point during the semester, everyone had to give a speech. The teacher demanded, however, that not just a speech be given, but also an outline submitted. Nusspickle had always thought outlines were a terrible and tedious waste of time, feeling that the spirit or effect of the speech upon the listener was the important thing. He asked the teacher if he could bypass the outline portion of the assignment and just give the speech. She said no. He then cut a deal with her that he would give the speech and let the class judge it. In other words, she could grade him based upon the reaction of the other students. To this she reluctantly agreed. He made his speech, received a standing ovation from the class, and an "A" from the teacher.

Nusspickle also took writing courses, where he expounded upon many of the virtues that his mother had long ago taught him and that Bob Zuppke had facilitated. For one class he wrote a paper entitled "Sportsmanship." In it, he detailed a philosophy by which he would live and die as he took the helm of athletic programs of the future:

"Sportsmanship means more than observing the written rules of the game; it means also observing the unwritten rules of fair play," he wrote. "Sportsmanship is a concern of the spectators as well as the players. Sport without sportsmanship has no more place in a society based on ethical principles than has work without workmanship in such a society."

In the paper, Nusspickle sights an example of a quarterback from Army who was injured in a game against Navy. He had to continue to play because there was no one to take his place. The Navy captain then told his teammates not to touch the hurt player the rest of the game. As a result, the quarterback was able to play without further injury.

"This little incident relates not only an act in the great game of football, but rather presents an act of sportsmanship in which the Navy football team refused to take unfair advantage of an injured opponent regardless of the cost to themselves," wrote Nusspickle. "This is an example of the highest type of sportsmanship."

He also related the example of American tennis great Bill Tilden purposely giving up a point in a world class match because his opponent felt that a call had gone against him wrongly. Another anecdote recalled was of two campuses who responded differently to their powerful football teams coming home losers. On one campus, the welcome-home parties and celebrations were canceled, and on the other, the celebrations were held with even greater fervency in an effort to communicate to the players how much they were appreciated, win or lose.

"The spectators, student body, and officials can and must be influenced by the type of play of their favorites," wrote the 24-year-old. "They also must stand for true sportsmanship and back their teams in defeat as well as victory. Not only does true sportsmanship take place in great amphitheaters and before immense audiences, but it also takes its just place in other branches of sport. A hunter will never shoot an animal that is standing still, but will make it run to give it a fair chance for its life. The fencer does not rush in to make as many points as possible when the opponent has dropped his sword. He will wait until his opponent has retrieved his weapon. The boxer does not take advantage of his opponent when he has fallen to the floor. He will go to the neutral corner and wait until his opponent has risen.

"Sportsmanship then, is not only a written law but rather is an unwritten code that should be encased in the minds and hearts of every person. It is an attitude that when carefully observed tends to raise the moral, social and physical standards of nations."

He finished by quoting the famous proverb by the greatest sports poet of his (and probably all) time, Grantland Rice: "When the Great Scorer comes to mark against your name, He writes not that you won or lost, but how you played the game."

No one ever doubted how Nusspickle played the game. And, as was his nature, not every game he played was all that serious anyway.

What was billed as the first-ever organized "Basketball Game on Ice" was played as part of an ice skating exhibition for the entertainment of the "Farm and Home Week" visitors in the winter of 1931. About 1,500 spectators packed the new University rink in Champaign to watch this unique game, plus figure skating, barrel jumping and stunt acts.

Rink manager Beekley Miller came up with the idea of "Ice Basketball" and Nusspickle, of course, had to get in on it. He, Miller Hotchkins, George Mills, Al Hazzard, Ed Faust and T.T.

Carr made up the Gray team. Bob Hotchkins, Ivan Schustek, R.G. Maloney, Cliff Hyink, Joe Bartulis and V.J. Bert were the Blues.

A cross between basketball and hockey, the game had no free throws, but when a foul was committed, the guilty party would have to leave the ice for a predetermined period of time, although he could be replaced by another. Also, a player could skate with the ball for the count of five, but then had to either dribble, pass, shoot or stop.

Although Miller took this new-found sport fairly seriously, it is not clear that anyone else did.

"The first basketball game on ice that any audience was privileged to see," wrote *Daily Illini* sports writer Ken Holt, "was fully as interesting as a game on the hardwood floor, and much more amusing. The laughs provoked by much scrambling and sprawling on the ice were, however, tempered by the anxiety lest some player have a fancy figure carved on him by the blade of an uncontrolled skate. There were no casualties."

No casualties, indeed, but there was a winner. After a hard-fought, yet somewhat disoriented first half, the Blues led 8-4. The Grays stormed out at the beginning of the second half, though, and took charge for good. Behind the sharp shooting of center Al Hazzard, who finished with 12 points to lead all scorers, the Grays went on to nip the Blues, 22-20. Chipping in four points for the winners was that flashy guard sensation, Ray Nusspickle.

As the college years wore on, of course, amid all of the fun, frolic, and responsibility of campus and married life, Ray and Maggie Nusspickle had begun to consider what they would do after Ray's graduation. During his senior year Ray asked for Coach Zuppke's advice, and began aggressively seeking interviews for coaching positions.

Meanwhile, LaRue Van Meter had taken over a struggling athletic department at small Illinois College in Jacksonville. The new athletic director was seeking to revitalize the Blueboys' sports programs, in part by bringing in an Assistant Athletic Director and new coaching blood. When he came to the Illinois State High School Basketball Tournament finals in Champaign, Mr. Milt Olander of the University of Illinois Physical Education Department told him he had, "exactly the man."

Van Meter received letters of recommendation on Nusspickle's behalf from the likes of Illini Athletic Director

George Huff, who called Nusspickle, "an exceedingly promising young man   … He is a hard worker and very conscientious and his habits are the very best . . . He is loyal and a team worker." Wrote baseball coach Carl Lundgren: "I do not know of a young man of whom I have a higher opinion . . . You will find him full of life and vigor and possessing unlimited enthusiasm. No player on the baseball squad is better liked and esteemed. He surely will be just as popular and respected elsewhere." Olander added, "(Nusspickle) will work industriously and leave nothing undone to prove his worth. I consider him to be one of the best qualified men who has ever graduated from our Coaching Course."

When he met with Nusspickle, Van Meter was immediately taken by this man who spoke with such humility, yet with confidence and conviction. The more they talked, the more he realized that Nusspickle had the spirit he wanted to infuse into his department.

In the spring of 1932, Van Meter made Ray Eliot Nusspickle his assistant and gave him the start to his legendary coaching career in collegiate athletics. Beginning the next fall, Illinois College would be Nusspickle's training ground and a short, small and hidden snapshot of that spirit, which would soon burst upon the nation.

6

Blueboys

Dawn stretched its fiery hand over Jacksonville, Illinois, on this cool autumn morning in 1935. Two figures made their way down a quiet street to the field west of the college buildings.

The smaller, a 10-year-old boy, carried two large tomato cans, one under each arm. The other, a tall, well-built man of 30 walked beside him with a sack of lime slung over his shoulder. They talked as they went, and now and again they would laugh. The young boy's name was Charles Bellatti, and he called the other "Coach."

Their feet left imprints on the dewy grass as they made their way across the field. The two stopped at one end. The man lowered the lime to the ground and the boy put down the cans.

The coach shaped the edges of the cans into spouts and poured the chalky, white powder into each. Tipping one can just enough, he drew a straight line as he backed his way across the field. Soon the boy picked up the second can and did the same, exactly ten yards away.

An ordinary field soon became a football field—a field where virtually every week in the fall two rivals clashed. Usually the most inspired team won. Usually, the most inspired team was the Illinois College Blueboys under its passionate head coach, Ray Nusspickle.

Illinois College is a small, quiet and historic school in central Illinois, its pretty campus nestled in the slight hills that roll through Jacksonville. Founded in 1829 by an itinerant minister and some Yale associates, I.C. is the oldest college in the state, and was the first to award a baccalaureate degree. The college boasts many important graduates, including the famed lawyer and statesman William Jennings Bryan, who received his diploma in 1881.

LaRue Van Meter and Ray Nusspickle walked into I.C.'s history in 1932. The two would form an unbreakable bond of friendship and, in their brief time at the home of the Blueboys, leave only legend in their wake.

In the 1930s, the Great Depression had its grip on most of America, although Illinois College remained fairly insulated from the worst of it. This is not to say the college had a lot of money, but it was able to stay afloat in the sea of despair that characterized much of the period.

Athletically speaking, however, Illinois College was in the throes of its own "great depression." School spirit and the morale of the college were down. Not coincidentally, I.C. hadn't won an athletic championship in any sport since the baseball team took the Little 19 Conference title in 1929.

It was because of this pervasive apathy and doldrums that Van Meter announced before the 1932-33 athletic season: "Illinois College needs a championship!"

In response, the school newspaper, *The Illinois College Rambler*, declared: "The effect of the morale of the college is evident to the casual observer or the newcomer. Naturally the whole of the condition cannot be laid to unsuccessful athletics, but it's probably true that a championship in a major sport would do much to foment a spirit of cooperation and unity now lacking."

Enter Ray Nusspickle.

The *Jacksonville Daily Journal* called him "the best imitation of a charged wire, equipped with a full set of first-rate brains." Whatever they called him, he was just what the doctor ordered.

Van Meter was a coach himself, and hired Nusspickle to not only assist him in the athletic department, but with the football team until Nusspickle was ready to take it over. Van Meter also made Nusspickle head coach of the baseball team. In addition, Nusspickle assumed charge of the swimming team and started the wrestling program during his tenure, which lasted through the spring of 1937.

What began in 1932 ignited "an unusual string of victories in almost all intercollegiate competition," wrote Charles E. Frank in his book *Pioneer's Progress-Illinois College, 1829-1979*.

However, in the fall of 1932 and the winter of the same, there was yet no championship for the Blueboys. The spark came when Nusspickle's first Blueboys nine made good on Van Meter's challenge, winning the Little 19 baseball championship (The Little 19 actually had 21 teams from colleges all over the state. To win the conference was akin to winning the state championship, because most of the small colleges in the state were in the Little 19 and only large schools like the University of Illinois, the University of Chicago and Northwestern were not). The Blueboys were beaten only once that year, and the domino effect was set in motion.

Nusspickle led the baseball team to second-place finishes in 1934 and 1935, and another conference title in 1936. In his last year, 1937, his charges finished 18-6. That season, the coach became the first to take an I.C. baseball team on a southern trip to play early games in a warmer climate. Nusspickle organized a barn dance to raise the money, and a motion was made and adopted to make the barn dance an annual affair in his honor.

The Blueboys' cumulative record under Nusspickle was 71-9, and with the talent and spirit Nusspickle left behind, the Blueboys won championships in 1938 and 39 also.

On the gridiron, Nusspickle spent his first year at Illinois College technically as Van Meter's assistant and the last four as the head man. Actually, according to some of his former football players, he did practically all of the coaching the first year under the watchful eye of Van Meter. The athletic director trusted the young mentor, but at the same time wanted to ease him into the position.

In 1934, Nusspickle's third year, he led the Blueboys to a 6-1 mark, their best record since 1915. One win away from the Little 19 conference championship, the "Nussmen," as a writer once called them, lost the final game to Macomb on a long pass in the waning minutes.

They finished the 1935 and 1936 seasons with winning slates and a 23-8-1 record over Nusspickle's five years. Nusspickle is also credited with laying the foundation for the Little 19 championship won by the Blueboy gridders under new coach and Nusspickle protege', Alf Lamb, in 1937.

Over the years, I.C. swim teams had barely tread water, and no team existed in 1934, but Nusspickle took one freshman athlete, Dewey Morberg of Chicago, to the conference meet and he alone scored enough points to give I.C. a third-place finish. Morberg then convinced his Chicago buddies to attend Illinois

College to swim for Nusspickle and the Blueboys. This they did, and went right to the top of the proverbial pool, although the pool was not their own. Illinois College never did have swim facilities. The team had to borrow the pool of the Illinois School for the Deaf, also located in Jacksonville.

Thus the Blueboy tankers were called the "pool-less wonders" when they won five Little 19 championships in a row, the first three coming under the tutelage of Nusspickle from 1935-37. The Illinois college swim team had never won even a single conference championship before.

Besides Nusspickle's achievements, others experienced success as well. Van Meter's basketball Blueboys won their first Little 19 conference championship ever in the 1934-35 season, and the tennis team only lost two matches that year. The golf team got into the act in the fall of 1935, winning the conference championship.

In religious jargon it would be termed a revival. And the preacher that lit the flame was Ray Nusspickle—not only by turning his teams into winners, but by infusing the whole student body with his positive and unifying spirit.

"Without the loyal backing of everyone on campus," he was quoted, "it will be impossible to win the highest laurels."

Nusspickle asked for enthusiastic cheering sections for Blueboy contests, and advised the girls to give the athletes a gentle slap on the back, and a word of encouragement to cheer them on to victory. He also suggested that it would be good for digestion to sing the college song before meals at Baxter Hall. If that were not enough, he urged all of the musicians on campus to try out for the band and a special deal was made to refund the 10-dollar activity fee to band members as an incentive. The campus responded.

It was a time when legends were made and it was, and still is, the single most successful and exhilarating period in Illinois College athletic history. The spirit of I.C. was higher than anyone could remember. *The Rambler* stated in 1935 that "Illinois College could point with pride to a complete reversal of this (previously poor spiritual) condition."

Dubbed the "Dutch Compliments" by students, Van Meter and Nusspickle received equal credit in the eyes of most for this "reversal." After all, as athletic director, Van Meter originally hired Nusspickle and set the high standards that allowed the athletic programs to succeed. Nusspickle supplied the spirit.

Both men are in the I.C. sports Hall of Fame, and the Blueboys football field was dedicated to both men over a decade ago. Each went on from I.C. to very important careers: Nusspickle to Illinois in the coaching profession and Van Meter to a federal judge post in Washington, D.C. They never lost touch. Today, plaques with engraved images of each reside side-by-side at the entrance to the Blueboy gridiron.

The athletic success, those wins in the "arena of play" as Nusspickle called it, was only part of the story, however. Indeed, the Nusspickles had a life outside of the arena as well.

They called him "Butch" Nusspickle at Illinois College. "Butch" was a name he got because he called everyone else "Butch." Of course, the reason he called everyone else "Butch" was because he could not remember their real names. Later at the U. of I. he called everyone "Coach." Same reasons.

"Next thing you knew in Champaign everyone was calling each other 'Coach,'" said Charles Bellatti, who became Sports Information Director at the University during Nusspickle's (Eliot's) tenure there. "And it all started because Ray couldn't remember anyone's name."

When first starting out, few couples are financially well off, and "Butch" and Maggie Nusspickle were in the same boat. Their first home at Illinois College was an apartment on campus above the old wooden Club House on Mound Avenue. Nusspickle's starting pay at I.C. was about $800 per year. Maggie had worked for a couple of years in the zoology department at the University of Illinois, but, with the hope that they would soon start a family, she did not work in Jacksonville.

The Nusspickles had to be a no-frills family, and I.C. athletics was a no-frills department. Nusspickle, in an old truck with a rusty bedspring trailing behind, dragged his own baseball infield, in addition to lining his own gridiron.

His coaching ingenuity even revealed itself in this regard, when late one autumn there was nothing but snow covering the football field. Charles Bellatti tells the story: "Ray decided that we should line the white field in black," Bellatti recalled. "We went to his house and got buckets full of coal dust and shoveled off where the lines were to be and lined the field with black coal dust. The lines didn't last too long, but we did beat Parsons (College) that day."

Nusspickle and Illinois College's thriftiness could also be seen when the coach began his career wearing his old Fighting Illini baseball uniform for both baseball and football.

Comical as that may have been to see a football coach in an old baseball uniform, Nusspickle wasted no time in gaining the respect of his athletes. Practices were tough—often Nusspickle would scrimmage the squad hard at Russell Field and then have them run up the long hill to the college campus—but his players "would do anything Butch asked them to do," said former Nusspickle assistant coach Ernst C. Bone to the *Jacksonville Daily Journal*. Said former player Jack Hartong to the same paper, "His own enthusiasm instilled the will to win in everyone he coached." And Forrest W. England, who played for Nusspickle at Illinois College and later was the Jacksonville High School coach, told the *Journal*: "He's my ideal of a coach . . . all the players and everyone that knew him liked him. I never knew anyone to criticize his work; not even the players that didn't have the ability to make his teams."

"Really," says John Doyle, a student manager on Nusspickle's baseball teams, "he was a coach that treated everyone the same from the least to the greatest."

The coach never hesitated to get involved with his players on and off the field. It was not uncommon for him to suit up, pads and all, and jump right into a football scrimmage himself when he had too few athletes.

In the same way, off the field, unmoneyed as they may have been, the Nusspickles' hospitality, which would become famous later in Champaign, was nothing short of astonishing. The coach and his wife had an open-door policy for anyone, especially any student.

Ira Clark, in those days a catcher for the Blueboys, experienced their kindness firsthand when the Nusspickles took him in to live with them when he first came to I.C. and had no place of his own.

One of the things for which Nusspickle always seemed to have time and money was taking a friend to the movies.

"He loved the movies," Clark recalls. "I can't tell you how many times he would spontaneously come up to me or another friend or athlete and pay our way into the movies. It was only a dime, but it was one of his ways of showing that he cared."

"He was a legend," says another of his athletes, Sam Pinson. "He was a legend because he would do anything to help anybody."

Not only did the Nusspickles open the door of their little apartment, but they got deeply involved in the campus and the community. They were one of the most popular couples at I.C., and were constantly in demand for chaperoning dances. They were also the sponsors of the Class of 1934, and gave abundant time to community projects.

In addition to his duties as coach and physical education instructor (where he won the esteem of the rest of the faculty because of his high standards in the classroom), Nusspickle began a "Coaches' Club" at I.C. to help prepare those interested in the coaching profession. The club would meet regularly to discuss different elements of coaching, and students would be given actual hands-on coaching experience.

From Kiwanis to Rotary to church groups and athletic banquets, Nusspickle spoke to any group in the community that asked. Toward the end of his stay in Jacksonville, he even began his own radio show called "News Behind the Sports Curtain." It was one of the most listened-to features of the newly-inaugurated Jacksonville studio of Springfield radio station WCVS. Maggie Nusspickle, however, was perceived by some as having a little bit more of a difficult time than her husband in their new surroundings.

"You have to understand that here is this New York girl coming out to the Midwest and getting thrust into a position and environment that she wasn't used to," says Clark. "It took a little time, but she warmed up."

Another possible explanation to Maggie's initial standoffishness may be that the years subsequent to their coming to Jacksonville were personally tragic. At the age of 61, in the year 1931, Maggie's father had passed away. The very next year she lost her mother. The impact of losing a parent can only be known by those who have been through it, but to lose both parents in such a short span of time, just a few short years after losing her beloved sister, was almost too much even for a strong woman like Maggie. On the heels of these terrible circumstances came the upheaval and move to Jacksonville. Ray and Maggie shared some very intimate hours during those years, and she adjusted.

Time may heal all wounds, but sometimes God has something even better in mind. No sooner had Maggie come back from the East Coast, where she went to bury her mother, than she found out she was going to have a baby. On March 1, 1933, just before Nusspickle would inaugurate his baseball career in Jacksonville with that first conference championship, Jane Child Nusspickle was born. She arrived at Our Saviour's Hospital in Jacksonville at 4:30 in the morning, weighing in at a hefty 10 pounds, 11 ounces. In the coming years, Ray and Maggie would try to have another child but suffered through more than one miscarriage. Thus, Jane would be the Nusspickles' only child and she would ever be the apple of her daddy's eye. After the final miscarriage, Ray comforted his wife by saying, "We have Jane and that's good enough for me."

Mom and Dad called her "Queenie." Queenie was taken everywhere, including at times to her father's classes. "She was a great excuse not to study," remembers Clark. She was also the reason Ray Eliot Nusspickle changed his name, or more accurately, dropped his last name and assumed his middle name as his last.

"In a little while you'll be Mrs. Nusspickle," Van Johnson tells Judy Garland of the mystery man she expects to soon wed in the movie "In the Good Old Summertime."

"Nusspickle!?" Garland gasps.

"Well, that's his name, isn't it? That's what he told me."

"Nusspickle...yes..."

"He's a nice fellow. I congratulate you."

"Why . . . thank you," Garland stammers, her eyes and voice trailing off together in fear and dread.

"You're a very lucky girl."

Judy Garland was not the first future Mrs. Nusspickle to be aghast at the name. When Maggie and Ray were engaged, Maggie tried to unofficially trim the name to Nusspick, thinking even that was better than the original. It didn't stick, however, and she had to grin and bear it, at least for awhile.

Doc Greene of *The Detroit News* once wrote that Ray "overcame the name before he changed it." Proof of that is how he was able to take the teasings and ribbings in stride.

The name Nusspickle was ripe for picking on and it had been, even to the point that Nusspickle good-naturedly accepted being named to a college football "best name All-American team" four years running when he played at the University of Illinois. There is even a question in the game Trivial Pursuit involving the original last name of Ray Eliot.

A publicist named L.M. Tobin tried everything to dissuade the coach from making the change: "Eliot, Eliot," protested Tobin teasingly. "There are millions of Eliots. Anyone can have a name like Eliot and lots of them do. But Nusspickle? Run that over your banjo, will you? You'll be the only Nusspickle in the history of coaching. What a name to publicize! Think of the headlines! 'Nusspickle in a Pickle.' 'Nusspickle Ponders Problems.' It's a publicity man's dream. Ray, you wouldn't do this to me!"

Actually, he would joke later that he changed his name to Eliot for the press because "it fit better in the headlines." Whether some media would be happy or some sad, the reasons for the change were much more serious. He had contemplated it for a long time.

"When Queenie was three or four he (Ray) came to me and confided that he wanted to change his name from Nusspickle to Eliot and asked me what I thought," Ira Clark related. "'Well', I said, 'Coach, you've been known as Nusspickle and are thought of as a successful coach by that name. Changing it now might not be a good idea.' I asked him why he wanted to do it.

"He said it was because of his little girl. He didn't want that name to hang like a millstone around her neck. He knew the jokes that were made about him, and he did not want to see the same thing happen to her as she grew up."

He changed his name at the end of his stay in Jacksonville. He came to Illinois College as Ray Nusspickle and left as Ray Eliot.

Some say that when God shuts a door He opens a window, and it is strange how fate sometimes works things out even in the face of initial disappointment.

In 1935 the job of head football coach came open at Cornell University. Nusspickle aggressively applied, even to the point of having "in his mind's eye the boys he would like to take along with him as assistants," reported Ernest Savage of the Jacksonville *Daily Journal*. Nusspickle wanted to be a head coach at a major college someday, and the salary of nearly $5,000 per year appealed to him as well. Newspaper reports indicated he was close to landing that job, but, alas, it went to somebody else.

Cornell's loss was the eventual gain of the University of Illinois at Champaign-Urbana. Two years later, Nusspickle's old mentor at Illinois, Bob Zuppke, needed a coach to assist head line coach Justa Lindgren. Seeing this as a great opportunity to return to his alma mater, where he said he "knew the ropes and most of the coaches," he once again pursued it vigorously. Though he would have to take a pay cut to go, the realization that the job would be a great learning opportunity and a step to a possible head coaching position at a larger university made his enthusiasm that much greater.

As well liked as he was in Champaign, and even with the great success he had had in everything he had tried at Illinois College, he was no shoo-in. As a matter of fact, he was the third choice for the job.

First choice was the former head coach of the Iowa Hawkeyes, Burt Ingwerson, who had been an Illini letterman from 1917-19 under Zuppke and was, at the time, line coach at Northwestern. Obviously Zup was looking for experience first, but Ingwerson turned him down to stay in Evanston.

Still looking for major college line experience, Zuppke offered the job to a line coach from Duke. He, too, turned down the position. So, though not the seasoned veteran that he was looking for, Zup turned to Nusspickle and offered him the job.

On paper the decision for the young coach was academic. But Nusspickle's decision to seek and then accept the position at Illinois caused a tearing in his emotions and in the emotions of the well-wishers that would bid him farewell.

A mass meeting was called in I.C.'s Jones Chapel in the spring of 1937 to say good-bye to the Blueboy coach and teacher. The *Daily Journal* said the get-together was a "pep meeting that featured yells and songs, (with) the Illinois College men's octet (singing) for the group."

Athletic Director LaRue Van Meter presided over the gathering, which, in addition to the afore-mentioned pomp, consisted of short talks by representative members of Illinois College personnel. Judge James M. Barnes opened the program representing the fans in Jacksonville. Tom Kline the co-captain of the

1937 baseball squad followed and he by Professor H.Q. Fuller speaking for the faculty. No doubt Illinois College President H.C. Jaquith spoke for everyone when he said in his speech: "The only thing we can give you that you can keep always is the eternal friendship you have built up with every member of this campus group."

With that final word, Nusspickle, friend and mentor rose to speak. As the guest of honor took the podium, the emotions in each extreme tore like a cotton sheet. "There isn't a student on the I.C. campus who won't celebrate his advancement," Ernest Savage had written, "although it will mean an almost irreparable loss to the college." Indeed the "celebration" and the "irreparable loss" were both felt that night.

In his years at Illinois College, every time Nusspickle spoke people leaned forward on their chairs to listen. Never more so than now did they bend an ear to hear this man who had meant so much in such a short time to all of Jacksonville.

"It has been a pleasure to work in an institution that has been so capably directed by a person of the caliber of President H.C. Jaquith," he began. "His clear vision, his sincere cooperation, and his able guidance have been of the same inestimable aid in my department as they have been in all other divisions of the school.

"My emotions have been a mixture. When my wife and I received the final word about the appointment, we didn't know whether to be happy or sad. The spirit of friendliness here at the college has been overwhelming. The sorrow of leaving at this moment overshadows the happiness in receiving a promotion."

A few years later, when Ray Eliot was to receive the head coaching position at the University of Illinois, the *Jacksonville Daily Journal* had this to say about their "Butch" Nusspickle:

"Men out for football at Illinois College tried valiantly to work as hard as (Nusspickle) did, but they never quite made it.

"He was at home on a muddy gridiron at a practice session which lasted until the lights at Baxter Hall were turned on. He was the master of the situation in the gymnasium—before the game and at halftime, as well. He could take defeat or victory with an air which marks a champion.

"In the classroom, he was thorough and insistent on a high standard of learning. He had the respect of the most conservative faculty members. When he took the platform at chapel—it was time to listen. And on campus he was strictly a human being, playing no athletic favorites and taking a genuine interest in the entire student body.

"In the brief years he was at Illinois College, he carved out a record which has become a legend—part of which was a definite belief that here was a man who someday would be tops in the coaching profession."

7

Minnesota

"And when I walk onto that field, why . . .
I guess there's no time that I feel closer to God.
My soul is wide open to the world."

—Ray Eliot

A few quiet conversations and a nervous joke or two laid a background to the silence. Athletes, clad in full uniforms and pads, sat pensively on the hardwood benches in the meeting room adjacent to the Illinois locker room. Alex Agase rocked back and forth slowly, rubbing his hands and fingers together. Jimmy Smith picked intently at the peeling paint on the bench under him, and Art Dufelmeier paced the floor. Finally, head coach Ray Eliot walked in.

In the locker room across the way sat the Minnesota Golden Gophers. It was October of 1942, and while Illinois had not won a Big 9 game since 1939, the Gophers had not lost one and were the two-time defending national champions. In most people's book the two teams had no business being on the same field together.

Eliot made his way to the front of his team dressed in a dapper brown suit coat and slacks, his wide-brimmed hat held in his hands in front of him. Whispering and fidgeting stopped and every athlete stared at his mentor. Eliot paused and looked them in the eye. The X's and O's stood still on the chalkboard behind him.

"Anything you think you can do, you can do," he began quietly. "Anything you think you can do, you can do," he repeated.

The night before at the Champaign Country Club, Eliot related the story of Illinois' great upset over Michigan in 1939, a tale that most of the players had never heard before. He spoke of an opportunity that lay before them and of the payoff for sacrifice, hard work, and belief in oneself. He reminded them that it was "not how big you are, but how big you play."

"We were inspired to a man," says Alex Agase today. "He had grown men crying as only he could do."

Now, moments before the great battle, he said, "You are human beings playing human beings. You are not playing gods today, gentlemen. They'll make mistakes. The team that makes the least amount of mistakes will win."

These men, these Fighting Illini, clung to every word and watched Eliot's every move. They believed him.

"It was really impressive," says Mike Kasap, another starter on this underdog Illini football team. "We were fired up. We could have walked right out the side of the damned stadium, we were so fired up."

Dike Eddleman, a member of the 1947 Illini Rose Bowl team, says that he would always stand in the back when Eliot rolled into his pep talks. "I didn't want to get stampeded when all of these big guys got fired up and went charging out the door."

A warm, confident glow burned in Eliot's heart that cool autumn afternoon. And 24,276 Homecoming fans waited anxiously to see what this young man and his Fighting Illini were made of . . .

The only way Eliot knew how to live was with all of his irons in the fire. That was true in Jacksonville, so too in Champaign-Urbana.

While the thirty-two year old was hired by Zuppke as an assistant to Lindgren and by the University as a Physical Education instructor, he also became an assistant on the baseball diamond, where he was instrumental in bringing future major league hall of famer Lou Boudreau to Illinois.

In addition, Eliot, in his first year back at Illinois, formed the first Illini hockey team. Hockey was so unknown to the Illinois campus in the winter of 1937 and 1938 that newspapers had to run complete exposes on the rules of the game as explained by Eliot.

Nearly one hundred prospective hockey players showed up at George Huff Gym in December of 1937 for a get-acquainted session. It was an opportunity for Eliot to find out what kind of experience his candidates had and give them a chance to get to know him. The *Daily Illini* reported that Eliot was satisfied with the turnout but expected "many more boys" to report later.

Over the Christmas holidays, the tennis courts west of the library were flooded and frozen for practice. Workouts began on the ice the day after vacation, but on days when it was too warm to have a good surface Eliot would lecture in Huff Gym. Through the month of January he pared his large numbers down to his varsity fifteen.

On February 21st, 1938, the Fighting Illini took to the ice for the first time, hosting the Fighting Irish of Notre Dame. Floyd Neckrosh and Dick Fee of Chicago, Dick Babbitt of Riverside, Johnny White of Monticello and Tiger Kusz made up the Illini starters in front of Chicago's Jim Beaumont in goal. Three periods and, as Perry Blain of the *Daily Illini* put it "two rousing fights" later, the Irish skated off with a 2-1 victory, but not before this new sport had lit a fire under the 1,200 spectators that packed the university's ice rink.

"To say they were nuts about (the game) is underestimating to the nth degree," Blain reported. "The game became so popular with the fans who witnessed it last night, that there probably was not a person there who wouldn't have rather been seeing that game than a basketball game."

As for the Illini, Blain was impressed.

"Illinois has a good team," he wrote. "Coach Ray Eliot has brought his men a long distance in this first year of the sport. He deserves a hand for putting a scrapping, hard driving, rough riding bunch of pucksters out on the ice to represent Illinois. It is a typical Fighting Illini team."

Of course, as much as Eliot liked baseball and hockey, football was his future. He took to his job as an assistant with as much gusto and energy as he had his positions at Illinois College. At I.C. he had learned from innovative and experienced coaches like Bradley's A.J. Robertson and William McAndrew of Southern Illinois. But now he would get the opportunity to be tutored further by one of the most respected head coaches in the country, Bob Zuppke.

Unfortunately, Eliot walked into a tumultuous situation when he came on board in the fall of 1937, as Zuppke's success on the field and popularity with some alumni and "the brass" was on the wane. The last truly great season that the Illini had had was in 1934 when they finished 7-1 and were second in the Western Conference. The decline was largely because Bob Zuppke still refused to recruit or give scholarships. Since the offers were better, many quality football players took their services elsewhere.

In Eliot's first year as an assistant, the Illini finished 3-3-2 and patience continued to grow thin. As the 1938 season approached, Athletic Director Wendell Wilson and others tried to pressure Zup to resign. This he refused initially. But by November of that year, after the Illini had concluded a 3-5 campaign, Zuppke gave in. The athletic board, chaired by Professor Fred Russell, accepted Zuppke's letter of resignation. All of this jockeying for position went on completely unbeknownst to the University's Board of Trustees, however. They swiftly rejected the resignation by an 8-1 vote after an emotional speech delivered in defense of Zuppke by Harold Pogue, who was an All-American halfback for Zup's 1914 Illini and was now a trustee.

Zuppke was back in the saddle, but success in the board room did not translate to success on the field. Illinois would not have another winning season under Zup, and his last two years would end with a combined 3-13 record.

The year 1938 was difficult for Bob Zuppke off the field and out of the board rooms as well. In the spring, his younger brother Herman was killed when he was struck by a car in St. Paul, Minnesota. This was the last of a string of personal tragedies for the coach over a short time. Just before the 1936 football season began, Zup lost Fanny, his beloved wife of 29 years. Weeks later, Illinois Athletic Director George Huff died too. Huff had hired Zuppke 23 years earlier, and the two became very close, both professionally and personally.

When times are tough on the head man he must have those he can count on to help shoulder the load. Eliot had shown himself worthy in this regard, and Zup was impressed with this young man. When Zuppke's brother died and he had to leave spring drills for a week or so, he showed the confidence he had in his assistants by leaving the team in the hands of Ray Eliot and Justa Lindgren.

There may not have been a lot of victories on the football field during those years that Eliot assisted his old coach, but there were some highlights. One that especially stands out Eliot used to rivet his listeners during speeches later:

"It brings me back to 1939," he would begin, "when a little band of kids at Illinois had to meet the most powerful juggernaut in the nation. And I am referring to the University of Michigan team that had five All-Americans on it. The year before they had won the national championship, and here they are coming now, the same group of men . . . oh what a powerful bunch of men!

"At Illinois we had no All-Americans. We were a bunch of babies. We had one good leader, a kid named (Mel) Brewer—a real fine football player.

"What had Michigan done? In their first four games they beat Michigan State by a big score; in their second game they beat a great Iowa team, the only game Iowa lost that year, by a big score. Then they went on and beat Chicago by 85 points and they beat the 'Toast of the East,' Yale, by a big score.

"What did we do in our first four games? Well sir, in the first game we tied Bradley nothing to nothing, in the second game we lost to Southern Cal by a big score, the third game we lost to Indiana by a big score, in the fourth game we lost to Wisconsin by a big score. And to make matters even worse, the Monday of the week we were going to have to play this Michigan team we lost the services of our Captain Brewer, our inspiration, our leader, who was called home because of the death of his mother. Gentlemen, he had just lost God's most precious gift to man—his mom. He went on home.

"It was our custom in those days to take the boys to the Champaign Country Club before all home games, where we could feed them and house them and Coach Zuppke would talk to them. It was a custom to meet at about 8 o'clock with the boys. And I'd like to bring you into that room for a moment because the boys were all sitting around in their wicker chairs, no lights on in the room, just the light from the fireplace casting its flickering rays across the face of the boys. (Zup) was talking about the reminders of the next day, when all of a sudden the door opened in the corner of the room and Captain Brewer came in and sat down on the floor. When Zup saw who it was he went over to him and offered that boy beautiful fatherly condolences. He turned to go back to the platform but he never reached there because there was a rustle in the corner of the room and Captain Brewer stood up. And in a voice that could be described as trembling and tearful he said, 'Fellas, my sister and my daddy join me in saying many thanks to you for your beautiful flowers and telegrams.' And then his voice almost became rasping when he said, 'I didn't travel this 250 miles for nothing. If you feel the way I do right now we'll go out and beat the hell out of Michigan tomorrow!' He sat down and the boys turned to the front of the room and I wish you could have seen it, I wish you could have been in that room! Electricity. You could have cut it! The feeling in there ... tears coming from the eyes of these boys. Zup saw that anything he would say from then on was anticlimactic and he stopped and said, 'Dismissed.'

"And when it's usually hard to get these boys to bed at ten o'clock, every boy was in his bunk at five minutes after nine and nobody asked them to be there. When I walked down the long line of cots I couldn't believe myself—no pillow fights, no kidding, nothing going on—just kids staring at a ceiling or laying on their fronts. And as I approached the light switch they said, 'Good night coach.' I turned around and I went on home. I knew something had to happen.

"We came back the next day. We went in the dressing room and we dressed. We went on the football field and loosened up. We came back in and something happened in that dressing room that I had never seen before in a dressing room. When Coach Zuppke called off each starter in the game, everyone else in the room came to his feet and gave that guy a tremendous ovation and charged him with his responsibilities of the day.

"I was the last one to say good-bye to the eleven starters. And usually they come by and say 'don't worry we'll take care of it,' and they didn't say a word—they went by.

"You know the rest of the story. That afternoon one of the greatest upsets in the history of the Big 10 took place when a little band of Fighting Illini beat the finest team in America 19-6! And the guy who started us off kicking three points through the bars, who had never kicked a field goal in his life, was Brewer when it came to that fourth and nine down there on the eighteen yardline— he put it through to start us off. Tom Harmon (the starting Michigan tailback) has told me many times he never was hit so hard and so often in his life as he was that afternoon: 'I played pro ball, I've played Big 10 football, I've played everywhere, and I've never been hit so hard in my life.' He did this, you know—he averaged 165 yards a game before he came to Champaign. That afternoon he walked out of the stadium minus nineteen yards."

A great and powerful speaker Eliot was, a historian he was not. If the reader is picky, he should note that the Illini had not lost by quite the margins in their first four games as Eliot implied. They did tie Bradley and lost to Southern Cal 26-0, but they lost to Indiana 7-6 and the fourth team was not Wisconsin but Northwestern, who beat them 13-0. The final score of the Michigan game was also 16-7 not 19-6, but his point was made, and the writer is not picky.

Grateful for those flashes of team brilliance in tough times, Eliot took mental notes and his popularity continued to grow with Zuppke, the players, fans, and alumni. Zup learned to appreciate more and more his football sense (he became Zup's "First Lieutenant" on the coaching staff his last year), the athletes liked his ability to communicate with and motivate them and he was becoming more and more a hot ticket on the speaking circuit across the state.

Opportunities came knocking for the young coach to move on from Illinois but, when it came time to make a decision, Eliot always concluded that he preferred to work for Zup.

Meanwhile, things had not gotten better between Zuppke and the administration. After taking a leave of absence from his athletic director post in 1940, Wendell Wilson and the University Board of Trustees had a mutual parting of the ways in the summer of 1941. That was an apparent victory for Zup, but as Wilson left, the board gave the coach only a one-year contract. In addition, fans remained on Zup's back and his power struggle with the former athletic director and others had taken its toll. Finally, five days before the last game of 1941, Zup called it quits. He had wanted to coach until he was at least 65 years old, and he had.

Reporters and photographers from all over the country came to record, and 35,000 fans came to witness the final curtain drawn on what still stands today as one of the greatest coaching treks in the history of college football. On his last day, Northwestern shut out Illinois 27-0. A legend was gone, an era ended.

The day Zuppke resigned, Doug Mills, who was made interim athletic director when Wilson left, was given the post permanently. Immediately the search was on for the first new head football coach at the University of Illinois in almost 30 years. There was a lot of alumni and student pressure to search the United States for a proven coaching genius, no matter the cost. In response, Mills, with the athletic committee of the Board of Trustees, scoured the countryside.

There were a lot of suitors. Burt Ingwersen, after turning down Zup for the position Eliot got in 1937, wanted it. So did Carl Marvin Voyles of William and Mary, and Jimmy Phelan, the former Washington mentor. All three were seasoned, top-notch coaches of their day.

Some at Illinois had another idea, however. Within a week of Zuppke's resignation, a delegation of Illini players confronted Chet Davis, chairman of the athletic committee. Led by lettermen Jim McCarthy and Ken Cheeley, they told Davis that the players to a man wanted Eliot.

"We campaigned for him anywhere and everywhere," says Alex Agase. The board's response to the players was quite chilly except for one trustee, Jim Cleary, who wanted Eliot from the beginning. He didn't know the young coach at all, but, if nothing else, Eliot was an Illinois man.

There was another force at work for Eliot, too. Justa Lindgren, who was not only a longstanding line coach at Illinois but also a highly respected member of the University's chemistry department, had begun an unofficial campaign for Eliot at the Illini Club banquet held in Chicago after the final game against Northwestern. During the long search for a coach, he had been heard often to say, "This Eliot fellow is one of the great young coaches in the country. He is the logical choice to succeed Zuppke."

"I never got my hopes up too much," said Eliot later. "I'll tell you though, I wanted that job as much as I ever wanted anything."

In mid-January the board had narrowed the choice to three—Ingwerson was one, along with Phelan and Eliot. After 72 days of restless anticipation, on Tuesday, January 27, 1942, the answer came. Eliot was working in his Huff Gym office at 10 o'clock in the morning. The athletic association board and Athletic Director Mills were meeting at that moment, and Eliot knew that a decision was imminent.

Suddenly there was a push at his office door and a secretary asked Eliot if he would please step down to Mills' office. Palms damp with nervous sweat, Eliot got up from his desk and walked through the doorway. Heart pounding, his eyes greeted a number of Illini players lining the hallway also awaiting the pending decision. The coach took hold of the doorknob of Mills' office, took a deep breath, and entered. He who had, in the end, recommended Eliot's hiring to the board would now give him the news. With a shake of Eliot's clammy hand Mills said, "Congratulations, Ray, the job is yours."

"With six words Doug sent me into a new life," Eliot said later. "I was thrilled at his utterance."

He wasn't the only one. Before Eliot could react, players, *his* players now, streamed into the athletic director's office in a tumult of celebration.

"Eliot was as serious as he could be under the circum-stances," wrote Eddie Jones of the *Evening Courier*. "He tried to play the part of the head coach and several times attempted to outline plans for spring practice."

But the players would have none of it. They hoisted their new head coach on their shoulders. "I forgot to grab my coat," Eliot recalled laughing. "So I was dragged halfway around the campus in the middle of winter in my shirt sleeves."

The players finally brought their coach back to his office, but were not finished with him quite yet.

"The players wrestled him around the room," continued Jones. "It was several minutes before he broke the boy's hold around his neck."

"We'll win 'em now!" exclaimed Joe Pawlowski, an Illini guard.

"This is just what the players wanted," Jimmy Smith, the Illini captain, was exuberant. "We've been for him one hundred percent. He's one of us. From here on we'll not concede a thing to any team."

All of this, and Eliot had not even been able to call his wife and daughter yet to tell them the good news. When he finally phoned, Maggie was doing house work. Three hours later, with the hub-bub growing, she said she was "still trying to get the beds made."

"The excitement is terrific," Maggie told the *Courier*. "But I enjoy it. I am so happy for Ray."

Others were just as excited about the selection, including

Bob Zuppke, who was having his automobile tires checked when the news was delivered to him.

"I'm thrilled," he said as he tugged his coat collar closed against the January wind. "Eliot's appointment is a very good and logical choice. He's the best young coach I've been associated with and the most loyal fellow I've ever known. He is a hard worker, a student of the game, enthusiastic and popular with the boys. The board couldn't have made a better choice."

One member of the community who was happy to give a comment to the local papers was one of Eliot's old bosses in college, Frank Robeson.

"Ray Eliot is one of the most capable boys I ever saw," he said. "He worked for us in a managerial capacity and did an excellent job. He's absolutely tops. Unless I miss my guess, he'll make an excellent coach. He has a big viewpoint. He sees the whole picture. He has tremendous energy and intelligence with it. I think he may be one of the best coaches in the country."

Royal Stipes Jr., president of the Champaign Chamber of Commerce went to school with Eliot: "(Eliot) has always been known as a hard-working boy," he was quoted as saying. "I hope this appointment, along with that of Dr. Mills, will serve to give impetus to a revived Illinois athletic program. I feel that every citizen of the state, and particularly alumni, should get behind these two men."

Eliot did not have to look far over his shoulder to find people behind him. His friends at Illinois College in Jacksonville were elated.

"That's the best news I've had since the war started," said Alf Lamb, who took over the Blueboys football, baseball, and swimming programs when Eliot went to Illinois. "If his players work as hard and are as sincere in their efforts as Butch is—and they will be, because his enthusiasm is contagious—Illinois will enjoy a new era of success in football."

In a telegram to Eliot, Lamb said: "Congratulations. This lump in my throat feels good. Best wishes. Lamby."

Professor of Mathematics, Dr. Earle B. Miller said, "His friends here in Jacksonville know the handicaps he overcame to achieve the success he has won. Surely the story of his success seems almost a fairy story to his friends here, and will be an inspiration to those who come under his direction in the future."

Orville Freeman, a Jacksonville attorney, understood the enthusiasm the players displayed for their new head coach. "Ray's experience working with young men and his universal friendship with boys with whom he has worked indicate that he has the makings of a real coach. His record as a coach indicates to me that the university made no mistake in his selection."

Still, in some corners, Eliot's hiring was received indifferently and even a bit coolly. "Who's Eliot?" some wondered. The *Jacksonville Daily Journal* blamed their confusion, in part, on his name change almost five years before.

After Eliot was able to calm his office enough to talk, he exhorted his players, "We've got a lot of work to do, boys. And we're not going to waste any time."

Terming his appointment "the best thing that ever happened to me," Eliot told reporters, "Of course I am happy to have my great ambition realized. I realize the heavy responsibilities the job entails, but I am confident, with the cooperation of all, we can build up Illinois football."

To the *Daily Journal* he said, "We will start right away to get things in shape for next fall. We have a great bunch of kids who love to play football, and it's going to be our job to mold them into a real team."

Later that night in the relative quiet of his home, with several journalists copiously copying his every word, he said quietly, "I don't know how I'll do in the big time as a coach. But I do know that my teams will want to win. That's my first coaching credo—to instill the will to win in every player. I know I can do it, too. Sometimes that won't be enough to take a title, but it'll be enough to cause lots of teams plenty of trouble."

In a week, Eliot returned to the Illinois College campus to be a part of "one of the biggest sports celebrations Illinois College has ever had," said the *Journal*. The first part was a banquet honoring Eliot, and the second was a benefit basketball game between the Blueboys and basketball power Chanute Field, proceeds to go to a special fund for the improvement of the I.C. baseball field.

Eliot arrived about 4:30 on a sunny Wednesday afternoon, February 4th, and the banquet began at six at Baxter Hall. Ernest Savage, the former sports editor of the *Journal*, was the toastmaster, and he presented Eliot to the guests.

"I've been just as thrilled this evening as when I stopped into Doug Mills' office last week and heard I was the new University of Illinois football coach," the *Journal* quoted Eliot. "I am so very grateful to Illinois College and the fine start it gave me. We had our ups and downs here—thrills, pleasures, and heartaches but," he said, setting his gaze on the students, "I assure you, that you have to have an opportunity to come back as I have come back tonight to appreciate how fortunate you are to be at Illinois College and to be associated with the people of Jacksonville. To be greeted by the men here who are so dear to me—it's tremendous. I'm deeply grateful from the bottom of my heart. It's great to call you friends. Thanks for everything you've done for me."

As for his promotion, he told the crowd, "When I heard the news I sat there amazed myself. Other than that, I can't remember anything that happened and what was said to me about terms, contract, and everything. I had to read all about it in the newspapers the next morning.

"To try to predict anything for the future is ridiculous," the coach said, turning his attention to his Illini. "There won't be any miracles, but we'll do our darnedest to win. We're in a tough league. It's a hard task, but I don't care how hard it gets—we'll do it somehow."

With that, everyone from the banquet headed over to the School for the Deaf gym for the benefit game. The Blueboys were beaten after giving a good struggle, but that loss took nothing away from the evening. At halftime, John Hackett, a Jacksonville businessman and former I.C. gridder, presented Eliot to the crowd and a group of Jacksonville fans gave the former Blueboy coach an all-weather wrist watch. "Butch" addressed the crowd and called his brief visit there "a real homecoming." The game, by the way, raised $350.

In all of the excitement and rush of well-wishers and stirred emotions, the largeness of the task in front of Eliot was not lost on him.

"In his quiet moments," wrote Lon Eubanks in his book *The Fighting Illini*, ". . . he and his wife would talk about the mind-bending pace of the new job. And he would admit, in those private, intimate conversations that a man shares only with the person closest to him, that he could almost feel the shadow of Zuppke's success hovering over him."

Some would reel under that kind of pressure, but not the future "Mr. Illini." The 35-year-old Eliot signed a one-year contract for $6,000, the same salary as Athletic Director Mills. He was determined to earn every penny of it right from the get-go, too. First and foremost were his boys.

"He immediately began to maneuver around," says Mike Kasap. "He had all of the players come in to see him."

Eliot had more than just an initial visit in mind.

"We had most of our classes around Huff Gym," Kasap says. "He told us that anytime we wanted we could come see him. And if he would catch us in the halls, he would invite us in. We'd sit down and he would talk to us about spring practice and where we would fit in. He kept us occupied for sometimes an hour at a time. We'd sit in there and just talk. He had an open-door policy I'll never forget."

As it was at Illinois College, this "open-door policy" was the foundation of Eliot's coaching style. In season and out, the conversations were often, as often as players wanted them to be, and informal.

There, of course, was never any question who was boss on Eliot's football teams ("Sure, I run my ballclubs in a democratic fashion," he would say. "We vote and sometimes I win 1-8."). But it is easier to listen to and obey a man whom you know loves you and relates to you as a person. As a matter of fact, most players never called Eliot "Mr." or "Coach," but "Ray." He was their mentor and he had a high standard of discipline to be certain, but he was their friend, too. To Eliot, "the boy was more important than the game."

Said Eliot to Lon Eubanks, "I liked to meet my players in my office or in their dormitory or fraternity and talk to them away from the practice atmosphere. I always tried to relate to them on a personal basis. If they were married, and they had marital problems, I tried to be a little bit of a marriage counselor. If they had grade problems, I tried to be a little bit of an academic counselor. I was their father confessor. And if it wasn't me, it was one of my assistants.

"Football is, above all else, an educational agency," he went on. "I think a coach has to have a closeness to his players, and I'm afraid a lot of today's coaches have gone downhill in that regard. I think too many head coaches in the country now are too aloof from their players. They think of themselves, their prestige, their television and radio contracts, where can they go to make more money. But the boy is still the most important part of any coach's job. I always felt I did a better job of coaching off the field than on it."

Former Illini player Micky Bates stated that, "Ray Eliot had what so many coaches do not have today—that interplay or tight relationship between the coach and the player. He wanted his guys to be achievers, not just football players and he was always willing to listen."

Said Jimmy Smith, "He had an intense interest in each of his players." And 1957 graduate Gary Francis stated that, "He made our problems his problems."

Football's immortal Red Grange, who became close friends with Eliot (they shared the same birthday and for over 50 years called each other on that day), summed up what everyone seemed to feel: "He had the qualities I liked in a coach. He was tough and he would go to hell for you."

Before he'd been hired, Eliot had already pondered like-minded men to be a part of his first coaching staff. When he got the job he immediately began bringing them in. He hired fresh blood like Charles Baer, Tony Blazine and Ralph Fletcher. Fletcher served with Eliot all through his tenure and then for Ray's successor, Pete Elliot, until 1963. Leo Johnson had been an assistant for Zuppke in 1937 and came back to join Eliot from 1942 until 1956.

Certainly the key figure to Eliot's staff, however, was the old plowhorse he convinced to remain as the only holdover from Bob Zuppke's band. Justa Lindgren was a Fighting Illini football letter winner four years running, from 1898 through 1901. He had played under George Huff, and began his coaching career at Illinois as one of four head coaches in 1904 along with Arthur Hall, Fred Lowenthal, and Clyde Matthews. When the idea of coaching by committee was abandoned the next year, he assisted, had a stint as the only head man in 1906 and then assumed assistant's duties again under Hall until 1912 and Zup until his retirement. From 1928-31 Lindgren coached Ray Nusspickle, and in 1937 he took a young Ray Eliot under his wing as his assistant. Now, the student was asking the teacher, already in his sixties, to hang on for a little longer to help steady the ship and pass along his vast experience to a new coaching staff. Lindgren agreed and stayed on through the 1943 season.

About 80 varsity candidates came out in the spring, one of the largest turnouts in Illini history. But Eliot had all of his ducks in order by then.

"This is your team—the coaches are only the guides," he told his players on the first day. "From the time you put on your suit until you take it off you ought to be a serious, determined individual. If this squad can improve 100 percent, and I don't think that's asking too much, you're going to tip over a lot of people. We've got a big job to do and some well-rounded practice will help us more than anything else."

He kept things simple to start, employing with a few variations Zuppke's single-wing offense. He used the bulk of his time getting an idea who would be major contributors the following autumn and convincing the boys that they could be winners. The younger players worked very hard because they sensed that they might get a chance to play. By summer, Eliot had a pretty good idea there would be new blood not only on the coaching staff but on the field as well. He kept all of the players confused as to what he was going to do, though, so that they would keep practicing as hard as they could, trying to win a spot.

Sure enough, when Eliot called out the starting lineup before his first game as Illini head football coach, he called out names like Agase and Kasap, Dufelmeier and Tony Butkovich. And he called out the likes of Mac Wenskunas, Frank Bauman, Joe Buscemi and John Genis—underclassmen all.

The youngsters were thrilled and eager to make the most of their coach's confidence. Eliot also had the wisdom to pepper in some experience with third-year offensive back and captain Jimmy Smith, senior end and team most valuable player Elmer Engle and, to help stabilize the line, senior Joe Pawlowski.

The Fighting Illini opened at home in 1942 against South Dakota and there could not have been a more appropriate opponent for Eliot's inaugural game. Eight years earlier the Coyotes had come to take on Eliot's Illinois College Blueboys. Eliot saw that game as an opportunity for his boys to step up to the next level by beating a very good team from a larger school. I.C. was one of the best in the Little 19, but the Coyotes had won their conference and were a new and unknown challenge for the youthful coach and his charges. Eliot enlisted the help of student groups to spread excitement about the pending match and they fired up the Blueboy faithful. The game was played in Spring-field, about 30 miles from Jacksonville, at the high school football field, and I.C. fans came out in droves. Eliot and the Blueboys were confident going in, but in a tough battle, the Coyotes put up the only score of the day in the third quarter and held on to win 7-0. Now the Coyotes came to prove themselves at the expense of a larger school and Eliot could turn the tables.

Later the coach would tell reporters, "my heart was in my throat as I wondered just what in the world the outcome of the game would be." But on September 26, 1942, in front of the home crowd, the Fighting Illini allayed his concerns by handing their coach his first victory at Illinois, blowing out South Dakota 46-0.

The next week Illinois dusted Butler 67-0.

Confidence warmed Eliot's heart and Homecoming the hearts of the Illinois faithful, but the Illini's minds toward the nation's number-one team were cold as steel.

Tony Butkovich predicted a win over Minnesota when he was on the rubdown table in the training room before the game. "If the other fellows feel the way I do right now, and I'm sure they do, we're going to win," his statement drawing on the previous night's inspiring tale of Mel Brewer's return in the Illini upset over Michigan in 1939. "Bet on it. It's a feeling I've never had before with a big game coming up. I wish we were out there right now."

They would be out there soon enough, but the only ones who shared his optimism were his teammates. Champaign fans had seen their team push South Dakota and Butler all over the field. But this was Minnesota. How would the Illini fair against All-Americans like halfback Bill Daley and tackle Dick Wildung?

Speculation aside, Eliot sent the Fighting Illini with a collective shout, roaring onto Zuppke Field with purpose in their minds and victory in their hearts. He said once that that day, the cleats on the cement runway leading from the dressing room to the field "sounded like thunder."

The Illini's thunder turned to a hollow clap for the Gophers in the first quarter though, when Daley struck like lightning. He broke free around end at his own 20 yard line, headed goalward, and was in the end zone before Illini fans could catch their breath. Minnesota led 7-0.

Not to be outdone, however, was a combination named Florek and Agase for the Illini. Minnesota had the ball at their own 39 yard line in the second frame, when Daley swung wide again. This time, linebacker Ray Florek read the play perfectly and drilled the All-American halfback. A split-second later Agase came on the scene, pilfered the ball from a stunned Daley and lugged 38 yards for the score.

"That was the longest 38 yards I ever ran," Agase said after the game. "I saw a good chance to grab the ball when Florek tackled Daley, and I did. The rest was easy. But I didn't wake up until I crossed the goal line."

"He wasn't kidding when he said he didn't know what happened," Don Griffin interrupted. "That's the first thing he said when we caught up with him in the end zone—'What happened?' And you should have seen the look on Daley's face—he had the most amazed look I've ever seen! He didn't know what in the hell happened either."

Unfortunately for the Illini, Jim McCarthy's extra point kick was off, and the Golden Gophers went into the locker room leading 7-6. But the Illini had established themselves as a worthy opponent for this potent Minnesota bunch, and Eliot's boys emerged like sharks smelling blood when they sprung from the locker room for the second half.

In the third quarter, the Illini drove all the way down to the Gopher three yard line. Inside the ten yard line many coaches tend to turn conservative. Not so Ray Eliot. On the next play the Illini lined up in their customary single-wing offense. But this time the snap went directly to the blocking back Florek. He lateraled the ball to Butkovich, who in turn lateraled to Don Griffin, who pranced in for the score. The underdogs led 13-7 as McCarthy's kick was good this time.

The Gophers did not become champions by laying down in tough battles, and, to nobody's surprise, they bounced back in the fourth quarter. This time they did it through the air, as Bob Sandberg gathered in a touchdown pass. It was their turn to miss a crucial extra point, however, and the game was knotted at 13.

Soon Minnesota owned the football again, pinned deep in their own territory. With a tad under four minutes left in the game on a fourth down, the Gophers were going to punt, but a bad snap from center allowed the Illini's John Genis to roar in from the right side and block it. The ball caromed into the endzone and a great scramble ensued as players from both teams chased it down.

In the pile, wrestling after the ball, were the Illini's Agase and Kasap. When the dust settled, the Illini had the ball, the touchdown, and the game.

Needless to say, as the final seconds ticked off the clock, jubilation broke out all over Memorial Stadium. Illini players mobbed each other and ran off celebrating into the locker room. Problem was, their coach was still out on the field. "Go get him!" somebody yelled.

Agase and Butkovich found Eliot and gave him a ride back to the locker room on their shoulders. The coach hadn't been jostled around so much since the players heard about his hiring nine months before.

"It's just too good to be true," Agase told reporters surrounding him by his locker. "I still don't believe it. This is the greatest moment of my life."

Butkovich, who had confidently predicted the victory, had displayed his brashness even further at halftime when he removed his hip pads because he didn't feel like he was being hit hard enough to need them. These he now showed to the writers saying, "What a bunch of farmers those Gophers are."

A shout went up when Florek raised the game ball over his head so that everyone could see it. Said Florek: "I made a dash for it just as the game ended. It was on the ground and a Minnesota player started for it too. I said, 'Get the hell out of here, Bud. This is mine.'"

Everyone started laughing, including a head coach who relished the win, but deflected the glory.

"Do not give me any credit for the victory over Minnesota," he told reporters, shaking his head. One hand ran thoughtfully over his balding scalp and the other held his hat. "The boys, everyone of them on this team, won the game from a championship team which they were given only a slim chance to beat."

The questions kept coming from newspapermen crowding the first-year coach until a final query came from the back of the pack. When the clamor quieted for just a moment, the voice and question came out of nowhere like a cold slap of water: "Are you concerned about an emotional letdown at Iowa next week Ray?" the reporter asked.

8

The Vanishing

"The youngster, the collegian, the boy, the scrub,
who all but burst his lungs and broke his butt
trying to put his team across."

—Grantland Rice

A letdown next week at Iowa was the last thing Eliot wanted to think about now. They had just knocked off one of the great teams in America in Minnesota—now was a time for celebrating.

The Eliots were a pretty unassuming couple. They also were a bit naive went it came to understanding a winning Big 9 coach's popularity. When Ray went home, he and Maggie figured that they would enjoy the evening together with a few friends. If he had taken a cue from the school's symbol, Chief Illiniwek, however, he could have put his ear to the ground and heard the buffalo coming. But the stampede that was to come took he, his bride, and his 10-year-old daughter completely by surprise.

After the game, Maggie cooked a turkey and made some sandwiches. The friends that they had expected came by, but soon people poured in from everywhere. Some were good friends, some people they barely knew or didn't know at all, but they came just the same. In less than an hour, all of the turkey and sandwiches that Maggie had prepared were gone.

"I went like a beggar from door to door in my neighborhood borrowing everything I could," Ray said later.

Congratulatory telegrams formed a mountain in the middle of the living room floor and before the night was over, the Eliots had served at least 500 guests. First-class hosts as they were, they did not complain.

Sunday came a little later for the Eliots, but when the coach awoke, he knew that it was time to tackle the question the reporter had posed after the big win the day before. He knew that his club, sporting a flashy 3-0 record, was indeed due for a letdown, and he knew that he must avoid that at all costs. He got help from a very unexpected source.

There is only so much a coach can do to prepare a team for an upcoming game. It is especially difficult after an emotional win to get them squarely focused on the next opponent. A coach worries about his team dwelling on the big win, being emotionally drained after such an expenditure of mental strength, about overconfidence setting in, especially with a young club like Eliot had. The coach also did not want them looking ahead to the Notre Dame game the following week.

The Illini were flat for the first three quarters against the Hawkeyes, but still managed to hold a 12-7 advantage going into quarter number four. Eliot was quite concerned still, because Iowa had a quarterback named Tom Farmer who had proven himself to be one of the best passers in the league.

Suddenly, though, the Iowa public address announcer's voice boomed through the stadium with the news that Notre Dame had just beaten the Iowa St. Seahawks 28-0. The paying customers at Iowa that day included 3,000 Seahawk cadets stationed in Iowa City, and they were angered that the Iowa fans laughed, applauded and cheered the Seahawk loss.

"There was already no love lost between the Seahawk cadets and the Hawkeyes," said Eliot later. "They were trying to date the same girls and so on. Well, the Iowa fans shouting for Notre Dame made those Seahawk cadets really mad. They were all sitting together in their uniforms and white hats, and, next thing you know, every one of them started cheering for us. It was just the emotional lift we needed in the fourth quarter."

Iowa threatened after that but never could score, and the Illini walked off the field still unbeaten after the 12-7 win. It was the first time since 1934 that Illinois had won four games in a row.

"Coach, we couldn't lose that game," some of the Illini players said to Eliot afterward. "We couldn't let those Seahawks down." The first thing the coach did when he returned to Champaign was sit down and write a thank you letter to the commanding officer of the Seahawks.

Notre Dame had played a small part in the psychological charge that the Illini got in their win at Iowa, but when the Irish came to Memorial Stadium, they would do Illinois no favors. Unlike Minnesota, the boys from South Bend had advance warning about this Fighting Illini football team. They knew that they would be facing a well-prepared and inspired club, and that they would have to be at their best.

Fans of the Illini were anticipating the first truly meaningful game at Memorial Stadium in eight years. They were still not sure if these Illini were for real, but they couldn't wait to taste the pudding and find out. Maggie was excited, too. Toward the end of the week she took a trip to the grocery store and bought enough food for a small army. She did not want to be caught unprepared as she had been after the Minnesota game. Among the spoils were two turkeys, two hams, a barrel of potato salad, various desserts and shrimp—lots of shrimp.

Unfortunately for Illinois, Notre Dame was as prepared as Maggie was. A great battle ensued, and the Illini got the upper hand only four minutes into the game, when Butkovich scampered into the endzone from the Irish 24 yard line on a reverse. Illinois held Notre Dame on their next possession, but then mistakes began to catch up with the young Illini. The Champaign eleven fumbled on their own 20, giving the Irish the ball at point-blank range. It only took them five plays before Corny Clatt dashed in from the five to tie the score.

There was fight in the Fighting Illini, though, and they roared back in quarter number two. Quarterback Dick Good hit Ray Grierson with a 24-yard scoring strike and Illinois led 14-7. But the Irish had a reply. Quarterback Angelo Bertelli poked the ball across the Illini goal line on a one-yard sneak and the game was tied again.

The warriors battled back and forth to a standoff in the third quarter, but by the end of the period, Notre Dame had the ball and was putting together its most impressive drive of the day. It was a drive that would finally end early in the fourth quarter when Jerry Cowhig slammed in from the one-yard line to give the Irish a 21-14 lead that they would not relinquish. Twice Illinois drove inside Notre Dame's 30-yard line in the final minutes, but they couldn't score. Exacerbating the problem for the Illini was an injury to Good that took him out of the game.

Eliot tended to get very melancholy after a loss, and this one was as painful as it got. But the coach mustered enough energy to head home and help his wife prepare for the expected multitudes to descend on their home.

"It was six o'clock, and there was nobody there," Eliot related. "And then it was seven and eight and the doorbell hadn't rung once. I looked at Maggie, she looked at me. We looked at all of that turkey and ham and shrimp. At nine o'clock we said the heck with it, and went out to see a movie."

One week the first couple of Illinois football was naive about their popularity, this week they learned that the inclination to party is much stronger after a win than a loss—even if it is a loss to Notre Dame in a close game.

"At least I won't have to take a trip to the grocer this week," said Maggie, looking at the bright side. Indeed, it would be quite a few turkey, ham, and shrimp sandwiches for the Eliots over the next several weeks.

After having played their first three of four games at home, these young Illini faced three straight games on the road. First was a trip to Ann Arbor, Michigan where the Wolverines dispatched the Illini 28-14. The third game of the road trilogy was played against the Ohio State Buckeyes, but instead of the game being played in Columbus, it was played at Cleveland Stadium in Cleveland. The Buckeyes were a powerful team anyway, but the Illini were both honored and awestruck at playing in such a setting. They stayed with the Bucks for awhile, but Ohio State rolled 44-20.

Sandwiched between these two defeats was a 14-7 triumph at Northwestern. The Illini had concluded the Big 9 schedule with a 3-2 record and a tie for third place.

Eliot's boys went out of the league the next week and suffered a 6-0 loss at home to Great Lakes, then traveled to Rockford for their final game of the season, posting a 20-0 win over Camp Grant. It was the Fighting Illini's third shutout of the year, and allowed Illinois to finish with its first winning record since 1936.

"He took a bunch of boys who lacked faith in themselves, who were defeatists, and gave them courage," Lindgren spoke of Eliot to reporters that year. "He couldn't give them superior playing ability. They weren't great players and they weren't, as a unit, a great team. He has talked common sense to these boys, they've believed him and they've acted on that belief."

A 6-4 record was an amazing turnabout for this young and tough Fighting Illini football squad, and they were gaining confidence every day. Expectations were huge for the next year, with many anticipating Illinois' return to the top of the Big 9 Conference.

Unfortunately, in a much more important battlefield than a gridiron, an aggressive enemy was afoot. The year before, the Japanese had attacked Pearl Harbor, and the war in the Pacific was now in full blow. Boys and girls, men and women from all over the country were responding to the call of Uncle Sam that soon would include youngsters from Illinois, athletes and non-athletes alike.

It seemed that the roll-call of the starting lineup from 1942 was the same list as those missing from the Illini at the outset of the 1943 season. Stars such as Tony Butkovich and Alex Agase were gone. So were regulars Mike Kasap, Frank Bauman, John Genis, Joe Buscemi and Art Dufelmeier. Lyle Button and other promising freshmen were disappearing to serve their country as well. In all, 58 Illinois veterans and incoming freshmen were gone come fall. Eliot long felt that if it weren't for the war, that would have been the strongest team in the history of Fighting Illini football.

As it was, only 47 athletes came out for football in 1943, and 32 of them would vanish by year's end. The bulk of the players that played for Ray Eliot that season were 17-year-old boys. When they turned 18, most of them would be lost to the service. Buck Correll, a senior halfback and punter, was the only available letterman from 1942, and he didn't come out for the first five weeks.

Some Big 9 schools were in the same boat as Illinois, losing players to the war effort. Three exceptions were Purdue, Michigan and Northwestern, each of which had Navy and Marine training programs. Amateurs or professionals who entered the service and were sent to West Lafayette, Ann Arbor, or Evanston were allowed to play football for those schools. Illinois had no training program except the Navy V-12, which was a noncollegiate service training. Those who participated could not go out for football.

Eliot was certainly sorry to lose his boys to the war effort, but he never complained. "Above all things we recognize that we are in an emergency," he would say.

As a matter of fact, Illinois almost lost more than its players—it almost lost its head football coach as well. Eliot tried every avenue to get into the service himself, but was rebuffed at every turn because of his bad eyesight. He even offered to go to work with service athletic teams on this side of the ocean, but he was denied. He was too young for the First World War and too blind for the second, and he always regretted not being able to serve his country in a way that he considered his duty. He especially felt the sting of unjustified guilt when he thought about those he knew who paid the greatest price of all.

If Eliot couldn't go to war, then he was determined to be faithful to pour himself into the young kids that remained under his charge. Those players that went into the service from Illinois were dubbed "The Vanishing Illini." Those that remained were called "The Kindergarten Kids"—appropriate names, both.

Opening the 1943 season, Illinois was to battle its final opponent of 1942, Camp Grant. This time the advantage would be decidedly in Camp Grant's favor. Not only did this game pit 17-year-old boys against experienced men, but three hours before kickoff, the cream of Eliot's 17-year-old crop, Eddie Bray, Chet Sajnaj, Hurricane Mitchell, and Ralph Serpico were ruled ineligible because their credits had failed to clear in time. The loss of Bray cost the Illini their chief running threat, Sajnaj was due to start at fullback, Mitchell at left end, and Serpico, a future captain of the Illini, was a reserve guard.

"As Doctor Eliot, professor of gridology, scanned his band of 17 year olds before the game," wrote Pat Harmon of the Champaign *News-Gazette*, "he appointed Edward Francis McGovern starting left half, gave the fullback's baton to Don Johnson, freshman from Charleston, and pulled a new trick off the shelf to solve the left end situation. He made Jim Srednicki, a right end, into a left end. This latter trick was perhaps the ole perfesser's neatest, for Srednicki played a bang-up game."

A desperate Eliot did find Eddie Nemeth, an Illini running back on a 21-day furlough from the army, and rushed him into a uniform. He came to town Friday to see the opener, and the coach nabbed him, fed him some new plays and used him for more than half the game on Saturday. Also Illinois had a 230-pound sophomore tackle named Bob Prymuski. He had been practicing with the Illini for about ten days, but would have to report back to the Army with Nemeth in a couple of weeks. While they were on furlough, though, they were Fighting Illini.

"Grant starts a lineup that boasts several outstanding college and pro players," said the Champaign-Urbana Evening Courier. "Illinois went out with a handful of 17 year olds, army privates, limping linemen, and ex-cheerleaders, who in normal years, might be lucky to get into the arena as water boys."

Needless to say, expectations that had soared at the end of the previous year plummeted. A few days before the game, sportswriters predicted the score at anywhere from 40-0 to 60-0. Fans were not optimistic at the prospects, either, and only 3,500 showed. It was believed to be the second smallest crowd in the history of Memorial Stadium.

With all of those dire predictions, however, Camp Grant only won by a 23-0 count, after leading just 9-0 at the half. The closest Illinois got to the Grant endzone was the 12-yard line, but, as the *Alumni News* reported, "Eliot-inspired, they scrapped every bit of the way (and) won the praise of everybody who watched them."

"Illinois' attempt to match the speed and power of Camp Grant yesterday was a picture of a race between the Burlington Zephyr and the handcar the section hands ride from job to job," said the *Courier*. "It is no contest so far as the score is concerned, but certainly there is no one who can chide the Illini for what might have been the most courageous exhibition the stadium has seen."

Maybe as impressive as the performance on the field by these peachfuzz-faced kids, were the players' responses after the game. It was obvious that they did not show up to get beat. Chuck Pollard, who just the year before was playing for Urbana High School, answered quickly when he was asked about the step from high school to the college gridiron. "It's tough to lose anywhere," he said.

Eliot saw it a little more clearly.

"Their (the Illini's) performance was superhuman," said the coach. "They tackled hard, held the line well, in many cases gave the veterans as good as they got. They played a great game. I'm darn proud of them!"

Camp Grant players, who were sure they would rip the Illini, were duly impressed. "Don't kid yourself about that team," said quarterback Reino Nori. "I know their schedule, and they shouldn't win a game. But if we pick up a Sunday paper sometime in the future and read where they've won we'll not be surprised. Those kids gave us more trouble than we anticipated. They have all the courage and all the desire that championships are won with. I know now why they called that Eliot a miracle coach last year. He puts something into a kid that he's never had before."

For fear of injury, the Navy had a rule that training school coaches should not start officers in a football game and that they use them only when necessary. It was obvious the next week when the Illini traveled to Iowa St. to take on the Seahawks that the gray in that rule made it imminently breakable and unenforceable. Some felt that if Illinois had just played against the cadets they would have had a chance to win, but officers not only started, but played virtually the whole game. Despite an 82-yard kickoff return for a touchdown by an injured Bill Krall for Illinois and the play of the now-eligible Bray, Sajnaj, Mitchell, and Serpico, the Hawks won 32-18.

Though they lost, the Illini scored early in the contest and Jill Drum, writing for the *Daily Illini*, thought it was a good thing.

"Since the draft board is so close on the heels of three of the boys, the Illini thought it best not to waste any time," she joked. "For fear that a little man might walk out on the field in the middle of the game and say, 'From the President of the United States to you, greetings,' and disrupt the team, they proceeded to score on their first drive."

After the game these young men were again severely dejected in losing. Effort and courage were fine, but they were not a win. Disappointment is the price one pays when he's taught to believe he can win and he doesn't. But then the teacher who made him believe must also have the remedy. Eliot always did. Suddenly, like a trumpet blast, came a curt command from the coach: "All right, all of you men! Into the lecture room!"

Slowly and wearily the boys filed into the stuffy room. They peered from their drained and battered bodies at their mentor.

"O.K. So we've lost the second game," Eliot gritted his teeth. "We're a long way from a good team. But we put on the greatest show ever seen in Memorial Stadium. You boys were great. You did something that you can be proud of. You scored three touchdowns against a professional team, against some of the best players in the professional field."

After Eliot's encouragement the players felt better, but who was going to console the coach? In the days when a good fight meant more then the victory itself, the press took up his banner. Said the *Alumni News*: "You want to cheer for the kids who could stay in there and play an alert, aggressive, heads-up game against the worst odds that ever faced an Illini squad. And you feel just as enthusiastic about the talent of Coach Ray Eliot who can teach youngsters that much football in so short a time and inspire them to play with such remarkable courage."

The Iowa State game would be the last of the season for Private Ed Nemeth and Private Bob Prymuski. Their furloughs were over and off they went from a kid's game to a war. "No coach had ever had finer from his players than Ray Eliot," wrote Pat Harmon.

It was musical chairs again for Eliot. From week to week he had to use whatever pieces he was left with. He had to appoint a new captain each game because personnel changed so much. Maggie suggested her husband adopt as a theme song, "You'll Never Know How Much I Miss You." Certainly it was funny to Ray, for a moment at least.

The brilliance of Ray Eliot has sometimes been limited, in the minds of people who did not know him, to his stunning persuasiveness and ability to motivate others. While that was his most noted strength, his football mind has been overlooked at times. Many of the upsets and big wins he orchestrated were only part motivation. He was one of the most astute students of the game and, in his day, one of its sharpest tacticians, strategists and innovators. Lou Agase, a former player and assistant coach of Eliot's, insists to this day, for example, that if Eliot did not invent the screen pass, he sure perfected it. There can be no doubt that he was indirectly responsible for bringing it to Illinois.

"I was in school in Boston in the early 1920s and attended a Harvard-Yale game," Eliot remembered once. "I'm not certain of the details, but it was a scoreless game and looked like it might end that way. Harvard had fourth down deep in Yale's territory. The Harvard quarterback—I think it was Gary Wood—was an excellent drop kicker who would hold the ball only about a foot off the ground and gave it a short boot.

"He lined up and bent over in an apparent try for a field goal. But at the last second he straightened up and passed over six onrushing linemen to a halfback who just walked across the goal line. That was the first screen pass. It made quite an impression on me and I remembered it.

"At Illinois College I immediately put in the screen pass. We had considerable success with it, and the Bradley University coach asked me to teach it to him. Well, because Bradley wasn't on our schedule, I showed it to him. Later I was on the Illinois staff under Bob Zuppke. We had a game with Bradley and, wouldn't you know it, they used that screen pass I gave them. Zuppke was impressed. He included it in our offense and called it the 'Peoria pass.'"

Eliot never did tell Zup where the play came from.

Eliot was also credited with plotting the strategy that overthrew the heavily favored Michigan Wolverines in 1939, and he convinced Bob Zuppke to use game movies to better and more fairly evaluate and educate the team (this after sneaking films into his own player meetings behind Zup's back). Actually, he has even been given credit for designing the bad weather ponchos that players wear on the sidelines and a one-piece pair of football pants with the pads built in. His specialty, though, was on the field, and his offenses and defenses were copied by many who went on to win championships at high school, college, and professional levels.

There was no better example of his strategic wizardry than in the two short weeks he had between the Iowa State game and the Illini's contest against Purdue. He sprung a surprise on the Boilermakers when he abandoned the traditional single wing and, in ten practice days, installed the "T" formation. Eliot saw the possibilities about the time he also realized it was hopeless to try to teach freshmen the intricate blocks of the single wing in a matter of a few weeks.

Don Greenwood, Eddie Bray, and Eddie McGovern were originally all candidates for left halfback. Utilizing all of the capabilities of these boys, Eliot turned Greenwood, formerly an end and a fullback at Missouri, into a ball-handling quarterback. McGovern was adapted to playing right halfback and Bray remained at left. His simplified "T" had just five plays that could be run to either side. Such simplicity was rank heresy in modern, high-pressure football, but in two weeks Illinois came out with a brand new offense, and the three former left halfbacks blossomed into an offensive trio that teams quickly learned to fear. Eliot was not handing any game to any team no matter what the odds.

"But this 'T' of Eliot's has a mild kick—it went for 234 yards, and 21 points against a rather powerful Purdue team," reported Fred Turbyville of the *Dayton Herald*.

Again, 21 points was not enough to give the Illini a win, they were beaten 40-21, but the "Kindergarten Kids" kept making heads turn by their play. Besides, Illinois was literally beaten by itself. In the starting lineup for Purdue that day were Agase, Butkovich, Kasap, Buscemi, Genis and Bauman—dubbed the "Purdue Illini." Sixty-one points were scored in the game and fifty were put on the board by Illinois boys.

In previous games that season, these players had written telegrams to Eliot wishing the Illini well in whatever game they were playing. They felt loyalty to their coach...to a point. Before the game, Butkovich had promised Eliot that he would be going all out. He did, running all over the Rossade Stadium turf and scoring four touchdowns, while rushing for 207 yards in only 12 tries. It was the game that stamped Butkovich as a star. Buscemi also scored a touchdown for Purdue, and Agase recovered three fumbles. It was an Illinois day.

"We probably played all the harder," said Bauman later, "because we wanted to make (Ray) proud of us."

"Fittingly enough," wrote the *News-Gazette*'s Pat Harmon, "every contribution the University of Illinois has made to the Purdue football squad through the medium of the Marine training program was a star Saturday."

These "stars" were also very fond of Eliot.

"Tony Blazine who sat in the pressbox to phone information down to the Illinois bench, sat up with a sudden start in the fourth quarter," reported Harmon. "'Who's that No. 69 on the Illinois bench with you, Ray?' he asked. 'Genis' came the reply. 'Send him in right away,' advised Blazine. Investigation proved that not only Genis, but Alex Agase and Tony Butkovich were sitting with the Illinois players in the fourth period. The Purdue second and third teams were holding forth at the time, so these first-team men came over to be with last year's coach. Eliot never sent any of them in, however."

In fact, all of the "Purdue Illini" starters were visiting their coach but, at one point, with the Illini threatening to score, Purdue's coach Elmer Burnham had to wave frantically for them to come back. They returned just in time to thwart an Illinois touchdown.

"They were just too good," Greenwood muttered to reporters afterward. "But I believe we could give them a good fight again." Asked about Agase's play he said, "Agase wasn't in his right position. He's a lot better guard than he is backing up the line. But he's a great ballplayer, all right." He then exhibited a cleat mark to prove it.

Eliot returned to Champaign proud—proud of his own Illini and his temporarily misplaced Illini. Still, he was discovered with "a faraway look in his eyes," wrote Bob Peabody in the *Daily Illini*. "He and the managers began gathering up pads and jerseys and the team wandered down to the cars. He was thinking perhaps of when his prodigal sons might return and a combination of young Illini and veteran Illini would sweep the country."

Illinois was not ready to sweep the country the next week but they were ready to sweep through Camp Randall Stadium, home of the Wisconsin Badgers, for their first win of the year. They finally were playing a team on a level playing field without service facilities. The Badgers were still viewed by experts as the team with the most experience and talent and were favored to win, but the Illini tuned them 25-7. It was their largest margin of victory over the Badgers in 10 years.

Wisconsin had come out in a 6-3-2 defense, virtually a nine man line, to try and contain Illinois' young scooters out of the backfield, but the Illini still rolled up 248 yards on the ground. "Tell 'em the Illini threw a party at Madison," said a happy Greenwood afterward.

Eliot was not amazed at the win, but very pragmatic. After he congratulated every single player individually, he said simply, "The kids tackled well. You can do so much when you are tackling right."

"A couple of backs named Eddie and a 'T' formation run the way it should be run were too much for the Badgers Saturday," reported the *Wisconsin State Journal*.

Of course, in these war years nothing could be counted on and a victory could only be enjoyed for so long. After the game, Eliot learned that halfback Don Anderson would probably get a draft call by October 25th, and Ralph Palmer, Illinois' starting left guard, had been ordered to report for induction at Rockford on October 18th.

Illinois came home the next week to ring up their second win in a row. They outscored Pittsburgh 33-25 behind the lightning and thunder of McGovern and Bray, who combined for all five Illini touchdowns and 218 yards rushing between them.

The winning streak was short-lived, however, as Illinois went back on the road again, this time to South Bend, Indiana, to take on the nation's top-ranked team, the Fighting Irish. Notre Dame was a powerful collection of athletes and had the benefit of servicemen, including the Illini's "Orange" Julius Rykovich in the offensive backfield. The conversational sparring between the two head coaches the day before the game was actually more competitive then what took place on the field.

"I've worried so much about this game I don't remember what team we play next week," Irish head coach Frank Leahy complained to Eliot. "I don't know from one week to the next whether I'll have my team in top shape."

"I don't know, Frank," Eliot replied, his eyes trailing off wantingly. "I don't know from one week to the next whether I'll have a team. You say you're worried when one of your players comes up limping at practice. How'd you like to have your right half come up to you on Thursday before the big game and say 'I got my orders, I won't be with you Saturday.'

"Now, if it looks too tough out there early in the game," continued the Illinois coach convincingly, "I'm not going to use those kids. I'm not going to risk injuries when we have games coming up that we have a chance to win. We'll be a match for Iowa and can win, and against Ohio State we'll have a chance. So I'm going to take care of those little halfbacks."

"I understand what you mean Ray," smiled Leahy, "but I'm not going to believe a word you're saying until about 5 p.m. Saturday after our game. We know better than to take any chances against an Illinois team."

If Notre Dame took no chances then they also took no prisoners. They ripped the Illini 47-0, with Rykovich scoring their first two touchdowns. Eliot did stay true to his word, though, pulling Bray and McGovern for the second half. Even after losing, he congratulated each starting Illini player personally after the game for their effort.

Pete Perez and Pete Kearney were a couple of new 17 year olds who played for Illinois, making it to Notre Dame in time for bed Friday night. By then Eliot had figured that he had lost 19 first-team players since the beginning of preseason practice.

Kearney would start the next week against Michigan because he had dared pop off to a Notre Dame lineman. On the next play, the freshman had to be carried off the field, following an application of what the Irish termed "football judo."

"Any kid who has got the nerve to sass a Notre Dame lineman can start the game for me any time," said Eliot.

Kearney started, but nothing was going to help these kids against another marine juggernaut. Michigan coach Fritz Crisler had inherited the likes of Bill Daley of Minnesota and Elroy "Crazy Legs" Hirsch of Wisconsin and, as expected, the Wolverines ran wild at Memorial Stadium. On a sloppy day in which Coach Eliot discarded his customary brown gabardine business suit and wore a football uniform because of the foul weather, Michigan buried the Illini 42-6.

Eliot did like the play of his end Max Morris but, alas, he became the next Illinois player drafted. "He was coming along fast," sighed the coach.

Still, the Illini remained an upbeat and fun-loving bunch. Going to Cedar Rapids, Iowa the following Friday, Illini gridders crossed the Mississippi to the tune of "Patty Murphy" and kept a bulging trainload of west-bound passengers entertained. On that trip, the *Daily Illini* nominated "Bray and McGovern as the most popular with visitors to the team. Greenwood as the biggest eater. Theron Bradley, who took a beating because of his wild west background, the most abused. And Bill Butkovich (the younger brother of Tony), the biggest realist—he thrilled to a story in a sport pulp entitled, 'Football Freshmen Come Through.'"

The Illini were even happier on the return trip. Against the Hawkeyes Eliot decided to "unleash their first sustained air attack of the year," said the *Daily Illini*. They threw nine times and completed three, but for these kids that was a sustained air attack. They also ran liberal variations off of their "T" formation by lateraling often, and took a lot of chances, going for it on fourth down and so forth. It all led to a 19-10 Illinois triumph.

That victory set up what Eliot billed as "The game for the Big 9 civilian football championship" the next week at Ohio State. It would be a day not soon forgotten by Illini and Buckeyes alike.

9

Ohio

"The field judge fires his gun to end the brawl,
The buzzing crowd moves slowly to the gates,
But hold! Those guys are back and playing ball,
And Illinois is cursing at the fates."

—James Doyle
Cleveland Plain Dealer
November 14, 1943

The Illini had not lost yet to a non-military team, and Paul Brown's Buckeyes had only been beaten by Indiana in the final seconds. The largest crowd (36,331) to grace Ohio Stadium in Columbus that year was on hand on that crisp 37-degree November day. "Kindergarten Kids" or not, championship thrill was in the air.

Through almost four quarters the Buckeyes showed grinding power, and the Illini, with their three scatbacks—McGovern, Bray, and Greenwood—displayed flashing speed to match the Buckeye strength. Illinois jumped out to a 12-6 lead after one frame and led 19-13 at the half. Ohio State took the lead in the third by one, only to see the Illini recapture it 26-20. The Bucks scored again but missed the extra point that would have given them the edge, and the game went to the closing seconds tied 26-26. It had been a great and exciting game, but it was about to become legendary.

"Certainly a 26-26 tie would, in itself, be enough to cause high blood pressure and delirium among Ohio State's biggest crowd of the year," wrote Milt Woodard of the *Chicago Sun*. "But the ending, albeit witnessed by a handful of the original gathering, put a touch of pre-war festivity to (the night's) homecoming in this rabid football community."

Eleven seconds remained, and Ohio State owned the football at the Illinois 21 yard line. Quarterback Bob McQuade faded to pass, then rolled slightly to his left under Illini defensive pressure. He saw a receiver in the endzone and let the ball go. The Buckeye dove for it but could not hold on, and the pass was incomplete as the gun sounded to mark the end of the game. Both teams congratulated each other and made their way off the field to their respective locker rooms, reasonably happy with a tie. Ohio State, however, went to their locker room without their coach. Brown was out on the field filing a protest with the field judge.

Fans were lining out of the stadium and pressmen were rattling their typewriters with game stories for the morning editions, but Benny Dempsey, who handled the down box and Joe McClure, who was in charge of the chain, held fast to their duties when they saw the discussion on the field.

Paul Walker, a sportswriter for the *Columbus Dispatch*, was on the sidelines close to the scene and explained, "On what was apparently the last play of a wild and wooly game, P.C. Goebel (linesman) tooted his horn for a foul. E.C. Krieger (field judge) saw that time was up and that the electric timer said no seconds to play. He fired his gun. Everybody, including three of the officials, thought the ball game was over and that the final score was 26-26."

When Krieger and Jim Masker, the referee, came over to the sidelines to pick up their jackets, Walker said he asked them about the horn on the last play.

"'I didn't hear a horn,' Krieger said, and he turned to Masker and asked, 'Did you hear a horn?'

"Masker said, 'No, I didn't.'

"Then he turned to me and said, 'Who blew the horn?'

"I told him I had seen Goebel throw his white cap to the ground to mark the spot of a foul, before McQuade threw that long pass into the end zone.

"Masker went out to Goebel and said, 'Was there a penalty on that last play?'

"Goebel replied, 'Yes sir! The defense was offside.'

"Masker, veteran of 40 years of football officiating and working his last game in Columbus prior to his retirement the next Saturday, said: 'We must call both teams out and allow them to run one more play.'

"He turned to Krieger and Don Hamilton, the umpire, and instructed them to call both teams back to the field ."

Illinois' Paul Podmajersky had been called offside on the play, and a game cannot end on a defensive penalty. There was a lot of talk that there should be two seconds left on the clock for Ohio to run one more play, but that was beside the point. Just the fact that it was a penalty on the defense demanded that the Bucks get another play, this time five yards closer, from the 16 yard line.

There was mass confusion, however. Goebel had called defensive offside, but another official had called defensive holding. It took the officials five minutes to sort it out.

The referee who went to the Ohio State locker room was the lucky one. They were more then happy to come back onto the field. As a matter of fact, they came running out like they were about to start a brand new game.

Illinois was not as excited.

"Another play?" they asked. "You've got to be kidding." Krieger was not kidding, and he had to tell the Illini to either come back out or forfeit the game.

Illinois players were, of course, in all stages of undress. "I was in the shower already," says Eddie Bray today. "I had to get out, towel myself off and put some sort of uniform back on again."

Eliot put a makeshift team together, and they straggled out, slowly and sullenly, for the final play. They were a dejected lot. It was obvious they did not want to see Ohio have another chance to win the game. Some of them came out shirtless, others pulling their jerseys back on. Many had already taken off their shoes in the dressing room. Podmajersky sat down by the goal posts and put his shoes back on, while Bert Levy stood back of the end zone in his stocking feet and watched the last play.

Several thousand spectators had gotten two or three blocks from the stadium when suddenly the loudspeaker blared out, "Hold everything, folks. It appears as if the game wasn't over."

As word spread that another play had been called, many of them ran back to their seats. The scene south of Ohio Stadium was a mob of running, overcoated men and women dashing back to see the final action. This only added to the confusion, as the fans became a milling mass, straining to see the last play. A small but hardy cheer went up as Ohio State's white-clad boys returned to the field.

The Buckeyes immediately gathered around their coach on the field of play, as he explained what he wanted them to do. This was a bone of contention for some because coaches have never been allowed to be on the field giving instructions to their team. Some felt (Ohio people included) that a 15-yard penalty should have been assessed to the Bucks. That would have put the ball back beyond the 30 yard line, out of field goal range.

As it was, John Stungis, a 17-year-old second-team player from Powhatan Point, Ohio, who had kicked extra points but never a field goal in his short career, lined up a boot. McQuade would hold from the 23 yard line, slightly to the right of the goal posts. Even the angle was controversial.

"I was screaming, but no one would listen to me," says Bill Butkovich. "I swear they placed that ball toward the wrong hash-mark. He should have been kicking from the left side. The wind was more in his favor from the right. I went to every referee and tried to tell them but they wouldn't listen."

The snap was perfect, and Stungis drilled the ball squarely between the uprights to give Ohio State a 29-26 win. A stunned radio announcer who apparently forgot he was still on the air screamed, "The son-of-a-bitch made it!"

Buckeye players and fans went crazy. The small crowd stormed the field and the spectators, along with the players, swept Stungis up on their shoulders and carried him off to the locker room. There, he was "beaten and pummeled by his fellow teammates who yelled about him and at him from all corners of the shower room," reported Perry Morison of the *Columbus Citizen*.

Some found it interesting that Goebel, who called the offside, was the same official who called an offside against Ohio State two weeks before that permitted a winning pass for Indiana in the final seconds. Many thought the official courageous, but a few did wonder if the call was a payback to even things up for Brown and his Buckeyes. Illinois fans probably thought it served Goebel right that after he threw down his white cap to mark the spot of the offside, somebody swiped it. Of course the officials had more to worry about than a stolen hat. Whether a real fear or imagined, they were concerned for their lives. The field was being overrun with rabid fans.

"I sure was glad to see those yellow helmets (of the security people) coming through the crowd," Masker admitted.

Speculations and questions swirled after what some began to dub "the famous fifth quarter." Besides all of the other controversies, it seemed that, with about a minute-and-a-half left in the game, there was an out-of-bounds play near the Illinois sideline. The clock was stopped. Seconds later the officials noticed the clock wasn't running, so two of them—Masker and Krieger—put an arm in motion to indicate to the timekeeper that the clock should be kept going. It was promptly started again, when it should have remained dead until the snap of the ball.

It was this that intrigued Eliot afterward, as he paced up and down the Illinois dressing room in the southwest tower of the stadium. "After Ohio had kicked its winning field goal," he said, "there (should still have been) time for us to elect to receive a kickoff. Who knows but that Ohio would have missed kicking out of bounds and the ball instead had gone to McGovern or Bray or Greenwood. Who would say there wasn't a chance that either of them would have gone for a touchdown."

"There wasn't much anybody could say to that," responded the *Columbus Citizen*. "Except maybe Ohio State wouldn't have elected to place kick...if there were more seconds to play. They might have gone for a touchdown, instead, and made it, thereby taking up more time. But nobody could deny that, with Bray or McGovern or Greenwood lugging the ball, there wasn't a potential touchdown in the making."

As disappointed as Eliot was, he remained, as always, graceful and congenial in defeat. It was clear that he was more concerned about the clock than he was about the offside or even the calling of his boys back on the field from various stages of undress.

"Ohio won," he said. "It's (their) game, but it was plenty rough all the way. They beat us 29-26 and that's the final score, that's all there is to it. Our boys fought hard and played as well as they could. Penalties are penalties. We cannot protest the decision of the officials. They called a penalty, giving State another play . That's that. We hated to lose it, naturally, but the officials' decision is final."

As for Brown, he understood the frustration of his opponent. "I feel for Ray Eliot," he said, "for what happened to him happened to us in the Indiana game."

Illinois players, who had trooped in gleefully only a few seconds before with a tie game to their credit, were not ready to let it die so easily.

Eddie Bray exclaimed that he was "mad enough to fight." Bray, praised by Brown as "a beautiful runner," muttered over and over: "It can't be. It can't be—we didn't lose." He sobbed as fellow players consoled him.

Greenwood was not sobbing but seeing red. "The damn gun went off, didn't it? The game's over," he growled.

"The officials' ears would have been burning if they could have heard what was being said 'Not for publication' in the Illini dressing room," wrote Lew Byrer in the *Columbus Citizen*.

In the end, what people wondered most was why it took the officials so long to make the call and decide what to do. The confusion could have been avoided if the penalty had just been assessed before the players left the field.

Actually, what would have helped the Illini more than better decisions by the officials was a little ball control.

"If we had the ball for as many plays as Ohio State, I think we could have beat the dickens out of them," said Eliot. Ohio had a whopping 90-43 margin in offensive plays.

Eliot's "T" formation continued to impress, however.

"It was obvious to even the most biased observer that Illinois was more than just a well-coached football team," wrote John Dietrich of the *Cleveland Plain Dealer*. "The fact was, many an old timer realized as the play unfolded, that he was seeing one of the most remarkable offenses ever turned loose in these parts. They were kept in the game by this offense and the never-say-die spirit of the Illini personnel from upback to water boy."

It was an all-time first for the Big 9, what transpired that day between Illinois and Ohio State. No other game had been decided after the two teams had retired to their dressing rooms and, as far as the writer can tell, it has not happened since. The controversy still swirls in the hearts of Illini and Buckeye faithful today, over 50 years later.

Appropriately, Art Robinson of the *Columbus Citizen* wrote, "The Ohio State-Illinois game of 1943 will never end."

10

Whiz Backs

"Take hold of this consoling thought;
If every ball that's thrown were caught;
If no one ever faltered; no one fell;
If every play we tried went well;
If gain with every venture came,
There would be nothing to the game.

And so with life—if all were plain;
If men perfection could attain;
If neither doubt nor loss nor fear,
Should ever test our courage here;
If we knew all, and all could see,
Then deadly dull life would be."

—Edgar A. Guest

The 1943 season ended the next week at Dyche Stadium in Evanston, where the military veteran-laden Northwestern Wildcats put a final licking on the Illini 53-6.

As one can imagine, Eliot was disappointed after the trimming Northwestern gave his boys. Closing a door to outsiders, however, Eliot told the squad not to take the defeat to heart. "You did the best you could and I'm proud of you," he said.

For Eliot, a very difficult and painful season was over. Seeing his boys go off to war, never knowing who would show up for him on a given Saturday, and dealing with the young unprepared psyches of 17-year-olds as they went up against veteran all-star teams most weeks (five of the top eight teams in the country beat them), was a colossal challenge.

"It's like getting a tooth out," Ray Eliot grinned wearily after the game and season had ended. "I'm glad it's over with."

Fritz Jauch of the *Daily Illini* glowed, though: "They're fine...in an immortal sort of way...these Illini of the war year, 1943."

Immortal were Bray, McGovern and Greenwood, turned loose by Eliot's bold switch to his innovative "T" formation. Bray led the Big 9 in rushing with an incredible 7.5 yards per carry average. Playing only five of six Big Ten games, he racked up 505 yards on the ground. McGovern finished with 366 yards in conference play and a 5.3 yards per carry average. Greenwood was rated by many writers as the most-improved quarterback in the conference.

"Just a lot of kids," Maury Kent, the veteran Iowa scout shook his head as he looked over the Illini that year. "Just a bunch of kids. We have a lot of them in Iowa, too. I looked on the training table the other day, and what do you think the kids were eating? Bread and butter, and sugar. I haven't seen anybody eat that since I was 11 years old."

Eliot, though, had the heart, patience and personality to get the most out of the "Kindergarten Kids." He assumed a father role like never before that year. He gathered them around him often on trips for informal talks on university life, war, typical young men's problems and, of course, football. Sometimes he even read to them. Once before a game Eddie Bray informed the media that he weighed 148 pounds. As Coach Eliot put a fatherly hand on the shoulder of the youngster he told a South Bend reporter, "I wouldn't trade Eddie Bray for Bill Daley."

The feeling was mutual. "Ray Eliot was one of the great, if not the greatest coach of his day," says Bray now.

Others agreed in 1943.

"It is all very well to speak of the success of those who have been gifted with veteran players from the beginning," Pat Harmon wrote in the *News Gazette*. "They have done a good job. But Ray Eliot has done a super job. No other team gave up so many players during the course of the season (Wisconsin, for example, lost about 60 players, Illinois over 90).

"Isn't it about time the coach of the year acclaim was given to the man who did the most unusual job? The successful coaches have been those who have carried on with a paucity of material. We know of no better choice for coach of the year than Ray Eliot."

Eliot was not chosen coach of the year (what 3-7 coach ever has been?), but don't tell Bill Schmelzle of the *Daily Illini* that he didn't deserve it. Schmelzle heard a Chicago sportswriter say that "If Ray Eliot wins ten national championships in a row, he'll never equal the job he has done this year."

"(The reporter)," wrote Schmelzle, "was pretty well expressing the thoughts of anyone who has watched this 1943 Illinois football team move from game to game...improving, scoring, and even winning. If there is any doubt that Eliot is the finest coach in America, then the only thing that will establish this fact is time. Illinois has hitched its wagon to a star. Bright days are ahead. Eliot and Illinois can't miss...Eliot knows boys, how to lead them, how to bring out every ounce of ability and spirit they possess. He could make a tackling dummy play good 60-minute ball. He has faith and trust in his players, gives them every chance to make good. The star of this tale of a short past and a long future is Ray Eliot, molder of men...the greatest coach in the nation."

There is no doubt that Eliot loved his men, who he affectionately called his "boys," and it mattered not how physically gifted they were or what color skin they had. Indeed, if the color barrier had been broken at Illinois in 1939 when Moline, Illinois, track star Floss "Flip" Anders became the first black to play football there, then in 1944 it was shattered.

Illinois had quickly gained a reputation under Eliot as an athletic program that would give a kid the same chances no matter his race. "He had no pets, no prejudice, 'may the best man fill a position,'" Jimmy Smith was quoted years later.

Thus, out of Chicago and Aurora came two young black men who became the wood that fed the Illini offensive flame of 1944.

Claude "Buddy" Young was a 5'5" sprinter out of Chicago's Phillips High School, who went to Illinois on a track scholarship. As a two-man squad, he and Ranie Thomas had taken the team state track championship in the spring of 1944. Young did his part by accomplishing the rare double: victories in the 100-yard dash and the 200-low hurdles. Eliot wanted Young to come out for football, though skeptical of his style of running ("In track he is a straight runner, and speed alone does not make a good halfback"). Young came out, and showed the coach that he had moves and toughness to go with his swift feet. He and Aurora's Paul Patterson teamed with Bray and Greenwood to make up one of the most dynamic backfields the Big 9 and the nation had ever beheld.

Unfortunately, although Eliot was an equal opportunity coach, not all whites held his views. After a white man refused to serve him in a restaurant soon after he arrived in Champaign, a concerned Young went to Eliot.

"Just score a few touchdowns and see what happens around this town," said Eliot. "And there's something else I want you to know—we don't have any jobs for whites or negroes on our football team. We only have jobs for football players. Don't ever forget that."

"Ray treated everyone the same," marvels Geraldine Young, Buddy's widow. "He and Buddy and Paul (Patterson) became such good friends. Buddy used to visit Ray whenever he went to Champaign and when Buddy and Paul used to get together in later years they would just sit and reminisce about Ray and all of the wonderful times they had at Illinois."

Buddy Young would concur with his wife as he spoke with Lou Engel of the Champaign *News Gazette* in the 1970s: "In 1944, my freshman year at Illinois, only eight people of color were playing football in the Big 10 and four of them were at the U. of I. It didn't take an act of congress, a Supreme Court decision or an act of the state legislature to make me understand what interdependence was all about. It is the true way of life the way Ray Eliot espoused it."

He continued his thoughts with Lon Eubanks for the latter's book *The Fighting Illini*: "We accepted each other as individuals and as football players," he said. "We had great camaraderie on the 1944 team, in particular. I've always felt a football team is a society within itself—it has to interact. The characteristics of the persons become the characteristics of the team. I have some friends from the 1944 team that I feel so strongly about it's unbelievable."

The Illini's great All-American, J.C. Caroline, says today that Eliot's evenhandedness is the reason he came to Illinois in 1952. "Southern colleges were still not accepting blacks, so my high school coach in South Carolina encouraged me to go to Illinois because he knew I would get a fair shake under Ray Eliot," says he.

Interestingly, Caroline's junior year was, record-wise, the worst season for an Eliot-coached team in any sport ever. They were 1-8. Because of his tremendous success in the years prior, Eliot was spared most of the usual roasting given to struggling coaches. But that did not mean the team was exempt from inane speculations as to what was wrong. Some aimed the accusation of racism at the Illini—not at Eliot—but at the players! The incredible suggestion was made by these "observers" that "The white boys won't block for the colored ball-carriers."

The day after the annual athletic banquet, the Champaign-Urbana *Evening Courier*'s Bert Bertine addressed the accusations publicly for the first time. "We heard that worn record played so often in past weeks," he wrote. "We disregarded it because the persons who told us, or asked us, included many who hadn't even seen Illinois play this year, much less be at practice as we were every afternoon for three months."

Eliot appreciated the responsible journalism.

The day of the banquet the players had met to elect their most valuable player and the captain for 1955.

"It was as outspoken of a meeting as I've attended," one player told Bertine. "The racial question was openly discussed with both races commenting."

The end result?

"Can't people ever believe that a team can be beaten just because it isn't as good as the other teams?" the boy asked the writer. "Why is that so mysterious? We just didn't have the horses this year. Last year when we did have them, we won."

Bertine concluded, "That's good enough for us."

It so happened that the players voted their best player on both sides of the ball captain for their next grid season. In what, just coincidentally, became a slap in the face to the racism speculators, J.C. Caroline became the first black captain-elect in the history of Illinois football.

"I'm honored to be here representing the University of Illinois," said the "Dixie Flyer" at the banquet that night. "I'm twice as honored to be a member of the Fighting Illini. I am very proud to be elected captain. I am very fond of my team and what we have done in the past."

Outgoing captain Jan Smid, one of those white linemen who had the responsibility to block for Caroline and the other backs said, "I wish next year's team and J.C.—the best running back in America—a lot of luck next year."

Unfortunately for Illinois, Caroline took his wares to the Canadian Football League the next year and was not able to fulfill his commitment as captain. Still, his election was a significant event that capped a difficult season in a very special way.

Eliot once said, "If I'm remembered for anything at all at Illinois, I'd like to be remembered for trying to put the best football players on the field every Saturday—black, white or red."

Sometimes he was chastised by fans for playing so many blacks. "Show me a white boy that's better and I'll put him in," he'd retort.

Under Eliot, Mel Meyers became the first black quarterback for the Illini, receiving his first letter in 1959. Ironically, that same year, a young Jesse Jackson (later the Reverend Jesse Jackson) attended Illinois and came in one day to see Coach Ray. A pretty fair athlete himself, Jackson said he wanted to be the first black quarterback that the University ever had. Eliot told him that he was too late—that Meyers had beaten him to it. Jackson never played for Illinois.

In 1972 Eliot was stopped for speeding by a black police officer. Eliot's treatment of blacks was so well known that the officer took one look at his driver's license, noticed who it was, and handed it back saying, "Mr. Eliot, you've done so much for blacks over the years, I can't give you a ticket."

The only time Eliot has ever been personally accused of anything the least bit racist was in 1993 by Bill Burrell in Loren Tate's column in the Champaign *News-Gazette*. Burrell, a black and Eliot's captain and All-American in 1959, questioned Eliot's sincerity toward blacks, using as an example, the fact that Eliot asked Burrell if he would like to have someone co-captain with him.

"I screamed bloody murder," Burrell was quoted by Tate. "I thought he was racially motivated, that he really didn't want me to be the captain."

It was all a misunderstanding. It must be pointed out first, that Eliot did not ask Caroline, another black man, that same question. Secondly, according to his secretary Margaret Selin, in the late 1950s Eliot decided that co-captains might be the best way to go. Previously he had asked a couple of white captains if they wanted co-captains. The truth was, Athletic Director Doug Mills did not want co-captains and so it never happened. When Pete Elliot took over as coach after Ray Eliot's retirement, though, he was allowed to have co-captains, and did, starting in 1962.

In 1944, though, there was no misunderstanding. After speaking with Eliot, Young felt better and bore down for his coach and Illinois, commencing a career that would make him an

All-American and eventually land him in the Pro Football Hall of Fame.

At a dinner gathering, Eliot once spoke of the dynamic halfback: "Eight or ten of us could station ourselves around this room and Buddy Young could scoot through this door before anybody laid a hand on him. He's the only back I ever knew who didn't give a darn whether he had downfield blocking."

Every journey, however, begins with one step and every running back's career begins with the first carry. In Young's case, it was four carries for 113 yards and two touchdowns in his inaugural game, as the Illini opened the 1944 season at home by demolishing Illinois-Normal 79-0.

The win was the 45th victory in 55 opening games for the Illini, and the score set a new record for Memorial Stadium, the old mark being 67 points when Illinois laced Butler under Eliot two years earlier. It also came within eight points of the Illini's all-time scoring high for openers, that being an 87-3 rout of Illinois Wesleyan in 1912.

After struggling to beat Indiana the next week 26-18, Illinois had to face powerful Great Lakes Naval Academy under their new head coach, Lieutenant Paul Brown from Ohio State. At the last minute Eliot decided to start almost his entire third team, including seven freshmen, against Brown's forces. The only bonafide firststringer in the lineup was Sam Zatkoff, who, with Jim Ellison, was playing his final game before answering his draft call. Eliot told the press that he didn't want his regulars to get hurt in the emotion of the first part of the game and that he wanted to get a look at the reserves under fire. Actually, he was ticked off at the performance of his first and second teams against Indiana. Eliot's discipline paid dividends. Young was a third-teamer at the time, and it was against Great Lakes that he and Illinois' high powered offense got into gear. The Illini gained 350 yards while the Bluejackets managed 334 and Young electrified the crowd of 25,000 sailors with a 93-yard touchdown run.

"Eliot and Brown staged another battle of football minds," wrote Eddie Jones of the *Evening Courier*. "Through the 60 minutes there was an abundance of strategy streaking from each bench. It was virtually a duplicate of that thing in Columbus last fall..."

Amazingly, Eliot and Brown (Illinois and Great Lakes) ended in another 26-26 tie. This time there was no "fifth quarter" for Brown's club but, Jim Mellow, the All-American from Notre Dame, almost gave Great Lakes the victory in the waning seconds.

"Mellow broke through the middle of the line and started goalward," Eliot would use the story in speeches later. "And the only thing between him and the goal line was this kid (Eddie) Bray. And when I saw those two bodies come closer together...I'm really wondering what I'm going to tell Mrs. Bray on Monday, that's about the size of it. But I looked up in time to see and to hear one of the greatest tackles I had ever seen or heard on a football field in my life, when that kid put his skinny ol' shoulders into the oncoming piston-like legs of that Mr. Mellow and picked him up and laid him back the way he was coming from—and laid on him 'til the clock ran out."

"Actually I think I got him by his nose," laughs Bray today.

Either way, with a group of kids, Illinois had tied a team that had beaten Purdue and was considered one of the best in the nation. Suddenly the Illini were 2-0-1 and people were taking notice.

"Illinois, with a blazing offense and an amazingly stout defense against both running and passing, vaulted to the top of the heap in the national collegiate football whirl today," wrote Jones.

"The speed of (Eliot's) backs at times confused the more mature service men," penned Wayne Otto of the *South Bend Tribune*.

"Illinois' 'Whiz Backs' dazzled Great Lakes and midwestern fans here today with a kind of offense that all the scouting in the world can't stop," *Daily Illini* sportswriter Glenn Roberts gushed. "Give Buddy Young or Paul Patterson the ball, throw a block, and 'Whiz,' another Illini touchdown. That was the case here today and from now on every team to meet Ray Eliot's 'Whiz Backs' will have due respect for them."

The next week, though, the Illini were beaten by Purdue 35-19. Frank Bauman was one of the few Illini still with the Boilermakers from the year before—most others had been called to action—and he said despite the loss, "That's the best offense I have ever played against."

Maybe Bauman was biased but Gordon Graham of the *Lafayette Journal-Courier* wasn't when he exclaimed, "Illinois has the greatest attack I have ever seen in football." And the Illini rebounded the next two weeks by pounding Iowa 40-6 and Pittsburgh 39-5 in their first trip out east since the days of Red Grange.

They were called the "Whiz Backs," the "Stopwatch Backfield" and the "Illinois Speed Kings." Young was called the nation's fastest football player (perhaps ever) and Patterson, shaking off a midseason injury and a bout with fumbleitis, was Young's perfect compliment. At one point Eliot commanded Patterson to carry a ball with him for 24 straight hours to cure this football-fatal disease of fumbling. It worked. The next game against Pittsburgh, while Young carried the ball eight times for 132 yards, Patterson also ripped off runs of 23 and 62 yards, without booting the ball once.

By the time Illinois had completed six games, they already had broken the team's single season scoring record by posting 244 points, with four games yet to be played. The previous mark of 227 points in nine games was Eliot's also, in 1942. In addition, the Illini were on a record pace in yards gained per game, averaging over 360.

Though his 17 and 18-year-olds had a record of 4-1-1, were confounding experienced defenses with ingenuity and speed, and setting records left and right, Eliot was not satisfied. He said as much after the Pittsburgh game.

"The boys were sluggish," the coach told the *Pittsburgh Press*. "They weren't overconfident, but they believe too much of the stuff the newspapers have said about them, and press clippings don't win football games. We can look for a trouncing from Notre Dame if we don't improve. Our offense will keep us in the game for a while, but I'm afraid we can't hold out against the power of the Irish."

The gridders from South Bend came calling, again ranked number one in the country. Eliot held his practices in complete secret all week as he prepared his Illini for the game of the year. An enthralled 65,114 fans, the biggest crowd in Memorial Stadium since 1929, witnessed another dog fight.

On Illinois' initial possession, and the first time he carried the ball in the game, Buddy Young broke over left tackle, beat the Irish safety in the first ten yards, and galloped 74 yards for a touchdown. Young held when Greenwood kicked the point after to make it 7-0. Just three minutes later, though, Notre Dame capitalized on an Illini fumble, Bob Kelly scoring, to make it 7-6 after the Irish missed their extra point try.

It was a source of some contention, among fans anyway, when Young got kicked in the head on the last play of the first half and could not play the rest of the day (Nothing dirty was proven against the Irish). Illinois had lost quite possibly the best runner in the nation and his replacement, Eddie Bray, also went out with an injury in the third quarter. Still, the Illini held on to their one-point advantage into the fourth.

Suddenly the Irish struck, seconds into the final frame. After a holding penalty had backed them up to their own 29 yard line, Kelly caught a pass in the flat. Faking like he was going to run, he lateraled the ball to halfback Chick Maggioli who sprinted down the sideline for a 71-yard touchdown. The point after was good and Notre Dame led 13-7.

Later in the quarter, Greenwood would gallop 70 yards for an apparent Illinois score, but an Illini was called for holding and the play was called back. It was the second touchdown of the day and eighth of the season taken away from Illinois for an infraction, and it brought the Memorial Stadium faithful to their feet in disgust, and Eliot face to face with field judge Bill Blake.

In Eliot's 11 years of coaching, including his stint at Illinois College, this type of confrontation had never happened before. As he had written in his college paper long before, the coach had always preached that true sportsmanship demanded taking what one may consider a bad call like a gentleman. Certainly one could ask an official a question or state an opinion, but to argue or raise a voice to a referee was, to him, unmanly. Today, coaches yelling, screaming, ranting and raving has become common-place. Many claim they need to stand up for their kids, defend them. Eliot was all for defending his players, but on the field he felt that the defending would be in the playing. He believed there were more important lessons in life to teach by example than to demand that one call be made right. Others could play an intimidation game with officials, fueled by their own egos, reasoning that an official will eventually make a call in their favor if harassed sufficiently. Not Eliot. He had enough faith in his kids' ability to overcome adversity without his bellyaching, and he would work all the harder to see that they did. If there was an advantage to be had, it was in class, he thought.

Besides, if the players' focus turned to a supposed bad call by an official, then the player would be distracted from the job at hand. To Eliot, bad calls often turned into poor excuses.

Of course, there are those coaches, too, who are just plain ill-tempered. As passionate as he was, Eliot always considered short fuses inexcusable, undisciplined and irresponsible. As a matter of fact, more than one official commented over the years that "Illinois football players are the finest gentlemen on the field of any school in the Big 10." And one official said, "There is more to coaching than teaching football, and to me Ray Eliot is the ideal coach."

But after Greenwood's touchdown was called back, Eliot took a couple of steps onto the field and told Blake, in no uncertain terms, what he thought of his call. For a moment, the forces at work played on Eliot's emotions. Illinois was on the cusp of knocking off the greatest team in America, it was the fourth quarter of an intense ballgame in front of a huge crowd, and Eliot's boys had a chance to establish themselves as a great team in their own right. But the coach could not forgive himself. As profusely as he argued the call, he apologized for it afterward. When the final gun sounded, after congratulating Notre Dame for their 13-7 victory, he found the official and was beside himself.

"He apologized to Blake a half-dozen times," wrote Eddie Jones.

"Ray," Blake calmed the anxious Eliot. "Any coach or player can be pardoned for flaring up in this game. Forget it. I appreciate the way you feel about it, but don't apologize for it. I'm not apologizing for calling the penalty."

Blake wasn't, but many fans thought he should. As they filed from the stadium, not a few paying customers could be heard insisting that the Illini had been "robbed."

More than just the call itself now, Eliot felt badly for his boys. "Looks like we've got to score about five touchdowns a game to get two or three to count," he groaned.

"Whew!" first year Irish head coach Edward (Tex) McKeever ejaculated to reporters after the game, wiping the beads of sweat off of his face with a towel (Frank Leahy had been called to service and McKeever had taken over in his stead). "That is a sensation. We haven't played a team anywhere near as good as Illinois this year. Every kid Ray sent out there wanted to play. You could tell it the way they came running in. Such spirit! I never saw the like. Great setup here at Illinois. A fine coach and I never saw a squad with as much overall fire. Not the first eleven, alone, but everybody who got into the game. Even the substitutes were up on their feet cheering about half the time."

Eliot was deeply moved by the effort of his young boys as well. "He didn't want to talk long," wrote Jones. "Eliot is a solid citizen, and sentiment in this football business is secondary to him. But you had the feeling, as you sat there on the bench beside him, that he might break down and bawl if you talked with him too much."

As he met with the press in the officials' headquarters, he mumbled words like "grand," "great," "couldn't believe it" and "it's incredible."

"Don't ask me to say anything about the way these kids played out there today," he pleaded with sportswriters. "If I talked all day I couldn't praise them enough. They were wonderful, marvelous, superb. I'm proud of every one of them. They played wonderfully, and they deserve a lot of credit. They're a bunch of fine football players—and swell fellows right with it. Tell (your readers) that I am proud of my team. Tell them that I am proud of the way they conducted themselves on the football field this afternoon. Tell them that the spirit, and drive, and brilliance of Illinois this afternoon will be an inspiration to all Illini in years to come. I am very proud of them."

The famous movie critic Gene Shalit, once a student at the University of Illinois and sportswriter for the *Daily Illini*, conveyed the pain the boys felt and the pride in the hearts of Illini onlookers when he told the story of the newly-retired Justa Lindgren and Buddy Young: "Buddy Young sat on the wooden bench in front of his locker. His mind aching, his heart broken, the brilliant little fighter sat and talked in a voice that sometimes broke. Standing beside him was Justa Lindgren, Illinois' great ex-line coach. 'Lindy,' one of the traditions of the University, had an autograph book with him. And that great man, with moist eyes, asked Buddy for his signature...asked him to sign his book."

While others can dwell on a great effort or on what they believe was a bad call, a football team must try to quickly put behind it defeat or victory and get ready to play the next week. In Ann Arbor, the Wolverines were more ready than the Illini, as they stacked a six-man defensive front to slow down the Illini's "Whiz Backs" and beat Illinois 14-0. The week after, the civilian, yet more experienced, Ohio State Buckeyes sent the Illini to their third straight defeat 26-12 in Cleveland. Unmoved by the final score, Eliot came into the locker room and simply said "Thanks boys, thanks."

The Fighting Illini capped their season by downing Northwestern 25-6. Despite the three-game losing streak, Illinois finished with a record of 5-4-1.

"I was proud of that 1944 team," Eliot would beam later. "We gave out 27 letters in 1944 and 21 of them went to 17-year-old boys and two of them went to 16-year-old boys. And that team led the United States of America in yards gained."

Eliot had learned not to get his hopes or expectations up too much in these war years, though, and when the core of his team disappeared to the war effort again after the 1944 season, including Buddy Young and Paul Patterson, he was chagrined but also resigned.

Nineteen forty-five did mark the return of Burt Ingwerson, a Lieutenant Commander in the United States Armed Forces, to Illinois. He who had lettered for three years at Illinois in the late teens, who had been the head coach of the Iowa Hawkeyes, who refused the line coach position at Illinois that Eliot took in 1937, and who Eliot beat out for the head coaching post in 1942, accepted a job as an assistant under Eliot. He walked into a crazy year at Champaign-Urbana.

Eliot was not as devastated as some may have been at the loss of Young and Patterson from his backfield. After all, he still had his crack backfield tandem from 1943, Bray and McGovern...or so he thought.

Before the season began, McGovern had an appendicitis attack that required immediate surgery. The doctors initially thought he might play that season anyway under the rehabilitation program of George Stafford of the University Physical Education Department. Stafford had been in charge of the Army and Navy physical rehab programs. Through a series of exercises that he could perform while still laid up, Stafford felt that McGovern could keep his uninjured muscles in tone and thus be in as good of shape when he got out of the hospital as the day he went in. McGovern missed the entire season.

In Illinois' second game, a clash against Notre Dame, Bray hurt his right knee and played only intermittently the rest of the year.

Injuries were certainly a big part of the story that year, as they piled up one after another. By their eighth game at Ohio State, the Illini had only three starters who had not missed a game. Incredibly, they even had another appendicitis attack when starting guard Larry Forst was stricken around mid-season. He was handling the sticks for the officials in Illinois' final game against Northwestern.

Unfortunately, after trouncing Pitt 23-6 in their first game, the decimated Illini offense became like the Three Stooges on ice. Against Notre Dame the Illini fumbled eight times (the Irish fumbled seven) and lost the ball six times. They also threw an interception. In losing 7-0, Illinois drives were stopped on the Notre Dame one-yard line, twice on the four, once on the 11, and once on the 15.

They were beaten next by eventual Big Ten champ Indiana 6-0 after fumbling three times and throwing two interceptions. The Hoosiers scored in the fourth while the Illini had a drive stall at the Indiana nine-yard-line in the last moments.

On the train to Madison, Wisconsin, the following week-end Eliot and his boys had some fun learning card tricks from half back Stan Stasica. Eliot even taught a few of his own. They could have used them Saturday afternoon, as they were favored to beat Wisconsin and racked up a whopping 490 yards of offense. But after fumbling nine times (losing eight of them), throwing an interception, having drives halted at the Badger 2, 11 and 13 yard-lines and freshman Robert Jones missing a 24 yard field goal with 9 seconds left, they settled for a gruesome 7-7 tie.

The Illini were coming home to take on Michigan the next week and Illinois Governor Dwight Green wrote Eliot a letter: "It goes without saying that I personally am pulling for you with all my heart and soul to beat the University of Michigan Saturday in football, but more than just my personal feelings I want you to know that I have been around the state quite a bit lately and on all sides I have heard people state how much they would like to see Illinois beat Michigan. I can say that the entire state is behind you to win on the eve of this game.

"I want you to know furthermore that I shall be on hand to

see it and I wish you the best of success and I shall be pulling for you and the boys every moment."

It didn't help. The Illini fumbled seven times and neither team scored until the fourth quarter when the Wolverines put up 19 points. Their first touchdown was on a blocked punt in the endzone.

When Great Lakes came calling, the Illini only turned the ball over twice but the Bluejackets scored 12 points in the first quarter and Illinois only six in the fourth.

Iowa gave the Illini some relief next. Illinois finally found some consistent offense in their 48-7 victory.

The speed and efficiency that they were lacking on the field they found in the air the week after, as the Ohio State game marked the first time an Illini athletic team travelled by plane. What many were calling "the finest college airport in the land," had just been built on the outskirts of Champaign and the U. of I. administration thought that flying in planes to games held great possibilities. It would at once decrease the student-athletes' time away from class and increase the scope of intersectional schedules by making it easier for the Illini to play teams farther away.

Everyone survived the first large passenger flight from the university's airport, though "Babe" Serpico's stomach did some flips. He blamed it on the glass of milk he had before he went. The Illini arrived at 2:30 Friday afternoon at the Columbus airport to a large crowd of writers and photographers interested in the original "Flying Illini."

"It was great—the only way to travel," said Eliot.

On Saturday afternoon, 70,257 fans at Ohio State saw the Illini down 7-2 after three quarters, only to have the Buckeyes ring up 20 points in the final frame to finish them off.

Illinois' loss to Northwestern to end the season was a perfect summation of a frustrating autumn. The Wildcats scored the winning touchdown in the fourth quarter after Illinois fumbled the ball away three times and was intercepted once.

It had been the toughest of the three war-year seasons, and it was over.

Still, through these years of growing pains, of heartache, frustrations, hard luck, of injuries, terrible odds, of youth and patched lineups, few doubted that the University of Illinois football program was headed in the right direction.

"The finest spirit imaginable prevails in Illinois' athletic department, with everyone from Doug Mills, athletic director, and Eliot down to the student managers working in perfect harmony," George A. Barton of the *Minneapolis Tribune* wrote. "With a set-up like this, augmented by 90 percent support from the University officials, alumni, and student body, Illinois, when peace is restored in the world, again will resume the place in the football sun it occupied during the years (Bob) Zuppke was one of America's top-ranking coaches."

In 1945 Dwight Eisenhower and his soldiers had done their duty in Europe, and Douglas McArthur and his had done theirs in the Pacific. Definitively and finally, the war was over and they were coming home. Ray's boys...all of them...except the stellar fullback Tony Butkovich, who was shot and killed by a sniper on Okinawa...were coming home. They all had offers to go else-where and play. Young and Patterson were almost snatched away by UCLA, Alex Agase was wooed by Purdue. But they all came home...every one of them, save one, was coming back to Illinois where his loyalty lay. They didn't have to—they could have gone anywhere—but Ray's boys, all of them, save one, were coming home.

Thorns

"Every man is given the warp for his tapestry
The woof of his legend he must choose and weave.
Recalled to Illinois, Ray was given the orange
And blue warp; the patterns of Zuppke and Grange.

The woof, tainted, in disarray to disarm and dismay,
Back it came from Asian pools and rice paddies;
Hidden traps, friend and foe indistinguishable,
Commonality found only in ruptured guts; faceless.
Luck meaning youth forfeit to neurosis and futility.

A nation stricken opened the halls of learning;
Unheralded to blur ghastly cost of human non-sense.
Metal hands could not be blurrred; constant reminders
That prosthesis postulates more than a plastic nose.

The old-time gospel of gridiron heroics collided
With unspoken rebukes, and sneers set to juke-box rondo;
The tinkling metal fingers playing on plate and bowl;
Out-moded visionary plays and paeans in a Rose Bowl.

As did the legendary weaver, if no one else,
Ray would scrape the grease and filth from the wool.
He drenched away the Asiatic slime, encrusted scabs;

The tracings of the leeches; he exorcised the evil
Miasmatic residue, the lassitude and sloth; dispirit.
The woof became elan woven among the threads of the warp.
Tapestry in splendor in Pasadena; a gleaming legend in Urbana.

—LaRue Van Meter

"This team is the most overrated team in the country," insisted Ray Eliot just before the start of the 1946 season. "And if you don't say so too, you're crazy."

But with Agase and Young, Patterson, Kasap and Dufelmeier; with Bauman, Rykovich and others returning from the service, Illinois was the preseason pick by many to win their first Big 9 championship since 1928 (they had not even had sole possession of first place in the conference since then). Some alumni thought a national championship might be in the cards. But Eliot knew that talent is a small part of football, and potential scores no points. As glad as he was that his boys were home, he realized there was a lot of work to be done to turn this group of big-name individuals into a team that would live up to its billing.

There were many problems when Eliot got on with pre-season workouts (workouts that started late because he was an assistant coach in the now defunct college all-star game), not the least of which was that an estimated 200 to 500 boys came out for football. Former servicemen, transfers, and incoming freshmen seemed to come from everywhere to play at Illinois. Eliot went from paucity to a glut of athletic flesh in just one short year. He and his coaching staff had to somehow weed through all of these try-outers and find a football team. The coach set up stations on the practice fields around Memorial Stadium and split the candidates up into smaller groups so that they would be more manageable. He put a lot of trust in his assistants to help him evaluate the talent, but as the whittling process began, so did the headaches.

Outsiders and so-called football experts terribly misjudged the time it would take returning veterans to adjust to civilian and college football life. These boys still had the same names of Agase, Kasap, Dufelmeier, etc., but they were not the same men. First, they were older. Many of them were married and some had children. Second, war is hell, and they had gone through it. They had become men at the shout of an officer and grew up suffering the annihilation of their buddies. The heroics that earned him a purple heart would change an Alex Agase, and eleven months in a prisoner of war camp would affect an Art Dufelmeier. They had stared at death and lived. They had won a war and came back feeling like they were their own men, that they didn't need much help from anybody.

"The war veterans were the most unpredictable, unsettling and—sometimes—unmanageable bunch who ever set a coach to strumming his underlip," reported the Saturday Evening Post. "Outright insubordination was rare enough, but there were other horns to the dilemma. No longer were coaches dealing exclusively with raw young athletes fresh from the prep schools, who could be pounded into the desired shape in drill-sergeant fashion. (Some were) fed up with jumping every time someone cracked the whip. Many a conscientious kid found weight-reducing agonizing, some showed a fine disdain for the class-room, others simply could not rekindle the old urge to play."

Then, of course, there were those who had remained at home. "We were apprehensive," says Alex's younger brother, Lou Agase, who joined the Ilini in 1944. "We didn't know what was going on or what would happen. Many of us had earned a place in the lineup and we wondered if these guys were going to come home and just take our jobs away. It was an insecure and uneasy feeling."

"We were 24-year-olds trying to mesh with some who were as young as 17 years old," explains Alex. "What a job Ray and that coaching staff had—they had the toughest job a coach ever had."

Eliot was not the only coach with a tough job. It is possible, however, that he ultimately handled it better than anybody else. Brilliant talent (four years worth) returned to most of the schools that did not have military programs. At many schools it created great ruckus, turmoil and bad feelings between coaches and players to the point where most teams never reached their potential. In fact, the great Brent Bierman of Minnesota finally ripped his men publicly, accusing them of gold-bricking, and said that they played worse at the end of the season than at the start.

Referring to the number of vets returning to Illinois and the expectations heaped upon them, the *Post* said that "Ray Eliot had the same miseries as other college coaches, only more so."

Eliot had long preached, "When you've got the boys in the proper state of mind sir, you've got a winner!" Now it was his job to put his team in the proper state of thought and make them of one mind and one cohesive soul. It was a minefield of egos and emotions, of psyches and spirit.

It was also no easier on the Illini when one of their key members, one who would be called upon to lead them to the expected heights, had not before been a Fighting Illini at all. If a position was weak at Illinois going into the 1946 season, it was quarterback. The prospects were young, and for the most part untested, so when Eliot had the chance to get help, he seized it.

Perry Moss was a largely unused signal-caller at the University of Tulsa. Eliot had seen him play, and then met him at the college all-star game and liked him, saying that he was the first quarterback he'd seen who could stand in the pocket and not flinch. Tulsa head coach Henry Frnka happened to be an assistant on that team, too, and Eliot asked him if he could talk to Moss about coming to Illinois. Granted permission, Eliot convinced Moss to transfer. It was a perfect fit—almost.

Some Illinois players resented the fact that Eliot had brought in someone from the outside to run the offense. They felt that Illinois had enough talent already and Moss wasn't needed. In addition, though Moss was described by the press as "genial and likable," he was perceived by some teammates as cocky and arrogant, playing favorites in the offense.

And a few Illini gridders were not the only ones who didn't like Moss's switch to Champaign. The quarterback was scheduled to start the Illini's first game at Pittsburgh, but did not play because the Big 9 faculty representatives were to vote the next week on his eligibility after an investigation. Other Big 9 officials and some newspapermen felt that Moss had not spent enough time on the Illinois campus to be eligible, even though he had completed the required summer work. Illinois rep Frank Richart and athletic director Mills decided to withhold him rather than appear to push things through without waiting for the conference's decision.

In addition to all of these mental strangulations (Eliot's veterans also had to adapt to the intricacies of the T-formation, a system new to most of them) the former servicemen had to get themselves back into physical football shape, which would take awhile ("Didn't realize we weren't in shape until that first half," a big lineman muttered after their game against Pittsburgh).

The Illini's preseason practices and scrimmages were described by the press as "slow," "punk," and "lethargic." And when one writer observed that this Eliot-coached team "lacked spirit," one knew something was terribly out of sorts.

So it should have come as no surprise to anyone when Illinois, leading only 13-7 at halftime, would open the season struggling against a young and inexperienced Pittsburgh club before prevailing 33-7.

Before the game, in the midst of all of the chaos, Eliot was touched by the first telegram that he had ever received from his mother. "Best wishes for a successful opening," Annie messaged. But afterward, sportswriters, who had billed that game as one of the three biggest in the nation that day, had a message for their readers. In columns across the country, they finally concurred with the coach that the Illini were overrated. Illinois' showing made them two-touchdown underdogs against Notre Dame the next week at Memorial Stadium.

Actually the Irish thwacked the boys from Champaign-Urbana by three touchdowns 26-6, and a record 75,119 still-hopeful fans went home bitterly disappointed. Though Moss had been declared eligible by the league, the 86-degree heat made life rough on the still out-of-shape Illini.

Excuses aside, Eliot began to get frustrated trying to bear the weight of a heavy favorite. At Illinois this was new to the 41-year-old coach; he had always been the underdog. In his first four years as the head man, he worked untethered by people's expectations, when any success was nothing short of miraculous. He would soon learn that, as forgiving as people could be when he did not have talent, they could be equally as brutal when they thought he did.

Adding to Eliot's dismal feelings was that this was not only a big loss, but another to Notre Dame. The Illini's series against the Irish came to an end with Eliot never having beaten them. Once more he had to make the trek to the middle of the field to congratulate Frank Leahy. As a matter of fact, even though these two schools had played some thrilling games, no Illinois team had ever beaten the Irish. They stood 0-9-1 against them, and there would be no opportunity to undo it the next year. The teams have played only once since, in 1967, a forgettable 47-7 loss by the Illini.

Even more disappointing to Eliot, though, was the lethargy and general disarray of his Illini. They were described by Joe Hendrickson of the *Minneapolis Tribune* as "fat and slow," and it was beginning to wear thin on the fifth-year coach.

"How do I feel?" snapped an out-of-character Eliot at a reporter who asked the ill-fated question. "How should I feel? What am I supposed to say? Don't ask me such questions!"

Whether he really believed it or not, a calmer Eliot said later, "We were licked by a better outfit—that's all." And then he gave himself some good advice when he stated, "It's best to forget about this game and go after the next one."

Ever the player's coach and friend, Eliot's countenance fell that day. Usually positive, upbeat and enthusiastic, he saw clearly that he was dealing with different men and attitudes than before.

"Frankly, some of those players who were older thought they knew more about coaching than I did," he said many years later.

So Doctor Eliot took the sugar out of the medicine. It was a "Get tough, be tough, I'm tough policy," wrote the *News Gazette's* Pat Harmon, and it began with a two-hour scrimmage on Monday. It was strange to see this fun-loving, personable fellow suddenly without a smile or a joke, but in his heart he believed in his boys, and he was going to see to it that they reached their potential one way or another. He didn't enjoy it, but Purdue was next, and by God, the Boilermakers would meet the real Fighting Illini!

"Stung by the crack of the whip throughout the week, Illinois was in shape Saturday for the first time this season," wrote Hendrickson.

Sparked by their first offensive play of the game, a 45-yard touchdown pass from Moss to Ike Owens, the Illini burned Purdue 43-7 to the delight of the home crowd. It was the worst Big 9 loss for the Boilermakers in 24 years, the first time Illinois had beaten them in 27 years (though they had only played four times in that span), and the largest conference win for Illinois since their 1939 46-0 shellacking of the University of Chicago in its last year of competitive football.

"One down and six to go!" cried Moss as he entered the locker room afterward.

Realizing that one win did not a season make, however, the Illini coach hardened his face. "Hard work is the menu again next week," he stated flatly. "It paid off this week."

Northwestern had whipped Wisconsin the same day 28-0, and the Wildcats, Illinois, Michigan and Ohio State were now considered the contenders for the Big 9 crown. Before Illinois would face off with them, however, it had to deal with an Indiana team that returned virtually everybody from its conference championship the year before, but that did not benefit from returning servicemen. It was not a day that the Illini cared to remember.

"Burn the tapes," the Illini players disgustedly blurted to Ray Hamm, their motion picture man, after they faced the Hoosiers.

"I wish I could," answered Hamm, "but I need to keep my job. I'm going to print the whole mess."

A mess it was.

An over-capacity crowd of 27,000 (largest in Indiana's history) witnessed the Illini score early, then flail in irons as Indiana came back and beat them 14-7. In the first five minutes the Illini gained 91 yards, but they gained only 78 the rest of the way. Injured captain Mac Wenskunas stayed in Champaign and listened to the game on the radio. It is said he could be heard by everyone in his apartment building pacing the floor and screaming out defensive plays in frustration.

"We just thought it would be too easy once we got that first touchdown," Mike Kasap said that day. "It was just like the Pitt game, only this time we couldn't recover."

Eliot didn't know what to say, and his players didn't know what to say to him. He sat on the equipment trunk with his head in hands.

That night Eliot did not sleep well. The wolves were howling and the demons would not let him alone. Although the newspapers did their best to represent the situation as it was, criticism of the coaching staff was growing. Some called the team "uninspired" and Eliot could not argue with them.

Some wondered what had happened to Buddy Young. The speedster's output was well below his 1944 and 45 levels and he hadn't scored a touchdown in four games. Eliot had gone into the season realizing that every defense he faced would key on Young so he decided to use him more as a decoy than an integral part of his offense. But that offense gained only 78 yards in the final 55 minutes against Indiana. Discontent grew, and petitions for Eliot's removal began to circulate among the student body and the alumni.

To whom much is apparently given, much is certainly required and the "best coach in the nation" was suddenly, in the eyes of some, a man who was failing at his mission. The Illini had settled back in the Big 9 pack with a 1-1 record in conference play, and their toughest games were still ahead. Their chances of a Big 9 championship were dubious and in their only big nonconference game they had been blown out.

These thoughts tortured the head coach. He had tried cajoling his players and that did not work. He then tried the tough-guy approach, but that was ineffective. He took it all very personally. He felt for the University, for the administration, but most of all, he felt for his boys. He wrestled with the demons, but could come up with no answers...except one.

On Sunday Eliot went to visit Doug Mills in the hospital (he had an eye ailment) and offered his resignation. The pride and reputation of the University were more important to him than his own career or ego, and, though he believed in himself, if the players could reach their potential under someone else, then so be it. Stunned, the athletic director rejected the idea out of hand. Hearing of this later, University President George D. Stoddard even offered to come out swinging publicly in defense of the beleaguered coach, but others advised against it.

Reinvigorated by the administration's loyalty and with his own faith re-stoked, Eliot, after some heavy-duty soul-searching, determined to do something about the situation.

First, on Monday before practice he called an unprecedented "gripe" session. Eliot listened, while the athletes talked. Few of the suggestions had practical merit, but the communication broke the tension. More importantly, the invitation to speak their minds appealed to the war veterans, many of whom held positions of authority in the service.

But afterward, to prove to them the foolishness of their hard-headedness and individualism, he showed them films of that Indiana game that never made it to the incinerator.

"I showed them on the films that they really weren't playing our defense at all," Eliot told the story later. "They were all out there playing whatever defense they wanted to. I told them that if they wanted input on the defense that was fine, so I said that they should get their defense together and let me know when they were all set. When they were ready we went onto the practice field and called over our freshman team. I told the freshmen exactly what I wanted them to do offensively and they ran right through the varsity defense like it wasn't even there. Without a word I walked off the field and went to the locker room.

"One by one, after the workout was over, they came by my office and said they wanted to go back to my defense, and play it the way I wanted it played. It was then that I knew I had them."

In the meantime, Mills was incensed about the attitudes

of the football Illini, and wanted to say some things that Eliot would not say in his own defense. Out of the hospital, he showed up after practice that day, came into the Illini locker room and sent all of the coaches, including the head man, out. He told all of the players to sit down and he lit into them.

"He told us how Ray had looked so forward to us coming home, how excited he was that his boys were here and that we were laying an egg," says Alex Agase. "He told us that Ray had offered his resignation and that we were letting down one of the greatest coaches and one of the greatest gentlemen in the nation. I think, from that day, we were determined to do something about it."

The tapestry was beginning to mend, and for the first time they all seemed to be climbing onto the same loom.

The *Saturday Evening Post* compared Eliot to the great General Omar Bradley, saying "Bradley was called 'the G.I.'s general' so Ray Eliot might be termed the ex-G.I.'s football coach." The *Post* described Eliot's brilliance and flexibility as "his rare big-brother coaching approach." Whatever one called it, he was determined to treat his boys like the men they were, and they to make up for their stubbornness by routing Wisconsin for their mentor. The facts faced, if the Illini had any realistic hope for a Big 9 championship they had to beat the Badgers.

"A finish that will rate as one of Illinois' all-time thrillers," Pat Harmon described the battle with the boys from Madison, "and the first quarter, the most startling played in Memorial Stadium since Red Grange ran for four touchdowns in 12 minutes against Michigan in 1924."

Illinois scored on the fourth play of the game when (guess who?) Buddy Young scooted into the endzone from 34 yards out. But Wisconsin answered on the ensuing kickoff, as Willie Dryer weaved 92 yards for a score. Two minutes and 15 seconds were gone and the score was already tied 7-7.

Two minutes later Young fumbled deep in Illinois territory and the Badgers punched in an easy touchdown from the six. Wisconsin led 14-7. On the Illini's next drive, however, they went 63 yards in 14 plays, and, before 10 minutes had elapsed, the score was 14-14 and neither team had punted.

In the second quarter, the Badgers' Jack Winks faded to pass and spotted Dale Bowers open behind the defending Illini

Julie Rykovich. Winks hit Bowers on the dead run and he went 56 yards for the score. The Badgers led 21-14 and Rykovich, a man already criticized by media and fans alike because his offensive running was not up to his prewar standard, could not be consoled. At halftime he sat, bent in tears and would not talk to anyone. He had been burned and the press was ready to pin the goat label on him, but he would remove the tag before it could stick.

Illinois stopped a Badger drive on the Illini five yard line and the third quarter was scoreless, but midway through the last frame, the home team began its move. They reached the Badger 20 yard line and Rykovich was given the pigskin. The blocking was shoddy, but guts and determination barrelled him down to the one. Moss plunged in from there with seven minutes remaining. But after being unsettled by waiting for the officials to quiet the crowd, not having enough men on the field and finally an offside penalty, Don Maechtle missed the extra point and Illinois still trailed 21-20.

Some say it was not a bad thing that Maechtle missed that kick, because, had he tied it, the Illini might have settled for that. Certainly, being behind by a point, the Illini's motivation remained keen.

The defense heroically stiffened again, the home team got the ball back at midfield, but were penalized back to their own 39. The clock and the Badger defense were duel enemies now. On their first play, Rykovich took a pitch from Moss, rolled to his right, pulled up and fired a 29-yard strike to Ike Owens. The Illini inched closer as the seconds disappeared. Ruck Steger, the big fullback, hit for five and then Moss speared Joe Buscemi with a 16 yard buttonhook. The quarterback rode the will of Julie Rykovich the next three out of four plays to the three yard line. With two minutes showing on the clock, Moss went to "Orange Julius" one more time, and the 205 pound back catapulted over the middle of the Badger front wall, scoring the touchdown that sent Memorial Stadium into delirium. Maechtle made the point after and the Illini defense thwarted Wisconsin's last-ditch efforts for the 27-21 win. Rykovich would never regain his prewar speed, but he did regain his pride. In the meantime, the gleeful Illini swarmed to the middle of the field and lifted their beloved coach on their shoulders, whooping it up as they carried him from the field.

"Ray deserved to win," shouted Art Dufelmeier to reporters over the celebration in the locker room. "I'm glad we won for his sake." Others echoed the sentiments of their teammate.

"We won this one for Ray," said the soft-spoken Young.

"I'm so happy I could hug that man Eliot," enthused big tackle Bill Franks. "He's the greatest guy in the world. I would do anything for him."

"Maybe this will quiet some of the talk around campus about changing the football coaching staff," stated Lou Agase firmly. "It was a good time to win—and to keep on winning."

Eliot wasn't down off the shoulders of his boys a second when he raised his voice in excitement, saying, "Never in my life have I seen a team put up such a fight to come back and win. It was wonderful. This is great. That was the fightingest Fighting Illini team I ever saw! You deserve all the credit for that game."

Later, to the press, Eliot's enthusiasm was not dimmed. "I'm so proud of the boys," he said. "Even if they had not won in the second half, you could never forget the impression they left you of a fighting, scrapping ball club. Those boys played football for keeps."

One sportswriter wrote that they played as "a unit" and Bert Bertine of the *Evening Courier* penned that "It was the first time this year the Illini looked and acted like they were really mad and wanted to win in the worst way. You could tell it by the way they tackled and blocked. There was viciousness in that Illinois team, the kind of hard-boiled, slam-bang stuff needed to win in this man's league."

Fierce was the play, and four Illini had to leave the game because of injury. Two of them, Alex Agase and Dufelmeier knocked each other cold as they collided in the third quarter converging on a Badger ball carrier. Kasap broke a finger and when Young was kicked in the head and had to be removed, emotions raged and a brawl almost broke out, Ralph Serpico coming to his teammate's defense.

The Illini sported new plastic helmets that day against Wisconsin, but more importantly, there were new men inside them. Suddenly this Fighting Illini football team was not fighting itself, but the enemy. Eliot's bold, sensitive steering through troubled waters, and the administration's support of him had paid off.

In other Big 9 showdowns of the week, the two unbeatens, Northwestern and Michigan, played to a 14-all tie, Iowa surprised Indiana 13-0, and Ohio State and Purdue ended deadlocked. With four games to go, the conference race was a four-team affair consisting this time of Northwestern and Michigan (still without losses), and once-beaten Iowa and Illinois. The Illini were the only ones that had to play all three of the other contenders, plus they had to tangle with Ohio State, a preseason favorite. Despite the thrilling comeback against the Badgers, some thought they would do well to win two of those games.

"We led Michigan 60-0. The boys got so tired making touchdowns they had to all be taken out—all the reserves were bushed too. So Ray had to forfeit the game because he didn't have any players left," Ruck Steger laughed as he related his dream to his teammates on the train to Ann Arbor.

The Illini hoped it was a precursor of things to come—the 60-0 part anyway—as they did when Dike Eddleman hit the unexpected jackpot that Friday at the Dearborne Inn. Eddleman was trying to make a phone call, when he got no answer and jiggled the handle to get his nickel back. Suddenly, there was a crash that could be heard all over the inn. Not only had Eddleman's nickel come out but 85 others with it.

Not many expected Illinois to get rich on Michigan, though, as the *Chicago Tribune*'s Wilfred Smith wrote, "Michigan's big test in its remaining games probably will come against Minnesota." The largest crowd to ever pack Michigan Stadium and the largest to ever see an Illinois team in action came with the same expectations. But the 86,938 fans watched the Big 9 rivals battle to a 7-7 tie at the half.

In the third quarter, Sam Zatkoff, who grew up 25 miles from Ann Arbor and had 19 family members and hundreds of hometown folk in attendance, intercepted a Michigan pass at the Illini 48 yard line. He angled away from his own blockers to the opposite side of the field, but still went in for his first-ever, and Illinois' go-ahead touchdown.

When he came off of the field, Eliot asked Zatkoff why he had deserted his own interference.

"Jeez, Coach," grinned number 38, straightening out the Illini's new white traveling uniform on his shoulder pads, "all my brothers were sitting on the other side and I wanted them to see me."

Maechtle's point-after was blocked and Michigan picked up a safety later to make the score 13-9.

In his excitement, Eliot found himself on his knees in front of the Illini bench for most of the fourth quarter. "No truth to the report I was praying," he joked later. "I didn't have time."

That final frame saw Michigan pounding constantly at the Illinois goal-line, having the ball for 25 plays to just four for the visitors. They threw their battering-ram to the 17, eight, and four yard lines on separate drives, but the Illini's bend-but-don't-break defense would not let the Wolverines in the endzone. When the dust had settled Illinois had earned its 13-9 victory.

These games were not for the faint of heart (there was a man in the crowd that died of a heart attack during the second quarter), but the radio people sure loved them. "I had to go to bed for three days after the Wisconsin game," said future Baseball Hall of Fame broadcaster Jack Brickhouse, who called the Illini games for WGN Radio in Chicago. "Today I got so worked up I think I've had a relapse."

Fans were worked up, too. About 300 hearty, appreciative souls had stood in the rain to see the Illini off at Champaign's Illinois Central depot on Thursday, but a spontaneous celebration broke out after the win, and when the Illini's train rolled into its home at 12:50 Sunday morning 6,000 wildly cheering fans were there to greet it.

"Old timers agreed," wrote Bill Scmelzle in the *News Gazette*, "that never before had an Illinois team been welcomed home at such an odd hour by such a huge crowd."

Seizing destiny by the throat, Illinois had beaten contender number one, and it was obvious to everyone that the selflessness that had characterized Eliot's teams in the past had re-emerged. When Ruck Steger fumbled in the fourth quarter to give Michigan another point-blank opportunity, for instance, several Illini immediately ran over and patted him on the back. Steger responded by making two tackles as Illinois held the maze and blue out again. Illini players talked about nothing but each other's exploits afterward. They preferred to applaud their teammates or coaches in their comments, and shun the glory.

Everything was "team" now, even to the point that superstitions became a group effort. For the trip to Iowa the next Thursday, the Illini boarded the same train they took to Michigan, left at the exact same time and stayed at the same hotel in Cedar Rapids that they had when they beat the Hawkeyes the last two times out. Friday evening, the same coaches that played a game of hearts at Michigan played again, sitting in the same order. In the trolley to Iowa City Saturday morning, Ralph Serpico wore Burt Ingwersen's hat for the third week in a row and in the back of the car, as at Ann Arbor, were Owens, Steger, Ingwersen and Bert Bertine, seated in the same positions.

Maybe the superstitions worked, or maybe the Illinois defense was just a little better than the Hawkeyes', but the Illini pitched their first shutout of the year, intercepting three passes in the process—two inside their own 20 yard line. The Hawkeye defense was just as impenetrable in the first half, but in the second, Eliot finally felt he had favorable field position to insert Buddy Young. Young only ran for 26 yards on his own, but his presence as a decoy stretched the Iowa defense and allowed Steger and Rykovich to bang inside for yardage. The Illini finally scored in the last quarter on Steger's first-ever collegiate touch-down.

Illinois won 7-0 and was alone at the top of the Western Conference heap for the first time since 1928. They had spent 18 years trying to re-ascend the throne, and now they had done it with the help of Ohio State, which knocked off Northwestern the same day 39-27.

Like giant dominos, two contenders had fallen at the hands of the boys from Champaign-Urbana and they had an open date before they had to take on the Ohio State Buckeyes (left for dead just a few weeks before, the Bucks had clawed back into the race with their win over the Wildcats) and finish up against a brooding band in Evanston. If they won both, they would be Big 9 champs.

Wrote Gene Shalit in the *Daily Illini*: "The reward is problematic but delicious—the Western Conference Championship, first since 1928, and a shot at U.C.L.A. in Pasadena's Rose Bowl. Pardon me dreaming."

For the previous 19 years, the Pacific Coast Conference (now the Pac 10) had voted their own representative to participate in the Rose Bowl and then invited whatever opponent they wanted from outside their conference. But now the Big 9 and the Pacific Coast conferences were working on a five-year agreement that would pit their two best in the "Granddaddy" of all bowl games. This agreement between them was not a done deal yet, but officials from each were to meet and finalize it at season's end.

If the Rose Bowl agreement was all but decided, the conference races were not. In the Pacific, U.C.L.A. still had U.S.C. battling it for the top spot. In the Big 9, Illinois, with a record of 4-1, was in the driver's seat, but the conference was still wide open with several teams still in the mix...including the Buckeyes looming around the corner at 2-1-1.

With rain in the offing the night before they were to host the Buckeyes, Eliot ordered the Memorial Stadium turf covered with the newly-purchased $25,000 tarp. But he showed up the next morning aghast at what he saw. Somewhere along the chain of command, his orders were lost, and the field was a quagmire. Some Ohio State fans accused the coach of leaving the tarp off purposely, feeling that it would somehow be an advantage for the Illini. The Buckeyes did have a couple of fleet backs that would be less effective running outside because of the soaked conditions, but the Illini had Young and Patterson, who they would have loved to cut loose as well. The facts were, Eliot ordered the tarp on, it did not get done, and the teams were left with no choice but to play in a stormy sea.

Besides, Ohio didn't have a problem moving the ball; it was scoring that eluded them. The Bucks had more first downs then the Illini (11-5), many more offensive yards (225-114), and more than twice as many plays (76-35), but the Illini had more points (16-7). When the chips were down, Illinois' defense was, once again, up. From a blocked punt for a safety, to a 99-yard interception return by Rykovich (a play some call the most electrifying in Illini history) to more late goal-line stands, the defense made the big plays for the orange and blue.

Once, late in the game, when the outcome was still in doubt, Ohio State had the ball first and goal at the Illini's five yard line. The big Buckeye fullback, Joe Whisler, pounded off the right side for two, then off the left side for two more. On third down from inside the one, Whisler was stopped cold. The Bucks decided to go for a fourth straight time with their fullback, who led all ball carriers with 123 yards on the day. The big man headed like a steam ship furrowing through the fog toward the right side of the Illini line. Illinois' great linebacker and captain

Mac Wenskunas broke with the huge boat and met it head on at the goal line. Whisler dropped one foot short of paymud. The Illini had preserved their victory.

Wind was almost as much a stopper on the day as Wenskunas. In the offseason, Eliot had tried to get a rule change through the conference rules committee that would give a team scored upon not only the decision of whether or not they wanted to receive or kick off, but also whether or not they wanted the wind.

"Give the team that is scored upon the option of changing goals," he argued. "You can score on a team and keep them in the hole for an entire quarter if you have the wind."

This Ohio State game was a case in point. The Bucks had the wind in the first quarter, and Illinois spent it at their own end. In each subsequent frame the team that had the wind knocked on the door of the other. His proposal, of course, was never made law.

For their part, Ohio State did not take this loss in stride.

"Naturally, no one ever wants to lose," first-year head coach Paul Bixler was quoted by the *Columbus Dispatch.* "But these are tougher to take when you earn yours the hard way and the other guy goes out and gets his the cheap way. That's certainly what Illinois did today. We ground through 'em and they scored on breaks."

Indeed, writer Paul Hornung of the *Dispatch* went as far as to say that Illinois had gotten their scores the "lazy way."

"Just among us folks," he wrote, with us eavesdropping, "Ohio State had the better football team. You could see it on the field. You could read it in the statistics."

But the Buckeyes were reading and weeping, while the Illini were cautiously celebrating, one game away from the Big 9 championship.

"We're not in yet," said Coach Eliot. "We're worried about Northwestern—they'll be hard to beat."

The race had come down to two teams on the final game day of 1946. Illinois was on top at 5-1 and Michigan was still panting right behind at 4-1-1. The Illini had a date with the 'Cats, and Michigan with Ohio State.

"There's one chuckle about the whole situation," penned Lew Byrer in his column for the *Columbus Citizen.* "It was only five weeks ago that they were circulating petitions on the Illinois campus about getting rid of Ray Eliot. Mr. Eliot's Illini are now about a 5-1 bet to win the Big 9 title and go to the Rose Bowl—and I can't find anyone in Champaign or Urbana who knows anyone who ever heard of anyone who had anything to do with circulating any of those petitions."

12

Roses

"Any team is a potential winner if it has the will to win. As far as plays and strategy are concerned, all major college coaches are much the same. The coach who succeeds is the one who best can inculcate his own will to win into his players. Some day, I'm going to take a team and pour into it such a desire to win one particular game that it will tear into a favored opponent and rip it to pieces. . . "

—Ray Eliot in his home on
January 27, 1942, the night he was hired
as Illini head football coach

Illinois capped the 1946 season by thrashing Northwestern 20-0 to capture its first Big 9 conference title since 1928. This did not, however, guarantee that the Illini would be the conference representative in the Rose Bowl.

It would seem unthinkable that the first place team (in this instance, Illinois at 6-1) would not be chosen by the Big 9 over the second place team (Michigan at 5-1-1), but it was possible. Only twice had the Pacific Coast sent someone other than the conference champ—still, it had happened (a school could also decline an invitation if they considered it too expensive or not in their best interests). Indeed, on the same day the Illini trampled the Wildcats, Michigan tried to build a case for itself by blistering Ohio State 58-6.

Illinois had strong arguments on its side, though: they were conference champs, they beat Michigan and the team that tied Michigan (Northwestern) they had walloped. The conferences were set to finalize their pact on Tuesday, and the vote on who would represent the Big 9 would come Thursday.

Eliot had been coy, almost superstitious, all week before the N.U. game about even mentioning a bowl bid, lest he jinx his eleven.

"Eliot accidentally let down the bars himself Friday night (though), on the diner coming up to Evanston with his team," joked the *News Gazette*'s Pat Harmon. "He ordered an extra bowl of tomato soup from the waiter. It was the only time all week he had mentioned the word B-O-W-L."

After the victory in Evanston, the ever-cautious coach grinned, "It's not official, until we get the official invitation."

The overwhelming majority of media and fans on the West Coast (and in the east) hoped no Big 9 team would be granted any kind of invitation. Until the Pacific Coast and the Big 9 had made their agreement, powerful and undefeated Army had been the leading candidate to face a Pacific Coast team in the Rose Bowl. With one game to play, UCLA was also unbeaten, and Nebraska, with a record of 3-5, was not expected to be a problem for them the next week. Fans and journalists on both coasts were dreaming of a matchup between the Cadets and the Bruins, who they were proclaiming as one of the greatest teams ever to come out of the west. As a matter of fact, Army officials had the impression right up to Illinois' final game that they would be invited. According to Major Paul Amen, the Cadets had received an unofficial bid from the West Coast.

"We were so sure of going to the Rose Bowl," said Major Amen to the *Daily Illini*'s Gene Shalit at the Illinois/Northwestern game, "that I was on my way out to the coast to scout UCLA and Southern California, but only got as far as Champaign because of the Big 9 tie-up."

A few days before, the Army players voted to accept an invitation to the Rose Bowl and were sorely disappointed when they found out they weren't going.

"West Coast officials had assured us we were going to receive the official invitation," Amen said. "Most people are mad at the West Coast. They were in control and could have insisted on Army. That is what most of the people wanted."

All of this was news to Big 9 officials, because the Pacific Coast had assured them that Army would only get the invitation if the Big 9 said "no." But the Big 9 was already on record as okaying the deal—a deal that would benefit each conference equally.

The Rose Bowl was not just the oldest college football postseason classic, getting its start when it officially replaced Roman-style chariot races in the Tournament of Roses in 1916, but, up until 1944 and 1945, it was by far the most prestigious.

However, the Sugar Bowl in New Orleans, Miami's Orange Bowl, and the Cotton Bowl in Dallas had begun to rival it for quality opponents and fan interest. The Pacific Coast had been trying to cut a deal with the Big 9 for years because they knew that the Midwest schools had one of the best brands of football in the country—thus they would be guaranteed a quality opponent each year and one from a densely populated region that would garner interest and fans.

The Big 9, at length, came to the conclusion that they would only gain by hooking up with the "grandaddy of them all." For 26 years, Big 9 officials had banned conference teams from postseason bowls because conference faculties said they prolonged the season and interfered with the boys' studies. They had eased their tough stand recently, though, and finally acquiesced with these stipulations: first, there could be no time lost from classes; second, no team could go two years in a row; third, every Big 9 school and the conference office would receive a share of the receipts.

But the critics were howling. The Illini, they said, were not worthy to take on the mighty Bruins of UCLA and stain the precious Rose Bowl with their inferior blood. These people saw nothing special about the Big 9, much less a Big 9 team that had two losses, as Illinois had. They even thought that many of the Illini wins were "escapes" rather than solid victories. They said Illinois got lucky in the last minute against Wisconsin, caught Michigan on a down day, and got help from the mud to beat Ohio State. They viewed Illinois as possibly the fourth best team in the conference, a team that had a rugged defense to be sure, but relied on opponent errors to win. They derided the decision even more when they found out that two Big 9 schools voted against the pact—and one of them was Illinois. If nothing else, the critics wanted the conferences to put off the deal until the following year so that Army could still come. But the Big 9 had made it clear: "This year or not at all," they said.

Sportswriters and fans screamed in the west and they screamed in the east, but that Tuesday the Rose Bowl pact was finalized, and Thursday the Big 9 voted that the Fighting Illini would be their first bowl representative in over a quarter of a century. Instead of the final vote quelling the media, it stirred it up all the more. The press on the west coast, especially, roasted the Illini, hoping they could somehow get Army in the game yet.

There was one writer who had a different point of view from the rest when comparing the toughness of this Illinois squad with Army, however.

"The Illinois squad includes a number of players who saw combat duty on all fronts," wrote George Barton, a writer from the east. "While they were facing hell on all fronts, West Point officials built up the greatest football team in the nation with a hand-picked squad composed of outstanding stars of numerous colleges who were promised immunity from the draft for four years."

Be that as it may, oddsmakers varied in their predictions from Illinois as 3-point favorites to UCLA being picked as 13-point winners. But you would have never known anyone thought the Illini had a chance by reading western papers. After all, the Bruins were the undefeated team, were playing at home, and outweighed the Illini 21 pounds to a man. While Illinois had barely slid through its schedule, UCLA had averaged five touchdowns per game and had vanquished Oregon State (the team most touted as the west's second best) 50-7.

"The Bruins have the plays and the players to whip the ears off the Illini," wrote Dick Hyknd of the *Los Angeles Times.* "And we care not whether the latter are champions of the Big 9, Terrible 10 or Dominating Dozen. They're going to be dead ducks in the famed Rose Bowl."

Rube Samuelson of the *Pasadena Star* asked visiting Illinois party members how many Illini players had voted against the Rose Bowl trip. When he was told that none did he was astounded and asked derisively, "Do you mean to tell me that none of them felt the Army should be out here instead of them?"

Ray Richards, the UCLA line coach, was quoted by another writer as saying that his players would make Illinois' Alex Agase (Big 9 Most Valuable Player and All-American for the third time) look sick. In addition, Buddy Young was voted one of college football's "flops" of the year in a nationwide poll of sportswriters.

Still another scribe queried, "Where is Illinois?"

The *Courier's* Bert Bertine wrote that Illinois was "the most unwanted bowl team in history." There was no disagreement from Frank Neill of the *Chicago Herald-American* who penned that Illinois was "the most highly-scorned champion ever manufactured in the Big 9 conference."

All of this put interesting pressure on the boys from Champaign, for they were not just carrying their own banner, but that of the Big 9. In reality, acceptance of the agreement between the conferences by the wide majority in the west hinged on an Illinois victory. Their opposition to the Illini was not because they disdained the Midwest so much as it was the want of a worthy opponent for their Bruins. If Illinois proved to be a worthy adversary, then the Big 9 would be considered a quality source of football teams to come to future Rose Bowls, and the rancor would stop.

"For the future of the Rose Bowl pact," wrote Leo H. Petersen of the *L.A. Times*, "most football leaders feel that an Illinois victory is imperative."

Eliot, of course, was not as concerned with the future of the pact as he was with the well-being of his boys, and the disdain, however spiteful, would play like a violin in the master's hand by the time he got done with it. But there were other obstacles not as simply dealt with for the coach.

The weekend after the vote that confirmed the Illini's trip to the Rose Bowl, Eliot and assistant Ralph Fletcher headed west to scout UCLA's final game against Nebraska. For years Rose Bowl teams had stayed at the Huntington Hotel in Pasadena, so Eliot and Fletcher decided to stay there on their scouting trip and at the same time make arrangements for the team.

Eliot proceeded to the front desk, asked for the manager and introduced himself.

"I'd like to get my team all set up to stay here when we come out in December," Eliot told him.

"Fine," said the manager. "And we'll arrange for your negro players to stay at another hotel downtown."

Eliot was completely caught off guard.

"I don't think you understand," the coach shot back. "This is a university TEAM. On this TEAM everyone stays together or we don't stay at all."

"But we've never had colored people stay at our hotel before," argued the manager.

"Well, I'll tell you this right now," Eliot fumed. "We're all 'colored' on this team. Some of us are white and some of us are black, but we're all colored." Eliot turned and headed for the door motioning for Fletcher to join him. "We're finding another place to stay!" he scowled.

"Okay, okay Coach," the manager stopped him. "If you feel that strongly about it, we'll try it."

A few weeks later the Illini broke the color barrier at the Huntington, but Eliot never told his players what had happened. (Incidentally, after the Rose Bowl was over, Eliot ran into the manager in the lobby of the hotel. "I just want to tell you coach," said the manager, "that this is one of the finest groups of young men we've ever had stay at our hotel. And that includes every one of them." Eliot would say later that that felt as good as any Rose Bowl victory could).

The coach finished his scouting trip and headed back to Champaign to commence preparations for the biggest game of his coaching life. He was already highly regarded in many places in the country and had coached some important games, but this would place him on the national stage like never before. This was the Rose Bowl, the most prestigious of postseason contests. The attention was already intense but the story line turned up the heat all the more: There was Army feeling slighted, UCLA sniffing at the prospect of playing what they considered twice-beaten semi-champions, and there was Illinois, beginning the season as the most overrated team in the country and now ending it the most underrated.

Obeying the pact rules, the Illini did not begin practice until December 15th when, because of severe December weather, they had to perform most of their drills inside the University of Illinois Armory on the hard dirt floor. The facility was a congested 70 yards long and Eliot didn't want anyone to get hurt unnecessarily, so they ran plays but did no real blocking and tackling. This left the coach with the feeling that they hadn't really accomplished much of anything. Thankfully, they soon would be heading to California where, the weather promised to be...well...California weather.

But University of Illinois Board of Trustees President Wayne Johnston was also a president of the Illinois Central Railroad, and apparently wanted the Illini to see every foot of his track because, instead of heading across the Midwest, they went south to New Orleans, across the plains of Texas and arrived two days late to Pasadena. To make matters worse, greeting the Illini was not the southern California sun, but rain...five days of rain. Game preparations suffered again.

Lousy weather, of course, was not the only distraction Eliot had to deal with when he brought his team to Pasadena. He had always been a coach who tried to shelter his boys from the distractions of the city when they traveled. Larry Stewart said it bordered on being a fetish: "He topped all of his other performances in this regard when he took a team to Seattle once. We got on the bus and went right through downtown Seattle and kept going. The bus didn't stop until we were in the middle of an absolute wilderness. And believe it or not, we spent that Friday night in a logging camp. A real logging camp. Ray even made a bed check of the players that night. They couldn't have gone anywhere if they wanted to."

There was no precedent for a Big 9 team preparing for a Rose Bowl, so Eliot and his staff were guessing as they went. They first thought the best way to get the team ready was to work them consistently hard, keeping them from the circus-like atmosphere that surrounds bowl games in California. One day, when the buses were sent to the hotel to bring the players to practice, though, none of them came down from their rooms. Eliot took aside a couple of the older players and asked what the hell was going on. They explained that the veterans in the group had just spent the last two or three Christmases away from home because of the war. Now they were away from home again over the holidays and they weren't having any fun. Every day was the same—practice and then back to the hotel. Eliot decided to gather all of his players together and worked out a schedule so the boys could see the sights of Hollywood after practices.

West Coast writers even used this to criticize Eliot. When he didn't seclude his team from glitzy Hollywood anymore, they wrote, "What a way to prepare a team for a football game!"

Eliot did try to keep the frivolities to a minimum, however, and he set a strict curfew so that the boys would get their necessary rest. Unfortunately two players, starting linebacker Ray Florek and Lou Donoho, broke the trust.

"We went out one night and were having a few drinks and laughs, when it was time to get back to the hotel," Mike Kasap tells the story. "Well, Florek and Donoho had met some ladies and wanted to stay out through the night. They said they would miss practice the next day, but were sure the coaches wouldn't notice. They asked me and a couple of others if we would cover for them if the coach said anything."

Florek and Donoho not only missed curfew and practice but curfew the next night too.

"At practice Ray (Eliot) asked me if I knew where they were and I said I didn't," Kasap continued.

By the end of the session the press had figured out a couple of players were missing and they began asking questions. When Florek and Donoho finally showed up, Eliot called them in. The coach loved his boys—but they had left him no choice.

"If I didn't send them home, I'd lose the whole team," he said years later.

"And because the press was suspicious, Ray couldn't very well not do anything," says Kasap realistically. "There was no hiding it even if he wanted to."

In scolding them, Eliot told Florek and Donoho that it wasn't the end of the world for them and that he would bring them back on the team the next year. Then, after informing them of his decision, Eliot gathered the Illinois press together, saying he had something to talk over with them.

"Men, we've had a couple of boys miss curfew, and I wonder what you think I should do about it," he began.

"Missing a curfew doesn't sound so bad," responded a couple of reporters. "For two days?" Eliot asked. He sent Florek and Donoho home.

In addition, Dike Eddleman had a conflict. Eddleman was a multi-sport athlete, playing basketball in the winter and the Illini had a game scheduled in San Francisco the night of the Rose Bowl game. Illinois' administration gave Eddleman the choice of playing in one or the other. As in keeping with his character, Eliot went one step further by insisting that arrangements be made for special transportation that allowed Eddleman to play in both games.

"Even though (Ray) had many players to use, I felt I was really needed," said Eddleman later. "And, as you know, with that feeling any player is going to give his all."

These difficulties did not help the Illini's mindset at all and they got a further scare when, on the 28th of December, Captain Mac Wenskunas went into a California hospital with what doctors thought might be appendicitis. It was a false alarm and he was in the starting lineup New Year's Day.

Of course, an appendicitis attack might have sounded pretty good to Eliot in comparison to his continuing ordeal with the West Coast press. As disrespected as the Illini were, one can imagine that their relationship with the scribes was not very good. It got even worse after their first workout on Pasadena soil.

"When we ended our practice, and I had talked with the newspapermen, I started back to the clubhouse to change my clothes," Eliot related to Lon Eubanks in 1976. "One of the newspapermen followed me over and said, 'Coach, I want to help you. I want to tell you what UCLA is doing since I've seen them in practice every day for the last week.'

"I couldn't believe it. 'We're such big underdogs,' I thought to myself, 'that even the newspapermen are trying to help us out.'"

Eliot looked at the reporter curiously and asked, "Are you sure you're a newspaperman?"

"He opened up his wallet and showed me his credentials," Eliot remembered. "I really shouldn't divulge his name. I said, 'Okay I'm going to give you a scoop. Just write down that all newspapermen from west of the Rocky Mountains will be banned from our practice sessions from now on out!'

"He said, 'Do you really mean that?'

"I said, 'Yes sir, I sure do. If you're willing to tell me what UCLA is doing, I don't think you're going to hesitate a minute to tell UCLA what we're doing. From now on the gates are closed.'"

The Pacific coast writers took offense to the decision to close practice and it fed the burning coals of indignation at this Illini club, even though Coach Bert Lebrucherie of UCLA had already been conducting most of his practices in private.

(Strangely enough, there was even a rumor spreading just before kickoff that Alex Agase and two other players had jumped the team. No one is quite sure where that rumor started, but Alex and the others did show up).

The game had not been played yet and the trip had already been tiresome. The five dollars and dried fruit that the Rose Bowl committee gave the boys for Christmas didn't quite fill the void. Several days before the contest, Eliot realized their spirits were low.

"So I sat them down in the shade near the practice field," recounted the coach later. Eliot had collected a manila folder full of press clippings from West Coast writers.

"I just let them start reading them," he said. "I made sure Alex got the one about how UCLA would make him look sick.

I remember him starting to read it, and I could see his face getting redder with every word. He started rising to his feet, and he threw the clipping down and yelled, 'All right, it's time we went to work!' That seemed to really get them fired up. They were not just preparing for a game now, they were preparing for a war. I remember that I had a heckuva time chasing the kids off the practice field every night after that."

That was the meeting that John Genis spoke of after the game when he said, "A few days ago we all got together and said, 'Boys, we're here to play football—let's go!' And we did." Eliot's men were focused now, and the excitement for the contest began to build.

In the 24 hours before kickoff, Eliot and his Illini received over 250 telegrams of good wishes from friends, family, and even Big 9 players that they had beaten during the season. The hullabaloo continued and, of course, Hollywood never did see a big act that it wouldn't join.

"I think it will be a tight game and the breaks will decide it," stated an uncommitted Bob Hope as he stood with Bing Crosby on the set of one of their "Road To"-movies. Hope was Grand Marshal of the Rose Parade. "No climbing on the limb for me this year."

"I think Antler Face is right," interrupted Crosby. "The breaks will decide the game, but Bert LeBrucherie's Bruins will grab the opportunities when they come along and I like 'em to win by 13 points. I'll slide out on that limb."

"I'm a Crosby fan myself," chimed in Dorothy Lamour listening nearby. "And I think Bing is right. The Bruins by 13 points—make a little room on the limb for me, Bing."

Abbott and Costello stuck together in picking UCLA by at least two touchdowns. Clark Gable also took the Bruins saying they "have what it takes to buy and sell the Illini." While Katherine Hepburn and former Michigan football great Tom Harmon picked the game even, boxer Jack Dempsey and Olympian Bill Tunney went with the West Coast team.

As for the coaches?

"If they think we are cheese champions, we'll show them they are wrong," vowed Ray Eliot. "I can't promise that we'll whip UCLA, for we are up against a mighty good ballclub, one of the best in the country. So I'd be crazy to predict victory, but I do want to say that we didn't come all the way out here to lose."

The Bruin's Bert Labrucherie said that his team "is ready for its best game and, win, lose or draw, there will be no excuses."

A hush fell over the streets of Champaign-Urbana on that chilly New Year's Day—nary a sound was heard. The black farm fields surrounding the twin-towns were smack in the dead of winter, yet radiant, crowned with unadulterated, sun-kissed snow. But the living rooms, dens and places of work were warm with Illini faithful gathered nervously around radios to follow their boys out west.

In Pasadena, rain finally gave way to a lovely California sunshine that bathed the Arroyo Seco with an arresting glow. A breeze waffled through the plush valley, moving a leaf or a palm here and there, the surrounding hills saying, "Welcome." Tucked in its blanket of green in the bottom of the valley, walls white-washed, its gallant pillars standing guard to its prestige, sat the Rose Bowl. And it began to bustle.

Many Illinoisians had paid 240 dollars or so to make the eight-day round trip to the Golden State and they helped fill the Rose Bowl to a boisterous, standing-room-only crowd of 93,083. Even then, UCLA fans made it known with pregame shouts and smug remarks that they were insulted to have Illinois there and that they still thought the Bruins should be playing Army.

Huddled in a locker room far beneath the raucous stands, were the resolute Fighting Illini and their convincing leader. The coach pulled out that manila folder and, as if putting hound dogs onto a scent, waved the newspaper articles of snide comment and derision in front of his boys one more time and gave them a "call to action," as Buddy Young called it later.

"When we went on the field," explained Alex Agase later, "we were determined to show the world that Illinois was a real champion and that Big 9 conference football is the best."

"The team had the most remarkable mental attitude I ever saw," said Eliot afterward. "Their pride was hurt and they wanted to win." He had taken his team and poured into it "such a desire to win one particular game."

Great occasions are rich soil for the fertile seeds of clever prose, and classic lines were written about this classic game: "(The Illini) blocked and socked and rocked the overrated Bruins with such ferocity," wrote Frank Neill, "that the echoes of bruising body blows still resound in the Pasadena hills."

Bert Bertine gloated that "the red haze hanging over Los Angeles tonight isn't the sunset, brother—its the reflection of coast scribes' faces."

Wrote John Carmichael of the *Chicago Daily News*: "Those folks out here who insisted that Army should have played in the Rose Bowl haven't changed their minds. Only now they think Army should have played Illinois."

And then there was this, penned by West Coast journalist Ned Cronin: "...the Bruins acted like a lost weekend trying to fight his way out of a revolving door."

From the first play from scrimmage, when Perry Moss fired a 44 yard strike to Julie Rykovich, the Illini made this contest no contest. They scored the first touchdown of the day a few plays after the Moss-to-Rykovich bomb, when the latter went over from a foot away. The Illini led 6-0 after a missed extra point.

The Bruins came back to take a brief 7-6 lead after a 51-yard drive was kept alive by a fake punt that went for 33 of those yards. But early in the second quarter, with UCLA still leading, the Illini drove into Bruin territory. Almost stymied, they faced a third down and 11 yards to go at the Bruin 38. It is here that Eliot took control of the game, for he had his team prepared strategically as well as emotionally. Moss called many of Illinois' plays on the field but Eliot called this new play, a play he wouldn't even run in practice for fear someone would see it who shouldn't. He devised it just for UCLA...and for Buddy Young.

Three Illini lined up wide to the right and Young set himself 10 yards behind them. Moss took the snap from center and shot him a long lateral. Young faked to the right then swept toward the left, just the opposite direction the Bruins expected. Blockers seemed to come from nowhere to assist him as Young zigzagged 16 yards to the Bruin 22 for an Illinois first down. It was that play that buckled the Bruins.

"The turning point in the game was Buddy Young's 16 yard surprise run which set up the second touchdown," said Labrucherie afterward. "It broke our spirit."

Young scored from the two a couple of plays later, and the Illini led 13-7.

The Illini's shifty offense confused the Bruins all game long. At one point, UCLA lineman Don Mike tackled Ruck Steger for the third time when he did not have the ball. "He got up," related Steger later, "and looked at me and asked, 'Boy, ain't you got the ball again?'"

Illinois hit paydirt three times and rang up 10 first downs in that second period alone to leave UCLA gasping. They followed Young's score with touchdowns after 52 and 50-yard marches. The first drive was capped off by Paul Patterson's four-yard touchdown run and the second by Moss' one-yard dive. Illinois had stretched its lead to an astonishing 25-7 and were all set to head into the locker room flushed with pride and happiness, when Al Hoisch, a little 139-pound Bruin scatback, fielded a kickoff on the bounce and returned it 103 yards for a touchdown. It was the first time in Rose Bowl history that a kickoff had been returned for a score.

"As I was running I was just trying to remember if Buddy Young was on the field or not," Hoisch chuckled later. "I was relieved when I realized he was not."

Eliot had also come up with a new defense for the Bruins. It was the first time the Illini had ever used the four-man line with the two ends dropping as linebackers (so effective was it that Bruin running back "Skip" Rowland, who came into the game averaging seven yards per carry, walked out with two total yards rushing on the day). They shifted in and out of this flexible defense as the situation warranted, and this helped keep UCLA off-balance and at bay as the score remained 25-14 into the fourth quarter.

But Young scored from the one on the first play of the last frame, Steger intercepted a pass and went 66 yards to paydirt, and Stanley Greene picked off another Ernie Case pass and ambled into the endzone from 15 yards out. UCLA was beaten.

"Illinois' greatest and most glorious athletic achievement of all time was arrived at here New Year's Day when the unsung, second fiddle, scorned and openly frowned upon football team took a gigantic but lumbering UCLA grid machine and demolished it piece by piece for an astounding 45-14 Rose Bowl triumph," trumpeted Bertine on the front page of the *Courier*.

Hoisch was not the only one to set a Rose Bowl record that day. The Illini set a couple of their own, including most yards rushing (320) and first downs (23). They just missed setting the record for most points, but still it was the worst defeat for a Pacific Coast Conference team in the history of the classic. Young and Rykovich, the most scorned of the Illinois backs, shared rushing honors with 103 yards apiece and MVP honors too. Appropriately, in 1993 they were elected together to the recently established Rose Bowl Hall of Fame.

At the outset of the game it was the UCLA fans shouting for Army, at the end it was the 15,000 or so fans from Champaign.

"We want Army! We want Army!" they sarcastically chanted as the fourth quarter wound down.

Even the midwestern sportswriters, some normally earnest old men, got into the act.

"Hey, do you still want Army?" they excitedly yelled down press row to their West Coast colleagues. "This team good enough for you?"

Illinois players also scoffed at these so-called bigger-than-life Bruins. During the game, the Illini line taunted the bigger Bruins saying things like, "Sorry, we're not Army." And Lou Agase stood over 230-pound UCLA tackle Bill Chambers after knocking him to the turf and cracked, "So you guys wanted Army, huh? What—for protection?"

After the game, the ribbing did not stop. "There are nine teams in the Big 9 that'll lick UCLA any day in the week," bellowed Alex Agase as he ripped off a dirty shirt and pushed into the locker room. "They were a poor team with a passer. We knew at halftime that we could take them."

"What happened to those odds?" asked a grinning Buddy Young.

"(West Coast writers) made us just mad enough to play a hell of a game," said Steger.

The other locker room, of course, was somber but honest.

"They were pretty tough," allowed All-American end Burr Baldwin. "They were fired up and socking like hell. That was about it."

Coach Labrucherie faced facts: "We did not play well," he said. "But I think if we played Illinois 10 times, I don't think we'd beat them once. They were just too good. They simply mowed us out of the line—that was all."

Labrucherie had the class to show humor in defeat when he was leaving for New York the day after to address the NCAA's coaches meeting on the subject of football defense. "I think I'll ask to be excused," he said. Asked further about the game, he turned and got serious, "Don't overlook the fact that (Ray Eliot) did a fine coaching job."

Alex Agase, himself a coach in later years, says the job Eliot did, not just in that game but for the entire season, was "miraculous."

His effort was certainly not overlooked by Gene Kessler, Sports Editor of the *Chicago Times*: "Eliot showed up a number of severe critics in his Rose Bowl strategy," he wrote. "Here is an unsung hero. He received little credit for coaching the Illini to their conference championship. Actually, most fans and newspapermen insisted all along that Ray failed to get the most out of his personnel this season.

"So allow us to point out how Eliot handled the situation, took criticism with a smile and proved it wrong on the immortal Rose Bowl gridiron with yesterday's one-sided win...Thus Ray Eliot finally received recognition for coaching mastery which he has displayed for years. One thing we know definitely; the next time Ray Eliot brings an Illinois eleven to the Tournament of Roses, it will be respected by everyone in California."

On January 2nd, Eliot went with Maggie and friends to the Santa Anita Racetrack, where he bet on a 90-1 longshot. The horse came in a winner prompting Grantland Rice to remark, "With this kind of luck, he ought to run for president."

13

Orator

"It's like Bing Crosby said to me once: 'Sing with your mouth? No, Ray, you don't sing with your mouth. You sing with your heart.'

"Did you ever hear him sing 'White Christmas'? Did you ever hear him sing 'Silent Night'? From the heart of a man.

"The great paintings of the world done by a man's bones and muscles? Yes, educated muscles and bones, but all from the heart of a man. . . the heart of a man. . . "

—Ray Eliot

In the midst of all of the daily business arranged and rearranged on Ray Eliot's desk in his Assembly Hall office, in between phone books, calendars, and pads of paper sat a book entitled, *Everything I Know About Public Speaking*. Inside, all of the pages were blank. That was meant as a joke, but that book spoke volumes about his philosophy on public discourse.

Eliot had no formal training as a speaker. He never took a speech course above required curriculum fare and beyond his stint in the Calliopean Society at Kent's Hill, when a private group of students gathered to further their debate and public speaking skills, he garnered no technical expertise. Even in that group, others were voted better speakers than he.

In fact, if one listened to Eliot's speeches, they were very raw, with many mistakes in form. Sometimes he talked too fast, or didn't complete sentences, sometimes he stumbled over words and repeated himself more than would seem ascetically correct. But, like Bing Crosby sang or DaVinci painted, he spoke from his heart. He could roar like Niagara Falls or quietly woo like a gentle stream. He had passionate emotion and drew listeners into his dramatic stories with precise and vivid portraits. His "rapid-fire, staccato delivery appealed to his listener's emotions almost spiritually," wrote John D. McCallum in his book, *Big Ten Football*. He spoke with a conviction, confidence and power that moved audiences, adult and child alike. He had no rules for speaking—he simply believed what he said and seized the listener with it. He used no extensive notes or prepared text, but filled up on his principles, carried them in his heart to the lectern, and poured them out on his audience. He was one of the great orators of the twentieth century.

"He speaks of the proper state of mind so honestly that one might think he thought up the concept himself," wrote Don Friske of the *Daily Illini* in 1975.

Already when he coached at Illinois College in the 1930s, some thought he was a better orator than the famed William Jennings Bryan. If nothing else, folks thought Eliot and Bryan would make a "whiz-bang debate team," Charles Bellati recollected in an article written upon Eliot's death in 1980. Jacksonville residents should know: Bryan was a part of Illinois College's 1881 graduating class. After finishing law school at the Union College of Law in Chicago, Bryan also practiced in Jacksonville for four years until 1887.

Some compared Eliot to Notre Dame's late, great Knute Rockne, calling him the "Knute Rockne of Illinois." Most who heard him speak thought he was better.

"Certainly the two are everything in common, even to being tops as after-dinner speakers," penned a sportswriter in the 1940s. "Rockne was smart, witty, versatile, truthful, clever, and was possessed with a flair for gridiron showmanship. Eliot is all of this...maybe more."

Wrote McCallum again, "Ray Eliot...had a style reminiscent of Knute Rockne. Like Rock, his harangues were 'like champagne from a battered oil can.'"

Whether it was a speech in front of a thousand at a banquet, a halftime pep talk, or a one-on-one conversation, his power of persuasion was renowned.

"I've been in the coaching business a long time," remarked Justa Lindgren, who had been in the Illini coaching ranks for 40 years until 1943, "and I might be excused if I did a bit of daydreaming when the head coach talks seriously and intimately with his squad. But when Eliot talks, explains and appeals, I find myself leaning forward, absorbing every word. That's the sort of compelling attention he commands."

Former Illini Ruck Steger was asked once if Eliot was a good locker room orator. "Is he?" shouted Steger. "Man, I used to come out of there ready to go through the nearest brick wall!"

"Ray was possibly the inspirational coach of our day," said former Michigan State head coach Duffy Daugherty to a writer in 1973. "He was great at getting teams with perhaps only mediocre ability to rise to great heights."

Chuck Flynn, the former Sports Information Director at Illinois, once said, "I've never known a more gifted speaker, one who could reach out and grasp the attention and the mind of anyone that listened."

Actually, former Illini Eddie Bray thinks Eliot might have missed his calling: "He would have made a million as an insurance salesman," he jokes.

Often it was not what Eliot said, but how he said it that affected his audiences so.

"Mr. Eliot spoke in the same manner that he must have played football in his college days, and in the same way that he molds Illinois lines today," said the Paris, Illinois *Daily Beacon-News* in 1941. "Those that heard him could readily tell why he has been a success as a college coach. Driving his ideas home with a force that nearly pulled the members of his audience to the edge of their seats, the speaker compared football with life in a manner that removed all thoughts from the crowd's mind that he was talking on a trite subject...(The speech) clutched at the heart of every member of the audience in the room."

"The forcefulness of Eliot's delivery is awesome, spellbinding," wrote longtime Champaign *News-Gazette* Sports Editor Loren Tate. "At some point you are so enraptured that it no longer matters what he says. You're caught in an emotional trap."

As Bill Schrader pointed out in a newspaper column, it was amazing that one school could be gifted with two coaches in a half century who combined coaching and oratorial prowess as well as Bob Zuppke and Ray Eliot.

"Zuppke's never-to-be-forgotten quips will go down in history," wrote Schrader. "Zup limited his words of wisdom to a few. Eliot is more verbose. Football fans all over the nation have marvelled at the way he tells a story. His fame is widespread."

Besides his scheduled speaking engagements, one could find Eliot in almost any setting—a party, a football clinic, a meeting—inspiring or entertaining people with his stories.

"To find the Illini coach (at these gatherings)," wrote Schrader, "it's just necessary to look around where a crowd is gathered, and in the center, gesturing wildly, will be Mr. Eliot."

The late Sam Mangieri, who played baseball and football for Eliot at Illinois College, puts it succinctly: "When he wanted to arouse somebody to do a job, he had no peer." Art Dufelmeier agreed when he said that, "If you had to pick one coach for one game it would be Ray Eliot."

He could even arouse a team when he wasn't there, as Mangieri and the rest of the 1937 Illinois College gridders found out. Alf Lamb took over as head coach when Eliot went to the University of Illinois that year, and the Blueboys won the Little 19 conference championship for the first time in 22 years, with no small assist from their former mentor.

The *Jacksonville Daily Journal* related the story as told them by Lamb: "The climax of the season was the homecoming game with (Illinois) Wesleyan here," Paul Findley wrote. "The Blueboys had won two games in the conference and if they could hurdle Wesleyan, the way seemed fairly clear for the championship.

"Lamb, realizing that a 'shot in the arm' from Eliot would help the boys win, wrote to him at the University of Illinois and asked him to come to Jacksonville and speak to the team before the game. Eliot was unable to come to the game, but wrote a letter which he asked Lamb to read before the contest.

"The letter from Eliot arrived too late for Lamb to read before the game started, but he read it between halves (the Blueboys were trailing 7-0) and it did the trick. Lamb and the entire squad were choked up with emotion by the note. Lamb couldn't finish reading it; Athletic Director (LaRue) Van Meter read the last few paragraphs. The squad streamed onto the field with tears in their eyes and mowed the Wesleyan team down the second half, winning 13-7.

"As a token of appreciation to Eliot the members of the squad—after they had won the title—wrote a note to Eliot. They also chipped in and sent Eliot a gold football, one similar to their individual championship awards."

Even when plans went awry, he still inspired. This was true in 1957 in what former Illini Rod Hansen called "the most famous pep talk of them all."

"Coach Eliot has a deep loyalty to the University of Illinois," said 1957's MVP to a reporter. "And he used this to inspire

Ray Eliot Nusspickle—with more hair than anyone remembers. This photo was taken in a Manhattan studio in 1910 when he was four years old.

Annie Nusspickle—
Ray's mother.

Around 1924—Ray (right) and a baseball teammate at Kent's Hill College Preparatory School, Maine.

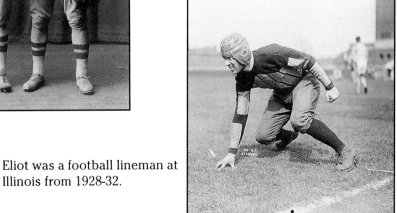

Eliot was a football lineman at Illinois from 1928-32.

Ray's wife Maggie and daughter Jane in their Champaign home on Springfield Avenue about 1940

From 1937 through 1941 Eliot assisted Bob Zuppke at Illinois. Here he is with Zup standing over his shoulder. Also shown are Ralph Fletcher (left) and Doug Mills.

Leaving the locker room for his first practice after taking over as head coach of the Fighting Illini in 1942. (University of Illinois photo)

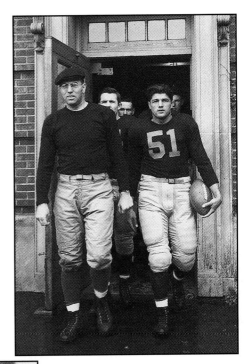

Even Eliot can hardly believe the 45-14 shellacking the Illini put on UCLA in the 1947 Rose Bowl. (AP Wire Photo)

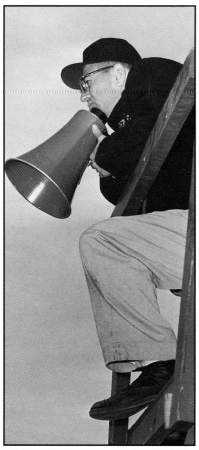

Watching over his Illini troops
at practice in 1952.

Where he loved to be: with his
boys. After they beat Northwestern to clinch the Rose Bowl
berth in 1951. (*Champaign-
Urbana Evening Courier* photo)

With good friend Bob Hope at the 1950 Illinois State Fair in DuQuoin. (*DuQuoin Evening Call* photo)

"Poor little lambs who've lost their way" —In 1955 Eliot leads friends in *The Wiffenpoof Song*, his favorite.

Two Illinois legends, Ray Eliot and Red Grange, mug for the cameras in 1944.

Los Angeles Times Sports Editor Paul Zimmerman makes the presentation to Eliot as 1951's National College Coach of the Year. (*Los Angeles Times* photo)

Displaying the Amos Alonzo Stagg Award with Big Ten Commissioner Bill Reed at Memorial Stadium in 1962.

Eliot's speaking took him all over the world, including Tokyo.

The intensity builds in one of the great orators of the twentieth century. Eliot trumpets his message to a banquet audience in 1975.

Mr. Illini

us in his pep talks. In the last game of the season, we were to play a good Northwestern team. Instead of a pep talk, Ray played the Illinois Loyalty song, which was a switch from the regular pregame talk. Right in the middle of the record, a tube blew out and the record stopped. Like the true champ he was, Ray unabashedly finished the song himself without missing a single word. He sang like he was the only person in the room. We went out and blew Northwestern off the field 27-0."

Eliot was a busy man on the speaking circuit during his coaching career, and even more so after his retirement from the gridiron. From Europe to the Orient and behind the old Iron Curtain, from the U.S. Air Force to the Illinois General Assembly to banquets and coaching clinics, he was in demand all over the nation and the world. Wherever Eliot went, standing ovations followed and newspapers gave him rave reviews:

"One of the most forceful speakers ever to appear..."

"His fiery talk drew a spontaneous ovation seldom heard at these events..."

"...the best football speaker we have ever heard."

The accolades went on and on.

His speeches were in such demand that, in 1962, one was made into a record album.

"It really isn't that good," insisted Eliot. "They taped me at a clinic and we discussed the idea of going into a studio and redoing it. But I never got around to it so they took the tape and made it into a record."

It may not have been "that good," but it remained on the market for close to fifteen years and it has been used to motivate thousands, including unnumbered athletes, on every level, whose coaches have played it for them. A version of it is still available at the University of Illinois.

"People talk about (Lee) Iaccoca," said John Doyle, a manager on Eliot's last two Illinois College baseball teams. "He (Eliot) was way before Iaccoca's time. He was way ahead of him."

This, however, was not always so. This man who brimmed with confidence and inspiration was not born with a silver microphone in front of his mouth. He almost didn't make it to the first public speech he ever gave as a coach. He was to speak during a banquet at Jacksonville High School shortly after he had graduated from the University and accepted coaching positions with Illinois College in 1932.

"I prepared for weeks," Eliot recalled later. "I made volumes of notes, threw them away, made new notes, agonized, walked the streets at night, asked Maggie to call and tell them I was ill and I couldn't make it, stood up and broke out in a cold sweat."

The great orator?

"To this day I have no idea what I said or whether anyone was still sitting there when I finished," he joked.

Still, Eliot worked at it. "I recognized that in my work as a coach, I would have to make many speeches," he said. "In my young days at coaching I took all of the speaking engagements possible for practice. I guess they say repetition makes for mastery."

Eliot had a wonderfully infectious personality and a terrific sense of humor, too, that made his speeches that much more palatable to the listener.

"A coach's job is hazardous because of one word: alumni," he would say. "I was told that if I wanted to keep my job, I had better keep the alumni disorganized. I always liked the letters I get from them, especially after losing a game. Of course, I don't know who to thank, no one ever signed one."

He talked of that Great Lakes team under Paul Brown that was so big "they couldn't play a six-man line—they had to play a five-man line because the field wasn't wide enough."

Or: "My kids fumbled 17 times in that game and I don't even coach fumbling. Once the leader of the band dropped his baton and I overheard one fan say: 'My God, he's even coaching the band now.'"

Eliot told the story of his quarterback who kept throwing interceptions. Eliot kept benching him. Finally he put him back in late in the game and, sure enough, he threw another interception. When he came off the field the coach asked him why he kept throwing to the guys in the white shirts instead of the guys in the blue shirts: "They are the only ones open, Coach," he said.

Eliot was once asked by Woody Hayes to speak at an Ohio State football banquet. After his opening thanks and greetings he began to reflect on the rivalry between the two coaches. "When I had the most talent, I won," he said. "When Woody had the most talent, he won. When the talent was even, I won."

One of his favorite tales was about the former Illini speedster, Buddy Young. "Buddy took the sweep wide to the right. He didn't see anything open so he reversed direction and came back the other way. Seeing nothing open that way either, he reversed directions again toward our side of the field. I looked and didn't see anywhere he could go so I waved him back the other way (Laughter). One Indiana player had fallen in pursuit and just laid there. An Illinois boy asked him if he wasn't going to get up and chase the runner. The Hoosier said 'No, I'm going to stay right here, he'll be back in a minute.'"

A speech was never routine coming off the lips of Ray Eliot. Sportswriter Eddie Jacquin termed his speeches "performances."

"Coach Ray has a great gift," he wrote the day after Eliot had visited Alton, Illinois. "I suppose I have heard Ray speak close to 100 times in the 30 years I have known him. He says it embarrasses him to speak when there is a person present, like myself, who has heard him so often. But I never cease to be thrilled in the presence of Ray's eloquence. It is his sincerity which helps to capture his listeners. He has lived the things he talks about."

In the midst of all of this verbose thunder, good humor and supreme confidence, Eliot was at the same time a most humble man. He would roll through his speeches and finish with his usual exclamation. The crowd would be aroused and listeners would always want to run up to him and tell him how great his speech was. They seldom had the chance.

Eliot had a habit of speaking and running. He would finish, thank everyone graciously, turn from the microphone and leave. Eliot was not one for attention. He was uncomfortable with the slaps on the back and the "great speech" comments and the "Gee, you were terrific" accolades. He would rather make the speech and get the heck out of there. He knew the listeners were trapped in their seats and could not chase after him.

His grandson did once, though. He was a manager on the Illinois football squad in 1977 and involved in the Fellowship of Christian Athletes. He had arranged for his grandfather to speak to them one night. There were maybe 20 people there, but there might as well have been a thousand because, as always, Eliot poured out his heart. He veered directions during his speech, just as Buddy Young had done with the football many years before. Toward the end, he began to talk about forgiveness.

He riveted his audience when he reached out and took the hand of the person next to him and quietly said "I forgive you. Is that so hard?" He went down the line and took several hands and said the same thing: "I forgive you. It's really simple isn't it?" Such wonderful spirit was in the room, but when he finished he immediately said thank you and walked out the door.

His grandson couldn't let this one go by. He pulled out of his imaginary seatbelt and chased him out the door. His grandfather was already partway down the stairs when he caught him.

"Grampa Ray," he called.

Eliot turned.

"Terrific speech." His words felt so trite.

"Was it okay?" asked the speaker.

("Was it okay?! Was it okay?!" he thought.) "Yes. It was great."

"Good, good," Eliot nodded as he turned to go.

It must be understood that Eliot did not spend all of his time talking Rose Bowls and football hype and banter. He only used those things to talk about the bigger picture. He spoke about what he called "the game of life." He spoke it to his players, to high-class audiences, at pep rallies, to children, to men, to women—to whomever wanted to hear. As it was when he coached, he used football to teach life. The game for him was simply a vehicle for, as he put it, "the real job of living a big life, courageously—studying and doing what you've got to do to be a better man!"

Describing his speeches once he said, "I try to build from an athletic experience what it takes to be great in the game of athletics and in the game of life. Stand up and be counted. Don't duck the issues. There is so much grumbling and criticism in the country today. We need people who are willing to step forward and become involved."

Eliot was concerned about the man. The goal in all of his speeches was to get to the man (or woman) in everyone. He talked about the spirit ("spirit, spirit—without it you're dead"), he talked about the heart ("The size of the man is in his heart") and he talked about life.

Brigadier General Earl G. Peck of the United States Air Force, who was the Commandant of the Squadron Officer School at Maxwell Air Force Base in Alabama, wrote Eliot in 1973: "Do you realize the actual significance of your total contribution to the education of today's Air Force officers, and how much we appreciate it? I want to make sure you do. According to our records, you have been speaking to our students three times a year since the beginning of 1956, a total of 54 classes. Although the number of the students in each of these classes has varied, I can safely say that you have talked to more than 35,000 Air Force officers at S.O.S. in the last 18 years. As you know, our students were selected from the most outstanding young officers in their respective units. This means that they are among those who are most likely to advance to leadership positions within the Air Force. In fact, some of the people in your first few classes now occupy those key positions.

"As you can see, your impact upon the Air Force, through its leaders, has been significant. Your inspirational speeches have helped us reinforce a sense of dedication and purpose in these officers. Through you these men have been remotivated toward their chosen profession, their country and the values which they stand for."

Eliot was an inspiration to the underprivileged, too. The day Illinois beat Syracuse 20-13 in 1953, eight-year-old Carolyn Hudspaeth was in the audience. Carolyn suffered from cerebral palsy and was there as a guest of the Illini head coach who also happened to be the Champaign County Chairman of The United Cerebral Palsy Association. "Ray Eliot has taken care of some of the fight and reward for (these) youngsters," wrote Bob Sonderskov of the Champaign *News Gazette*. "For a long time now he hasn't confined his famous pep talks to the football locker room. The results for Carolyn have been almost unbelievable in just one short year. She has learned better how to challenge the thing that holds her back from the other kids."

Later, in 1959, Eliot was the Illinois State Chairman of the Heart Fund Campaign and, in the 1970s, State Chairman of the March of Dimes.

Oh, Eliot loved the game, but he especially loved the education that the game offered, and defended its value in the education process to the end. Once a columnist blasted football for its lack of sportsmanship. Eliot responded in a speech: "He based his arguments on three incidents over a three-year period—out of over one million contacts a year in college ball. If people on the street showed the same good sportsmanship and interest in others as players demonstrate on the field, then 42 persons would not stand by on a street while punks beat up a helpless old man. I went shopping for a Christmas present for my wife about a week before Christmas. I was pushed and shoved by human animals—yes, human animals. What's happening in this world? Have we forgotten the amenities? You tell me about sportsmanship!"

"I wish we had the same high principles all over America today that we have in football," he preached another time. "There is a lack of discipline in our homes today. Why do we coddle our kids? Why do we haul them two blocks to school? Why can't they do things for themselves? We in the United States today lack discipline. One place where you do see it is on football fields."

Eliot would challenge anybody who was fearful of America's future to "look to (high school) sports because these are tomorrow's leaders. No finer young men and women are being turned out then those students who 'take a chance' and participate in athletics at the high school level."

"Loyalty to self, family, and community have made this country big and fine," he'd say.

Eliot loved his country, but he especially loved what he called "young America." Football was more than a game to him, it was life in a capsule to be studied and learned from. Life was the issue, and no one in the history of the game drove home the point better. He once said that, as a "preacher for life," he had the greatest job in America.

There was an anonymously written poem he often closed his speeches with that pulsated with the beat of his message:

"If you think you can, you can;
If you think you dare not, you don't;
If you think you'd like to win,
But think you can't;
It's almost a cinch that you won't.
For out of this world you'll find,
Success begins with a fella's will
It's all in the state of mind.

"Full many a race is lost
'Ere even a step is run.

And many a coward falls
'Ere even his work's begun.
Think big and your deeds will grow;
Think small and you'll fall behind,
Think that you can and you will
It's all in the state of mind.

"If you think you're outclassed, you are;
 You've got to think high to rise.
You've got to be sure of yourself
Before you can ever win a prize.
Life's battles don't always go
To the stronger or faster man,
But soon or late the fella who wins,
Is the fella who thinks he can."

Wrote Loren Tate in 1980: "Dynamic? And how! Inspirational? Beyond belief! Corny? Perhaps in the modern context. But the motivation of Ray Eliot came from the heart.

"In the history of football in this country, there was no one who better combined the qualities of loyalty, commitment, and inspiration. He demonstrated beyond question the awesome power of the spoken word."

14

USC

"Amid the broad green plains
That nourish our land,
For honest labor and for learning we stand
And unto them we pledge our heart and hand,
Dear Alma Mater, Illinois."

—Illinois Loyalty
(final verse)

Its screw propellers working hard against the bitter cold wind and gravity, the big plane labored and groaned skyward. In the cabin, he laid his head back and shut his weary eyes to rest, as the roar of the engines and the spit of the props almost drowned out the ache of the hull around him. His fellow passengers were the varying voices, thoughts and personalities scrimmaging in his head, warring their opinions, manipulating his feelings and disconcerting his thoughts. The aircraft made a hard, uneasy turn over Chicago and headed south to St. Louis for an eventual trip west to California. His mind faded back in time. A lot had happened that last week of January, 1951.

The University of Illinois had been Ray Eliot's love and loyalty, his life's blood. In nine years as head football coach he enjoyed great success through difficult times at the home of the Illini. Not only had Eliot rebuilt Illinois into a national football power, but he had been schooled there, was mentored by the great football professor, Bob Zuppke, and filled Zup's shoes as no one else could.

He had many friends at his university. Of course, as with any coach, some criticized his football strategy, but no one ever criticized his heart. He loved Illinois and, overwhelmingly, Illinois loved him. Indeed, if loyalty was the substance of his blood, then orange and blue were its colors.

Difficult it was then when, the week before his plane trip west, Eliot attended the NCAA convention in Dallas and was accosted by Willis O. Hunter, Director of Athletics at the University of Southern California. Hunter wanted Eliot to replace Jeff Cravath as head football coach at USC. The offer stunned Eliot. Maybe he was more surprised that he was actually considering it. He had had feelers from other teams, even offers, both college and pro, but never anything that really tempted him—certainly nothing this sudden and direct. He would have to think.

The possibilities were intriguing. The Trojans were the most successful football team on the West Coast in the first half of the 20th century, thus it was a prestigious, high-profile job. It was also in sunny southern California (no more harsh prairie winters), it was a new challenge, and the pay was better. On the other hand, the tradition he had rebuilt, the friends he had made, the boys he coached, and his own burning loyalty to his University and alma mater brought the weights of the scale back to even. Besides, he had an Illini team, at the time, that seemed to be on the verge of greatness.

Too, early in the week when the offer became public, it brought a shocking outcry from the west almost equal to the derision flung at the Illini in 1947 when they went to Pasadena. Though Hunter wanted Eliot, few others in California did, and the press and the broadcast media picked at him mercilessly. No one could deny that he had done, at the very least, a decent job in the Big 9, but to them this boy from Illinois was not worthy of the top coaching position on the west coast.

USC alumni secretary Arnold Eddy led the charge against the Illini coach, according to a broadcast report by announcer Bob Kelley of Los Angeles' KMPC. "Go back to Illinois!" they shouted through the media. The alumni's choice was Paul Brown, at the time owner and head coach of the NFL's Cleveland Browns (Brown never wanted the job, though it is said he did play along with it for awhile because he was flattered by the thought and he liked the publicity). Some USC alumni went so far as to wire Eliot, stating that if he accepted the position they would not recruit any talent for him. Of course, Eliot was a tenacious man. He had faced many strong, cruel headwinds before, and if he wasn't going to take the job it wouldn't be because of a bunch of scoffers and doubters at USC.

At Illinois the reaction was quite different. Every single one of Eliot's players came to his office personally and begged him to stay. It was as 1950 graduate Ron Clark conveyed to Eliot once, "I am sure that if you should ever leave Illinois, that a part of each and every fellow that ever played for you will leave with you."

Eliot had other considerations as well. He and his wife had made a home in Champaign, and his daughter had just made the University of Illinois her college of choice. With his mom in Manhattan and Maggie's family on Staten Island, a move to California would make the distance that much greater from their roots. His mom seldom saw his games as it was, and if he moved, the opportunities would be even less.

But this was USC calling. When another offer like this would come along, nobody could tell. This would be akin to coaching Notre Dame in the Midwest or Army in the East. On the other hand, the thought of his boys filled his mind too.

The arguments tumbled in his head like gridders chasing an elusive pigskin and his plane moaned on to the western shore. He was going to meet with Hunter, and Hunter was hoping to seal the deal.

Buddy Young was married and had a child by 1947, and thus forsook his last year of college eligibility, taking his wares to the NFL's New York Yankees after Illinois' Rose Bowl win. His running mate, "Orange" Julius Rykovich, graduated, joining the Buffalo Bills of the old All-American League, and the heart and soul of the Illini, Alex Agase, was also gone to the Chicago Rockets of the same league. They and other great names like Mac Wenskunas, Frank Bauman, Mike Kasap, John Genis, Stanley Green, Ralph "Babe" Serpico, Ray Ciszek, Louie Donoho, Ray Florek, Ray Grierson, Bill Heiss, Tom Zaborac, George Dimit, Eugene "Kwas" Kwasniewski, Bert Piggott and Bill Huber read like credits after a great moving picture. They had starred in one of the superlative big-screen epics in college football history. Now they were gone, and to some that fact was obvious.

"I thought Illinois was better last year," said "General" Robert Lee a halfback for Pittsburgh, as he rested his sweat-streaked body on the training table in the visitor's locker room.

The Panthers had just been beaten by the Illini 14-0 to open the new campaign. "Then we were always afraid of Young around the ends. This year we could concentrate on the middle of the line better."

Maybe the General was right. Michigan was the heavy favorite of most to strip the Big 9 crown from the Illini. But you would have been hard-pressed to convince the Illinois couple who, the week before the opener, wanted to buy 1948 Rose Bowl tickets, even though in their enthusiasm they forgot that Ray Eliot's boys could not go back to the Rose Bowl again a second year in a row because the conference prohibited it. And the Iowa Hawkeyes might have become as confident in Illinois as that couple after the boys from Champaign-Urbana crushed them 35-12 the second week of the season.

But before anyone could get too excited about the Big 9 race, there loomed ahead a nonconference mega-game with Army at Yankee Stadium, New York. Army was unbeaten in thirty straight games and were national co-champs the year before. This was the team that the West Coast wanted instead of the Illini for the Rose Bowl. Illinois and Army had not met on the gridiron in 13 years and the series was tied at two games apiece. In 1929 Bob Zuppke's Illini won 17-7. The next year Illinois had lost big to graduation and then to Army 13-0. Zuppke said they were so small in stature that year that "Three high school teams in Illinois were heavier than us." It figures that a young man named Ray Eliot Nusspickle was on that 1930 light brigade when they received a standing ovation from the throngs at Yankee Stadium for courageously holding Army to a scoreless tie at halftime. In 1933 Army won again 6-0, but the Illini squared the series in 1934 by beating them 7-0.

Navy, though, had been upset that Army was able to utilize post-graduates and, according to Zuppke, talked the Big 9 into not playing the Cadets anymore. So this game in 1947 was the resumption of a rivalry and considered the rubber game of the series. The collision could almost be heard before it actually took place.

Like 1930, this tribe of Illini were not very big and a New Yorker commented on their size when the players deplaned at Stewart Field. "That's what they said at Iowa too," Illinois' Ruck Steger answered back. Then, speaking loud enough for the West

Point enlisted men to hear, he said, "We may be small potatoes, bub, but we're awful hard to peel."

Since the game was to be played in her own backyard, Annie was able to attend and watch her son lead his Illini. She and Ray, of course, took the opportunity to visit. She was so very proud of what he had accomplished, and their times together were always warm and affectionate. Maggie's Staten Island family were fans as well, and they came out en masse to join 65,000 others at Yankee Stadium that Saturday afternoon.

In the end, the rubber game decided nothing, finishing in a 0-0 tie. Twice the Illini drove down to the Army seven yard line in the first half only to be turned back. At the end of the half, they kicked away a chance at a field goal because of a bad snap from center. In the third frame they cut their own throats again by fumbling the ball at the Cadet 12. By all accounts it was a thrilling spectacle, but the teams came in even and left the same.

The Illini were downhearted. Field position and statistics said they had won, but those voices meant nothing when the final score was tied. They took it as a loss—that is until Ray Eliot got ahold of them:

"Chins up!" he shouted as he stepped briskly into the dressing room, not giving the boys any time to sulk. "We are not out of anything. And we haven't lost a ball game. I thank every one of you for all you did. You boys played a good game—a good game. We're still in it all the way. Stick in there. Don't forget everything is ahead of you. Next week we've got Minnesota. Let's look to that baby."

Then he sent them on their way to have a good time in the city. "Tonight is yours, but take care of yourself," he said. "And be ready for Minnesota."

That night they took care of themselves and the next week they took care of Minnesota by a 40-13 score. Rose Bowl or no, with some holdover stars from the year before, they were still on top of the Big 9 conference and on pace to repeat as champions. Perry Moss had matured as a passer and Dike Eddleman was coming into his own as a runner. With the likes of established veterans Lou Agase, Art Dufelmeier, Ike Owens and Les Bingaman, the Illini seemed to be picking up where they had left off in Pasadena.

Of course, Eliot knew that there were always hidden pot-holes in the road. As a matter of fact, the first great coach in football, Amos Alonzo Stagg, was a hero of Eliot's, and was said to wring his hands terribly over coming games. Eliot would have made Stagg proud, then, if the old legend could have seen the Illini coach squirm when discussing their upcoming date with Purdue.

"We meet Purdue at a bad time," he cringed with worried creases over his brow and a large look in his eyes. "Last Saturday it was Minnesota and we had to be up for them. A week from Saturday it is Michigan and we certainly can't afford to be anything but keyed highly for them. So here's Purdue, right in between, which might easily sneak up on us. I certainly hope our boys don't take Purdue too lightly. It will be a tough game. Sometimes I envy those eastern teams which can have a breather between tough games.

"By golly," he continued aghast, waving his arms for emphasis, "you know who Army played after they met us? VPI! Who did we have to play? The biggest team in the conference. This Big 9 is tough."

The Thursday night before the game Eliot went to the movies. Oddly enough, he often disappeared after dinner to go to a movie theater so he could concentrate on the game. He said it got him away from phone distractions and he could sit in the dark undisturbed and ponder. Whether he could tell anyone the plot of any film he saw is unknown.

The trip to the cinema didn't help this time, though, as Eliot saw his worst fears realized—the Boilermakers beat Illinois 14-7. The loss was like a hard fist in the stomach to the Illini: it knocked the wind right out of their sails. The next week Michigan nipped them by the exact same 14-7 score, and before these Illini could scream "avalanche!" they had lost their grip on any chance to be repeat champions.

But, as always, Eliot saw beyond the score. Later that evening, long after the clash with Michigan was over, after everyone had gone home and Bert Bertine was putting the final touches on his stories for the Sunday sports section at the darkened offices of the Champaign-Urbana *Evening Courier*, the phone rang. It was Ray Eliot. "Bert," he began, "I wish you'd tell them that I was mighty proud of my boys today. You can say all you want about Michigan—they're great and everything—but let me tell you there are no better hearts in football than those at Illinois."

The Illini would not contend again until 1950.

The freshmen class of 1948, though, was considered a bumper crop—Eliot's best since 1942—and this time there would be no war to interrupt their progress. They even toyed with Pasadena in 1949 as sophomores only to be thwacked back to reality by Ohio State in the last five minutes of the second to last game of the season. But they were growing up. Their day of reckoning dawned with the new decade and, like a train out of a dark tunnel, they would suddenly emerge.

Now director Eliot had new stars on his Memorial Stadium stage led by the likes of Johnny Karras at offensive right halfback and on defensive linebacker Chuck Boerio.

In 1950 they won four out of their first five ballgames. Unfortunately, their lone loss came in the Big 9 to Wisconsin, 7-6, thus every conference game was a must for these improving Illini now if they were going to vie for Pasadena.

The sixth week of the season they traveled to Michigan to take on the always difficult Wolverines. The night before at the Dearborne Inn they discovered a wedding party there for a rehearsal dinner. Twice before, Eliot had kissed a bride for luck before a game. The result was a 1-1 record in those two contests. But Eliot must've felt that it certainly wouldn't hurt so he puckered up again.

Next morning, Illinois Senator Everett Peters sat in a barber's chair at the inn. As reported by Champaign *News-Gazette* Sports Editor Jack Prowell, the barber mistook Peters for the Illini head coach and asked him how he felt the game was going to go that afternoon between Illinois and Michigan.

"We're going to win," Peters replied flatly.

"How can you be so sure?" the barber demanded.

"Don't tell anyone, but I have eight Chicago Bears coming up," explained Peters. "After the uniforms get muddy a bit and you can't see the numbers I'm going to slip them in there. I'll tell you, we're here to win!"

The barber looked at the Senator reproachfully and answered, "Gee you shouldn't ought to do that. That isn't fair."

Out of nowhere, a blinding snow swept into Ann Arbor, but 97,239 fevered souls, the most ever to see the Illini play, witnessed the pivotal matchup between the Wolverines and their ancient Big 9 foe. A strong north wind, 30-degree temperatures, slushy underfooting, and the thick driving flakes of the early snow were a tougher opposing team than either Illinois or Michigan could be that day. The sudden drop in temperature was a surprise to everyone and before the game Eliot sent his managers out, trying to purchase 40 heavy long-underwear shirts but couldn't find any. Finally they borrowed Michigan sweat shirts.

In the second quarter the Illini slogged 74 yards to the Wolverine six yard line. Quarterback Fred Major had been inconsistent as a passer and with the conditions as they were, the Wolverines stacked their defense against the run. With all of Michigan's "defensive eggs in one basket," as Bert Bertine described it, Eliot had Major take the snap from center, wield around and fake a handoff to Don Stevens, who was playing for the injured Johnny Karras that day. Stevens slammed into the line and the Wolverines were on him like vultures on a carcass. Problem was, Major still had the ball and Tony Klimek was sloshing wide open through the endzone. Major lofted the short pass and the Illini led 7-0.

It was the only pass completed by either team all day and the only score. Michigan had been shut out for the first time in six years and beaten by Illinois for the first time since 1946.

Later, Illinois' United Airlines DC-6 broke upward through the snowstorm. Cruising at 16,000 feet, Eliot picked up the stat sheet from the game and chatted with his boys.

"Rocky, you played a great game," he said to Dick Raklovits, who had carried the Illini's rushing offense for the first three games of the season until Karras got on track. He had 122 yards in the snow of Ann Arbor. "That's great running under those conditions. You can feel proud of yourself. You had yourself a day. And most important, you didn't fumble that ball."

"I did, though, coach," Raklovits admitted meekly. "I lost it once."

"Well, then, don't," Eliot countered...with a grin.

His finger dropped down to the line opposite Stevens, who had 91 yards in 17 carries.

"There's another boy who stepped in and really did a job," he said.

He scanned the almost non-existent passing statistics and mused on the winner.

"I looked down the field on that play and saw Chuck Ortmann backing up the Michigan line. Then Fred threw the pass. I was afraid Tony might be out of the endzone when he caught it. But the play was perfect. Six big points."

His eyes next hit the team rushing yardages: 226 for Illinois and 119 for Michigan.

"You've got to have that running attack," he directed his comments back to Raklovits. "Always remember that. You've got to have the runners first of all."

Don Laz had averaged 32.3 yards per punt.

"That's good kicking in that weather," the coach said. "One thing you want to remember, Don Laz, is that when you're kicking on third down in this kind of weather, you don't have to punt. You can eat that ball and kick on fourth down."

Laz nodded his head. "I remembered, coach," he said.

"Kickoffs," Eliot continued down the sheet. "None for Michigan. Did you realize that we didn't receive one kickoff?! Fumbles...five by Michigan, losing the ball twice; two by Illinois, losing the ball twice. That's what you can't do! You can't lose that ball."

From his aisle seat, Eliot paused and looked thoughtfully across the view of one of his assistants and out the window of the aircraft. He turned back to his boys. "It means something to beat Michigan. Isn't that right boys?"

They all agreed.

At the end of the flight Eliot got up and walked to the onboard public address system. "I want to thank the whole squad for the wonderful game," he announced. "Believe me, a victory over Michigan is something. But remember one thing. Iowa is next and we've got to be ready for that game next week. We'll continue to play 'em one at a time."

When the plane was preparing to land, Eliot wandered back to his seat, bending to talk to some player about some play, and patting different boys on the back. He finally sat back down with a satisfied smile. "What a way to make a living," he said to himself.

The plane taxied on the runway and Eliot and his boys peered out the windows. Their hearts leapt suddenly as they beheld 6,000 Illinois friends and fans, shouting and waving their hands to greet them! It was overwhelming. Eliot did not have to walk to the team bus, but received a jubilant ride on the shoulders of the Illinois faithful.

After Illinois dispatched Iowa the next week 21-7, another huge crowd met them at the university airport. This time Eliot addressed them saying, "We—the team and I—appreciate your loyalty and spirit. But if you know any prayers please save them for next week when we have to play Ohio."

The Buckeyes were now the number one team in the country and 5-0 in the Big 9 conference, while the Illini were 3-1, Michigan 2-1-1, and the Wisconsin Badgers 4-2. The Bucks could not go to Pasadena because they had been there the year before, so Illinois had gained the inside track to the Tournament of Roses. That offseason the Big 9 had passed a rule stating that, unless there are unusual circumstances, the highest eligible team will go west. So now teams would only be subject to what was really a token vote. If Illinois won their last two games, against Ohio State and Northwestern, they would go. They were where every team wants to be, with their destiny in their own hands.

The United States Secretary of Defense General George C. Marshall and the governors of Ohio and Illinois were part of a sellout crowd at Memorial Stadium in Champaign. They watched Illinois' defense give up its first rushing touchdown of the season to the Buckeyes. But that's all it allowed, and Fred Major tossed two touchdown passes to Don Stevens, as the Illini knocked off the top-ranked team in the nation 14-7.

The crowd went wild, storming the field and the Illini locker room doors. It took Eliot a full ten minutes to get into the locker room and to a side office where he could breathe again.

The players spilled in, excited and ecstatic. "California here we come!" they sang. "Boy this is it!" others chimed in.

"Don't you guys forget, we still have to win one next week!" shouted Don Stevens like a drowned-out prophet in the midst of a tidal wave of emotion. The Illini followed each other into the meeting room and raised their jovial voices in singing Illinois Loyalty.

After a few minutes respite, Eliot made his way to his boys. As he walked in, they were singing and he joined in. When the players were about to roll into the song for about the third time, though, Eliot gestured for silence.

"Don't forget," he echoed the prophet. "We still have Northwestern to beat. Let's get 'em!" The players responded with a shout and the celebration was on again.

Underneath the sizzling emotion, there were a few cold facts that Illinois had to face before they faced the Wildcats. First, since the Illini beat them in 1946 to clinch the Rose Bowl berth, Northwestern had whipped them three times in a row. Second, the game would be played in Evanston not in Champaign. Third, winning two games already in the conference, this was not a bad Wildcat team. And fourth, it would be difficult to avoid an emotional letdown after conquering the supposed best team in the country, and the Cats would be keyed to the ceiling with an opportunity to make their entire season worthwhile with a win over Illinois.

Writers tried to resist handing the trip to Pasadena on a silver platter to the Illini. Excitement was building, though, and they found it difficult not to. The positive things written about Illinois all week had the effect of unintentionally minimizing Northwestern, and the Wildcats smartly used it to their emotional advantage. There was a huge pep rally in Champaign, where the administration even canceled classes the Monday of the game, and the Cats viewed that as a premature Rose Bowl party, even though it wasn't.

Still, at the beginning, the Illini dominated the game. On the very first play from scrimmage, Wildcat quarterback Dick Flowers faded back and let a long pass go down the middle of the field. A 25 mile-per-hour north wind caught the ball and then so did Al Brosky the All-American Illini safety. He intercepted at the Cat 42 and was tackled immediately. Seven plays later Illinois was on the board, a healthy Johnny Karras sweeping left for a 14-yard touchdown and a 7-0 lead. But Eliot and his men would not score again that season. Northwestern checked the Illini's momentum and then took it away, racking up two touchdowns in the second half to win 14-7. It was the most points the Illini defense had given up all year.

The loss cut Mr. Illini's heart, like the blade of a pruning sheer snips the stem of a rose.

Willis O. Hunter paced his office. It didn't matter to him that Michigan represented the Big 9 in the Rose Bowl New Year's Day or that Illinois lost to Northwestern. This Ray Eliot had proven himself a winner, taking a program from practically ground zero and putting it back on par with most others in the country. Not only that, but Eliot was a personable and honest fellow, loyal too, just the type of man that could reestablish USC's dominance in the west. He knew the complaints of the alumni about Eliot, he had heard them time and time again. Of course, if they were serious and would not work for Eliot, then it would be very difficult for the coach to have any success, no matter how great he was.

"Aw...their Trojan pride will get the best of 'em. I'm sure they'll come around," he thought as he heard a knock at the door.

"Come in," he said.

"Hello, Mr. Hunter," said a smiling, yet slightly flight-weary Ray Eliot as he opened the door.

"Hi, Ray," Hunter reached out and shook Eliot's hand while pointing to a comfortable chair in front of his desk. "Come on in, and have a seat."

Hunter poured two cups of coffee and sat down. He and Eliot talked for a long time.

Hunter had been so sure of inking Eliot to a contract he had scheduled a meeting with the media later in the day. Eliot didn't tell him that on his way over from the airport he was barraged with cries of "Go back to Illinois!" and "We want Paul Brown—not Nusspickle!" from USC alumni.

Hunter showed Eliot the prepared contract. Only one thing was missing—the salary. Hunter told Eliot to name his price and guaranteed him at least five years. Eliot was flabbergasted. It was all so enticing. Eliot looked the contract over, bowed his head in thought and then looked up at the Athletic Director.

"Let me be frank, Mr. Hunter," he finally said. "I have never backed away from a challenge in all my life. The reactions of the media and alumni out here are nothing that a few victories couldn't cure. I'm sure we would all eventually work out an amiable relationship."

He took a sip of his coffee and continued. "But, I did a lot of thinking on the way out here. USC is a great university and it would be an honor for any man to have the position of head football coach. But, the boys at Illinois..." and he didn't have the words.

"I love Illinois, sir," he said gathering his thoughts to-gether. "And I more relish continuing my friendship with them than moving on. Plus, I think by hiring me you'd be putting yourself in a very difficult position."

He left the contract unsigned and returned to his boys at Illinois.

"I thought everything was going to end (when Eliot was considering going to USC)," said Chuck Boerio. "But when (he) announced (he) was staying—I believe that was the happiest moment of my life."

Other offers would come over the years. Texas tried to woo him with another guaranteed five years and the position of Athletic Director. Nebraska and Florida would knock on his door, too.

Even businesses came calling with attractive job offers and big salaries. But, to the glee of his boys and all future generations, he remained, the one and only, Mr. Illini.

"Ray had dedicated himself to building something more than a football factory," Loren Tate wrote for the *News-Gazette* in 1979. "He was involved in constructing the 'whole man,' and that could be accomplished from a seat in Champaign-Urbana as well as anywhere."

Of course, most of the folks in California were pleased that he turned down the job as well. But it would take only one short year for Eliot to return west to make an unintended point to the Golden Staters and the entire country. He brought his show on the road again and played a perfect script to the most appropriate of audiences in the most prestigious of theaters. He left California (especially those at USC) dumbstruck in the 1952 Rose Bowl. But then, we'll let someone else tell that story, a story that if made up could not have been any more timely or dramatic...

15

Desserts

"For Taylor, Chuck,
Bring him much more luck
Than those before him had,
And keep Ray Eliot's husky lads
From getting too darn mad."

—Braven Dyer of the *Los Angeles
Times* in an open letter to Kris
Kringle December 25, 1951.

Five of the original Illini were given leave of Heaven to visit their old stomping grounds, where they had played college football in 1890. The skies were both white and gray with a mist enshrouding the makeshift field, and they couldn't see beyond it in any direction. They could barely make out the wooden, barn-like viewing stand across the way. As they walked in their weather-beaten, high-topped leather shoes across the damp turf, they knitted a perfect history, spinning yarns about their favorite subject: Illinois football. They fell to conversing about 1951, one of the greatest pages in Fighting Illini lore.

"Did he show 'em or what!?" enthused former guard Ralph Hart.

"Yeah, but I don't think he ever thought of it that way," answered Scott Williams, coach, captain and quarterback of that first Illini eleven. "Ray Eliot just wasn't that way."

"Maybe not," chimed in Jim Steele a tackle. "But it had to feel good to him when that radio announcer in L.A. said the things he did the day after Illinois pulverized Stanford in the 1952 Rose Bowl, 40-7!"

"What was it he said again?" asked halfback Royal Wright.

"Man, I'll never forget," answered Art Pillsbury another halfback. "I'll quote 'em verbatim. The guys name was uh...uh..."

"Kelley, Bob Kelley of KMPC Radio," threw in Williams.

"Right, right. Now listen," continued Pillsbury, hamming it up with a deep, phony radio voice. "You know, there's an old saying that every man gets his just desserts, and thus it came to be on the first day of 1952."

Pillsbury cupped his right hand to his ear and contorted his face for dramatic emphasis. "Ray Eliot Nusspickle—the man who was so disgracefully insulted that certain people even ridiculed his name—had proven that he truly is one of America's great football coaches; that he is indeed coach of the year. It was just last week that the *Los Angeles Times* named Eliot 1951's (national) Coach of the Year, in the face of Western factions who felt Chuck Taylor (of Stanford) deserved the honor. There can be no doubt tonight that the right man took home the bacon."

The other four were laughing at Pillsbury's melodramatic performance. He could barely keep a straight face himself.

"And I couldn't help thinking of Willis O. Hunter yesterday," he went on, "as the Indians of Stanford got a worse scalping than the Iroquois ever gave the pioneers of old. What was going through Hunter's mind? Perhaps the thought that he should have been watching Coach Ray Eliot of USC administer the Coast's first licking to the Big 10. And so, a year later, as we were leaving the Rose Bowl yesterday, we saw two contrasting sights. One was the slightly pale countenance of USC alumni secretary, Arnold Eddy, leader of the anti-Eliot movement; the other, the sight of the joyous Illinois players carrying Ray Eliot Nusspickle off the field after he had scored the third most decisive victory in the 38-year history of the Rose Bowl."

"Can you believe that?" snickered Wright. "One year he's practically drummed out of California, the next he romps in the Rose Bowl right before their eyes."

"Yeah, I guess you could say he showed 'em," relented Williams. "But I still don't think he ever felt that way. He was just happy for his boys."

The five walked across the old, soggy sod toward the viewing stand that was filled only with memories now. Of course, in Heaven they had had a great vantage point and so, between them, knew every detail of that glorious year.

"What a season that was," mused Steele.

"One of the best ever," said Hart very matter-of-factly. "It was the first unbeaten season in 27 years for our ol' alma mater.

They had a first-team defense that did not give up a single touchdown to a conference foe—out of six teams they shut out four. They won the Big 9 championship outright, the Rose Bowl championship and finished ranked number two nationally."

"Though even Grantland Rice said that they were the best team in the country," inserted Steele.

"That's right," Hart agreed.

They crossed the worn middle portion of the field, stopped momentarily, then continued.

"It was the hit that did it," Williams thought out loud.

"The hit?" Steele turned his head

"Chuck Boerio," Williams looked at Steele.

"The Wisconsin game!" Steele seized the thought. "Second game of the season. The Illini had wiped out UCLA in the first game like 27-13 or something. Anyway, it was the third quarter, the Badgers up 10-7. They had a first and goal at the Illini one-yard line. If they score they go up 17-7 and the game is, for all intents and purposes, out of reach."

"And so is a Big 9 championship for that matter," said Williams.

"Wait, let me tell this story," Royal Wright jumped in. "Eliot used to use this one in his speeches all the time."

"Yeah, let Wright do it," said Hart. "He does a great Ray Eliot."

They had reached the viewing stand across the field and Wright leapt up on the platform in front of the first row of benches. He stood between two wood posts, waved his hand over the imaginary crowd for silence and confidently started in.

"You know how far one yard is?" he asked in Eliot's quick, passioned and resonant tones, toying with his audience of four. "Thirty-six inches? Three feet? The shortest darn thing in the world when you've got to defense it and the longest darn thing when you're trying to get it. One yard.

"Johnny Coatta took his Wisconsin team back in the huddle and as Johnny was about to enter the huddle, this kid Boerio of mine, 187-pound linebacker of mine, hollered to Johnny, 'Hey Johnny, send (Alan) Ameche at me!' Send Ameche at me, he said. Can you see the audacity of a guy? Hell, most of us would hope he'd go north somewhere, wouldn't we?"

The four laughed just like audiences did so many times when the real Eliot stood before them.

"Do you get the impact of this thing, sir?" Wright waxed serious with Eliot's emotion, smacking his lips as Mr. Illini used to. "Do you get the impact? Send Ameche at me—70,000 people looking at us—one yard away from something. And Johnny sent him there and Chuck got him back for a three-yard loss. And when the four downs were over instead of that ball crossing that one-yard stripe it rested on the six yard line.

"Gentleman, one yard from the winning of the game, one yard from the Big 10 championship, one yard from the Rose Bowl championship, one yard from success or failure, one yard from distinction or nothing! And in the game of life that you play, that could well be one inch. Or not turning the right corner. Or not having the guts to open the right door! Or pitying yourself by saying, 'I can't go on—one yard, how can I do it?' Yes, one yard from being somebody..."

The goose bumps could be felt by each of them. Yes, Royal Wright did a good Ray Eliot.

"Eliot said that that goal line stand made them a team," Wright pointed out.

After a moment, a puzzled Jim Steele asked, "Wasn't it actually Rollie Strehlow who Boerio stopped with that tackle on first down?"

"Quit being a damned historian," said Ralph Hart, slapping Steele playfully on the head.

"You know, there was another play in that game that was equally important," Art Pillsbury offered.

"Which one was that?" asked Steele.

"Well, Illinois was still down 10-7 late in the fourth quarter, when quarterback Don Engels threw a desperate thirty-yard pass down the middle of the field," related Pillsbury. "Remember? That pass was intended for Steve Nosek. Well, Nosek reached for it and it went off his fingertips right into the diving, outstretched hands of Rex Smith. So the Illini had it, first and goal at the Badger seven. Some call that lucky. I call it opportune!"

"Johnny Karras scored the winning touchdown two plays later," added Hart.

"Exactly," said Pillsbury.

"I'll tell you the key to that season and even to that win over Wisconsin," deducted Williams. "It was a conversation Eliot had with his No. 1 quarterback at the beginning of the year."

"Wasn't the quarterback Tommy O'Connell?" wondered Royal Wright.

"Yep. He was a transfer from Notre Dame, and this was his first year of eligibility with the Illini," answered Williams. "Anyway, Eliot called him in at the beginning of the season and told him to 'cut it loose.'"

"What do you mean 'cut it loose?'" Wright looked confused.

"Eliot had the skill, as all good coaches must, to adapt his game plan to the ability of his players," Williams said. "He knew he had, possibly, the best passer he had ever had in his years at Illinois—certainly since Perry Moss—and so he told him to let it go; open up the offense."

"Yeah, they put in that spread offense, with one setback—usually Karras—and five receivers going out all over the place," explained Steele.

"And they think the 'run and shoot' is something new today," smirked Ralph Hart.

"The point is," continued Williams, getting over his chuckle at Hart's comment, "They came out with a very balanced attack that was very effective and dangerous."

"Dangerous for the defenses they faced!" Wright stated emphatically.

"You know what I noticed, too, about this team?" Williams quizzed the others. "Did you see how these guys took wins in stride compared to the year before?"

"Yeah," answered Wright. "There was not nearly the hype like there was after they beat Ohio State in 1950."

"They learned a lesson," Williams taught on. "Really, they just matured, gained experience. Like when they beat UCLA to open the season, they were gone out of the locker room in just a half hour. Chuck Studley, their captain, said it best, I thought. He said that that was just one out of the way and that they had tasted the gravy now and they had to keep going."

"The game I remember most is the one in the snow against Michigan," Hart changed the subject, pushing himself up in a sitting position on the same platform as Wright, feet dangling down toward the ground in front of him.

"Didn't they play in a snowstorm the year before in Ann Arbor?" Steele asked.

"Yeah, but this one in Champaign was even worse," answered Scott Williams.

"It sure was," continued Hart. "This time the wind was blowing like 40 to 50 miles per hour, there was a blizzard and wind chills were near zero."

"Memorial Stadium was packed out," inserted Williams. "Remember how most of the fans were dressed?"

"Yeah, they all had blankets or layers of real heavy winter clothes," said Hart.

"Remember the one guy with the blanket over his head and the eye holes cut out in it?" Steele asked.

"And the lady with the fur mittens, men's paratroop trousers and a mink coat," added Pillsbury. "What a combination that was!"

They all chortled at the memory.

"Weren't they 5-0 at that point, Ralph?" asked Wright, getting back to the game.

"Sure they were," Hart responded. "Anyway, as you might expect in that kind of weather, it was 0-0 after three quarters. Just when it seemed everyone in the stadium would be satisfied to go home with a tie, Illinois got the ball with about six-and-a-half minutes left at their own 17 yard line with that 40 to 50 mile an hour gale in their face."

"Michigan quick-kicked the ball down there," helped Williams.

"Right," Hart rolled on. "So Karras tried the left side and got nowhere, then O'Connell tried to keep it himself going to the right and got just three yards. Next came the play that they said gave the Illini courage. You remember?"

"Sure," Williams said. "Karras off left tackle for 15 yards, first down, Illinois at the 35."

"He was about a step from breakin' it too," added Pillsbury.

"Karras lost a yard then, and Pete Bachouros lost three," Hart picked up his story. "Now, before the drive, Eliot had told Tommy to let it all hang out, so on the next play he did something that nobody thought he could do in those conditions—he threw the ball. He drilled a pass to Rex Smith along the right sideline and Smith got shoved out of bounds at the Wolverines' 46. Maybe hoping that they could get it done on the ground, O'Connell went to Karras again, but for only two yards. So he went back up top to Smith for another first down at the 30."

"Weren't O'Connell and Smith old high school team-mates?" Steele inserted the question.

"Yep. South Shore High School in Chicago," confirmed Williams.

"Well, on the next play the defense covered Smith like one of those warm blankets in the stands, so O'Connell looked off and found Joe Vernasco at the 19," enthused Hart. "Now, they're knockin' on the door right? So the clever quarterback decides to change up and Bill Tate hammers right up the gut for 13 big ones to the six yard line. Bachouros tried right end then, and lost a yard. Now, like deja vu from the year before, Michigan shifts up and to the right, thinking Karras is going to get the ball. Wrong. With two minutes and ten seconds left, O'Connell faked to him and Smith was all alone in the corner of the endzone. Check and mate, touchdown—the Illini win!"

All five of them clapped and cheered as if they were seeing the game in front of them for the first time. The three standing on the ground bounced up the stairs of the viewing stand and took a seat on the old wooden benches behind Wright and Hart.

"Eliot was a happy and proud coach after that win," Hart continued. "He said it made him want to cry, the way his players fought back to win that game."

"Put yourself in their place," Royal Wright stood and went into an impassioned imitation of Ray Eliot again. "The ball is wet and slippery, their hands are cold, the ball is as hard as a rock, some of them are bruised and shaken, we're on our own 17 yard line and the Michigan defense has been in their hair all afternoon.

"You can't hold your footing, common sense says you can't pass or catch and a gale is blowing in your face. So what do we do? We score a touchdown and win!"

"Yeah, he was excited all right," agreed Williams.

"You think Eliot was excited, you should have seen Bert Ingwerson," exclaimed Jim Steele. "The ol' crusty coach went up and planted a big kiss on Tommy O'Connell's cheek!"

They all threw their heads back in laughter.

"You could maybe picture him bussin' a lineman, but not a back," joked Steele.

The five got a good hardy laugh again and then it was quiet for just a moment.

"So the next week they beat up on Iowa and now they are

7-0, but they go to Columbus and let Ohio State tie them 0-0," lamented Pillsbury.

"Wasn't that Woody Hayes' first year at Ohio?" asked Royal Wright.

"Yes. And the idea of the gentleman competitor went out when he came in, I think," answered Williams.

"What do you mean?" Wright queried.

"Well, you could just tell after the game," Williams responded. "He was quoted as saying things like, 'I told (my players) that Illinois was not a great team and I still say they're not.' And he apparently said 'To me Karras is just another back,' and then, when someone suggested that maybe O'Connell had an off day, he said 'Hell no! Our pass defense was great. And besides, O'Connell's record isn't that good. He's had a good percentage, but he's behind a lot of Big 10 passers in completions.' Before that, in the name of sportsmanship, almost all coaches and players generally praised the other team even if they had to stretch the truth a little bit to do it. The type of responses Hayes gave were almost unheard of at the time. Some call a guy like him honest. I call him ungentlemanly. That was his beginning and we all know his end."

"Yeah, there is a lot that has changed," lamented Ralph Hart. "Like during the Syracuse game—what was that, the third game of the season?"

The others nodded.

"An official actually asked Illinois' Rex Smith if he had caught a ball that was close to the ground. At first Rex said, 'Sure I did' but then he smiled and admitted that he had caught it on the short bounce. Can you imagine that type of gentlemanly conversation going on in the 1990s?"

They all concurred that they couldn't, and let the subject saturate their minds just as they soaked in the little bit of sun that had begun to filter through the hazy clouds. The warmth felt good.

"You know they won that Syracuse game 41-20 and buzzed the coach afterward," Wright broke the silence.

"What do you mean?" the others wondered.

"Sure. They stopped at a novelty counter at the airport on their way home and John Bauer bought one of those hand buzzers and nailed Eliot with it. That cracked everyone up, including Eliot."

All five belted out in laughter again.

"Yeah, well they may not have clinched the Big 9 championship against Ohio, but they sure did the next week," Jim Steele brought them back.

"Well, they got very serious after the tie at Ohio, having to face the same darn team that kept them from the Rose Bowl the year before," interjected Williams. "Usually they met on Sunday mornings for the next game but this time Eliot called a meeting for 6:15 Saturday night as soon as they got back from Columbus."

"That's true," Wright agreed. "And on the flight home Eliot got on the public address system at the end and said that there would be no joking that week. He said, 'We've got a big job—let's get out and get it done!'"

"Eliot was not giving occasion to Northwestern at all after what happened the year before," said Pillsbury. "Do you know, he didn't even send scouts to California to watch Stanford in their last game? And each year the Big 9 would ask teams that still had a chance to play in the Rose Bowl to supply travel and practice schedules for December, just in case they go—he wouldn't do that either. He didn't want to give Northwestern a thing."

"They didn't give them a thing—they shut them out," quipped Steele.

"Can you believe it was a 17-yard field goal by Sammy Rebecca in the second quarter that held up until the end!?" exclaimed an amazed Ralph Hart. "You know, Sammy said once that he and Eliot almost never talked before he went in to kick but merely catching Eliot's eye as he entered the playing field would light a spark of determination."

"He sure was sparked that day," Steele came back. "Three to nothing; against Northwestern no less. What a nemesis they had been."

"They also say that Rebecca was possibly the first specialist in football," Pillsbury noted. "No one had players that just kicked before. I guess he came to Illinois as a quarterback, but really didn't have the size for it so Eliot suggested that he concentrate completely on his kicking. And that's what Sammy did. He practiced and practiced and practiced."

"It sure paid off," Steele said.

"That's exactly what Sammy said to Eliot after the game," said Williams.

"You know, the Cats had beaten Illinois four times in a row," Wright said.

"That's what I meant: nemesis," responded Steele. "Mr. Humble—Eliot was asked afterward about breaking that jinx and he just said that the law of averages was working for them, that's all."

"I think there were a few more things working for him than that, eh?" Williams suggested.

They had gotten quite relaxed in their conversation now, lounging around the viewing stand, as if on a picnic on a perfect spring afternoon.

"What a scene that was," Wright mused aloud, staring at the blank sky.

"What's that?" Hart asked.

"After that game was over," answered Wright. "The band rushing onto the field to play Illinois songs, the rush of fans after their heros, the hugging and backslapping by the players. There are few feelings on earth like that."

"True," Williams thoughtfully responded. "Too true."

"And Eliot finally let himself celebrate that night," Wright interjected.

"Yeah he went out to that fancy Edgewater Beach Hotel," Art Pillsbury picked up the story. "Hildegard was singing and Eliot convinced her that she needed a new song to improve her show. 'Something with class,' he said. 'Something like Illinois Loyalty.' So they sang it together there in front of everybody with Eliot telling the great Hildegard the words as they went. Most of the audience joined in, too. It brought down the house. Someone called it a night to end all nights."

"That Eliot knew how to live, didn't he?" marveled Wright.

"Indeed he did," agreed the others.

"Did you know that Eliot's daughter, Jane, rode on the Big 9 float in the Rose Parade?" Ralph Hart tested the other four.

"Yep. She was Miss Northwestern," said Pillsbury with a wink.

"That's true!" insisted Hart laughing. "It's no joke!"

They all chuckled at the irony.

The five Illini pioneers knew that it was almost time to go, but they chatted like their time was never going to end.

"There is something few know about that Rose Bowl trip," mused Wright.

The others looked at the speaker.

"Illinois' Bob Ryklowicz reinjured his knee in one of the last practices before they left to go west and wasn't going to be able to play. Ray Eliot took it upon himself, in the midst of all of his own game and trip preparations, to get the businessmen in town to pitch in and send him along with the team to Pasadena. Ryklowicz said that that was the kindest and most wonderful thing that anyone had ever done for him."

They all took in the compassionate act by a coach on behalf of one of his boys.

"Illinois was a seven-point favorite going into the Rose Bowl against Stanford," Steele broke the silence.

"Even Bob Hope admitted that he picked Illinois this time," Hart laughed.

"And he laid down a little wager with Bing Crosby, too," Wright added.

"You know," Pillsbury said, "Eliot got all those West Coast writers stirred up again when he banned them from his practices like he did in 1946."

"But he did go downtown almost every night for press conferences," Williams explained. "Besides, some of these guys were still kind of out to get him. One day, a writer asked him if he cared whether or not Stanford practiced against a pro team that was training close by. Eliot said no, that would be okay— whatever Chuck Taylor wanted to do to get his team ready. Next thing he knows he gets a call from some San Francisco scribe, accusing him of encouraging Stanford to practice against a pro team so all their players would get hurt."

"Can't win for losing," moaned Pillsbury.

"I'll bet he really needed his hair restorer after that one," Ralph Hart joked.

"Hair restorer?" the others looked at him.

"Yeah, his players gave him one that year for a Christmas present," Hart laughed.

"Actually, the whole alumni association and football staff learned something from being out there in 1946," Williams said. "Eliot got that hair restorer at a big Christmas bash put on by the association. Not only that, but all of the players and coaches received watches and other grab-bag presents. Even St. Nick stopped by."

"And did you guys know that this was the first nationally televised football game by a major network?" asked Steele.

"Yep...NBC...Mel Allen doing the play-by-play," Wright threw back.

"And what a game for Illinois," marveled Hart.

"I thought our boys would win, but have more trouble with that Indian passing combination some thought was the best in the country," Steele cocked his head in wonderment.

"Gary Kerkorian to Bill McColl," Pillsbury said. "But it didn't mean much in that game."

"Stanford did lead 7-6 at the half you know," Steele raised his eyebrows.

"Yeah, but unfortunately for them Eliot did his thing at halftime giving, what Sam Rebecca once called, 'the most inspirational talk I've heard,'" Hart blurted. "From the time Stan Wallace picked off that pass in the third quarter..."

"And returned it all the way to the Stanford 13..." Wright interrupted.

"That's right. It was all Illinois," Hart finished.

"Who was the MVP of that game?" Steele quizzed the others.

"Bill Tate. 150 yards rushing," answered Hart smartly.

"You know, safety Al Brosky tried to talk Eliot into letting the defense play offense when the game was out of reach," said Williams. "But the coach pooh-poohed that idea."

"40-7," Steele shook his head. "And the USC naysayers were left with their mouths gaping."

"Stanford had an ironclad excuse for losing, though," Pillsbury drawled sarcastically.

"Oh, yeah what was that?" the others inquired.

"Milkshakes...remember?" Pillsbury raised his eyebrows.

They all laughed as the memory instantly flashed back to them.

"Dick Hyland used to play halfback for the Indians and in 1952 was writing for the *L.A. Times*," Pillsbury, chuckling, pictured it for the others. "He wrote that Chuck Taylor let his players drink too many malted milkshakes during training, so they were fat and flabby. He said that it especially showed up in the last 18 minutes of the game."

They laughed harder.

"Boy, the telegrams and congratulations sure poured in for that one," Wright finally shook his head.

"Yeah, Eliot especially liked the ones from his mom and from his ol' high school buddies," added Hart.

"His mother's sure wasn't very fancy," Steele commented.

"No, but it was from his mom," Williams knowingly answered. "'Congratulations in winning Rose Bowl game,' it said."

Recollected Pillsbury, "The other one from his pals from Massachusetts said, 'With prayer and hope for your team's success. From the boys of Bennett school, 1919 and Brighton High, 1923.'"

"Guys that play together don't forget each other," Williams noted. "It's kind of like going to war—they're buddies for life..."

He looked at the other four and the other four took a long look at each other.

"...And beyond," he said.

They knew it was time to go. The five got up from the different places where they were prone. Wright and Hart made the short jump from the platform on which they were sitting to the grass below. The others stepped slowly down the stairs and met up with the two. They strolled across the gridiron to the other side.

But as they approached the boundary of the field, down in the corner near the old, rickety fence, flickering in the rays of the intermittent light, they noticed a young rose blooming in a breathless flush. 'Twas a gift and a thank you from one generation to another. They looked at each other, smiled knowingly, and left.

16

Michigan State

Eliot sat alone in his den, lights dark, with only the flickering lamp outside his second-floor window casting movement within the small room. He was nestled uncomfortably in his feather-cushioned chair, sock feet resting on the matching ottoman. He chawed the events of the day and the thoughts hit his stomach like lead. Losing never came easy for the coach—especially like his Illini did that day; in the final game of the season and the final play of the game, to his worst rival, Northwestern.

The 28-26 loss ended a disappointing 1952, leaving a squad with a puzzle of expectations a couple of pieces short. The Illini ended a blasé campaign with a blasé record of 4-5 and it gnawed at him. Eliot refused all inquiries and phone calls, preferring to sit alone and contemplate the past and the future. Only his daughter Jane had access, and she, as always, comforted him.

The season did have its interesting moments. The injury situation got so bad, for example, that at one point the coach had his great end, Rocky Ryan, playing running back.

But nothing could match the fiasco that played itself out in the seventh week when the Illini visited Iowa. In the fourth quarter, in what became known later as the "Fruit Bowl," the visitors were beating the home team pretty badly. Throughout the game there had been bad blood between both clubs, and each thought the other was playing dirty.

"I played across from a guy that kept cheap-shotting me time and time again," recalls former Illini tackle Pete Palmer. "He kept it up and kept it up and finally I had had enough and I hauled off and slugged him. Well, the next thing I knew, I felt a firm slap on my shoulder pad and the ref said, 'Number 78 out of the game!'"

Amid the mixture of boos, cheers and jeers from the crowd, Paul Luhrsen replaced Palmer at tackle and got the same treatment from the offensive lineman.

"About three plays later Luhrsen hits this guy and all of a sudden the place went up for grabs," Palmer continues his story.

Iowa first year head coach Forest Evashevski stormed onto the field in protest. Suddenly, fans started hurling apples, oranges and bananas, along with bottles and any other loose thing they could find, down on the Illini players. Some of the fans began to overrun the field, and that brought the police to confront them. One Iowan popped off to Rocky Ryan and Ryan broke his jaw with a punch. Players and coaches that weren't fighting ran for cover as the police tried to break up the brawls and remove the people that didn't belong.

At last, order was restored and the Illini got away with a 33-13 victory, but the ramifications of the near-riot were still reverberating. First, the fellow who had his jaw broken by Ryan threatened to sue, and would have, but Eliot was able to smooth it over with the Hawkeye coaching staff. Second, the Illinois administration, in reaction to the out of control crowd in Iowa City, refused to play Iowa again and took them off of their schedule indefinitely. Eliot's teams had played Iowa all eleven years of his tenure at Illinois and had never lost to them. For all Eliot knew, a guaranteed victory was removed from the schedule each year for the remainder of his coaching career. The teams did not play again until 1967—fifteen years later.

Yes, it had been a strange and trying season. The day after his daughter commiserated with him in his den was a November Sunday, and Eliot lounged in the sun room on the east side of his home, away from the bustle of Springfield Avenue. His view was the driveway and the towering bare oak and green pine trees surrounding his house on the outskirts of Champaign. The grass was almost brown, trimmed by a white picket fence, and the air crisp, but the sun warmed the room in which he rested. Jack Prowell of the Champaign *News-Gazette* stopped by in the afternoon.

After some quiet conversation about the game and the season, Eliot looked up at an attentive Prowell.

"We must condition the people," he said thoughtfully, "that this is only the first of several lean years. This is not a condition which can be corrected immediately, because I don't believe the stuff is here.

"But one thing I promise," to Prowell his eyes flashed with the familiar blaze. "We will play the kids next year that want to play football. And I mean hard, rugged football. We will play the kids who want to play that way all the time. We will have no part time football players."

At the same time Eliot and Prowell were visiting, the Big 9 athletic directors announced that they had voted to send Wisconsin to the Rose Bowl instead of Purdue, who had tied them for the conference championship. Each had fairly dubious records for a bowl team. Wisconsin was 6-2-1, but 4-1-1 in the Big 9, while Purdue was 4-3-2, but also 4-1-1 in the league. Schools voting for Wisconsin besides itself were Michigan State, Ohio State, Iowa, Minnesota and Michigan. Purdue voted for itself along with Illinois, Indiana and Northwestern.

The folks at Purdue were very upset. They could not understand, for example, how Ohio State could vote for Wisconsin when Purdue beat the Buckeyes 21-14 and then the Buckeyes beat Wisconsin 23-14. They also were perplexed as to why Michigan State voted for the Badgers.

"We gave Michigan State a tough 14-7 game—could have won it—and Wisconsin won't even put Michigan State on their schedule. Yet they vote for Wisconsin," beefed Purdue head coach Stu Holcomb to reporters. "Look at your future schedules and you'll see that Wisconsin is the only Big 10 school that hasn't put Michigan State on their schedule yet."

This the Boilermakers would not forget when the Spartans officially joined the conference the next year. On October 24, 1953 in West Lafayette, Indiana, with Michigan State rolling toward an undisputed Big 10 championship at 3 0 in league play (4-0 overall) and having won 28 straight collegiate football games, Purdue beat them 6-0. The Boilers threw a fired-up defense at the Spartans, fueled by the memory of the vote the year before.

Meanwhile, reporters had agreed with Eliot in assessing the Illini's chances for a Big 10 championship as nil. Most predicted a second division finish, and their minds didn't change much when Illinois opened the 1953 season by tying Nebraska 21-21. But some eyebrows were raised when they popped a pretty good Stanford club 33-21. It was in Columbus, Ohio, though, the third week of the season, when the nation's collective head turned completely around.

Nineteen fifty-three was to be Ohio State's year. It was the third autumn in the reign of Woody Hayes, and his people and system were in place now. Experts felt the youngsters, like running back Howard "Hopalong" Cassidy, were ready for a run at Pasadena.

Several items had not been taken into consideration when most viewed the Illini's chances, however. One, of course, was Eliot's motivational ability to make his boys play better than they really were. Second, was his ingenuity as a strategist. Third and fourth, were a couple of sophomore halfbacks named J.C. Caroline and Mickey Bates. But then Eliot had made sure nobody knew about them. When they were looking good in freshman practices Eliot, to protect them from unfounded expectations, had ordered that it be kept a secret.

"Don't let those goll-darned newspapermen know about them so they can blow them up before they've ever gained an inch for Illinois," he commanded his assistants.

As soon as the Illini were done with Stanford, they went to work on the Buckeyes. On Sunday the coaches locked themselves away for 18 hours and Eliot drew up an offense and a defense, special deliveries for Woody Hayes' club.

Defensively, Eliot first looked to stop the run. Secondarily, his strategy was designed to stop the pass, not by loosening up and relying on coverage, but by putting pressure on quarterback John Borton.

"It's a gamble," Eliot said before the game. "Maybe it'll work, maybe it'll kill us."

He described it to reporters as a sort of 5-2-2-2 alignment: five men in the line, two coming off the line to back it up, two playing a quasi-outside linebacker or medium deep halfback and a double safety.

It was on the other side of the ball, though, that Eliot did his best handiwork. It was this that gave him confidence as he sat alone with Larry Stewart the night before the ballgame. "We would always play Gin or something like that (the night before a game)," Stewart says today. "Finally I said, 'What do you think about tomorrow—how bad is it going to be?' He looked at me—he was always succinct in his thoughts—and he made sure nobody was in the room and that the door was closed. He turned to me and he said, 'Larry, I'm gonna tell you something. If Woody stays in that same defense that he has used for the last two, or three games,' he said, 'we'll just beat the hell out of them.'

"I looked at him and I thought he was crazy. I said, 'You've got to be out of your mind.' He said, 'Well, you wait and see.'"

Illini quarterback Em Lindbeck explained to a reporter later: "(Ohio State) was ahead of most people defensively. They were one of the first to loop their defensive linemen. We worked on it and with Mickey and Caroline going for us we caught them looping at exactly the right time—when the gaps were four yards wide."

Lou Agase, who in 1953, was an assistant coach at Illinois says: "It was brilliant. We were all amazed. Woody Hayes said that that offense taught him a lesson about defense that he would never forget. He said it was responsible for much of the success he had later."

Hayes commented that week that he had spent most of his practices fine-tuning his looping defense, but on a beautiful 71 degree September day in Columbus, J.C. Caroline ran for 193 yards and two touchdowns, while Mickey Bates romped for 152 and four scores as Illinois derailed the Ohio train before it could pick up steam, 41-20.

The Buck's three touchdowns came in the second quarter, two after Illini fumbles and one on their only sustained drive of the day, which was aided by a 28-yard pass interference penalty. Otherwise, Eliot's custom-made offense was devastating and his defense impenetrable.

Jack Prowell called it, "Organized destruction of the gigantic Ohio State myth."

Besides the brilliant strategy employed by the Illini, there was an incident before the game that didn't hurt their chances either.

"It was common practice to check with an opposing coach before a game to find out at which end of the field they wanted us to warm up on," Eliot remembered many years later. "Well, we went looking for Woody and we couldn't find him anywhere. So we took the field and went to the near endzone and started getting loose. Next thing we know, Ohio State comes out and completely encircles us and starts doing their exercises. That really made our boys mad. Then some Ohio State people told us that that was their endzone and that we should move to the other one. When we went back into the locker room Rocky Ryan exploded in anger and had our guys fired up. I guess you could say we were in the proper state of mind for that game."

The Illini kicked it into overdrive the next week, whipping Minnesota 27-7. (At halftime Eliot gave Pete Palmer, a music major, permission to become the first Illinois gridder to stay out on the field and entertain the crowd, singing a new Illini fight song. Later Palmer, with wife Aniko, went on to a celebrated career on stage and television.)

Then, on the same day that Purdue upended Michigan State 6-0, Illinois slid by Syracuse 20-13. In that win Eliot found a new offensive weapon, as Caroline and Bates were bottled up but fullback Stan Wallace busted loose for 115 yards on only five carries. Ryan, thought by some to be the best offensive end in the country, added a touchdown catch. Even though they played a nonconference game, the Illini suddenly found themselves the league leader because, along with the Spartans, Michigan and Wisconsin, both unbeaten to that point, got pinched.

Still, Eliot was not at all pleased, describing his team's performance as "Rotten, (the) worst of the season."

The following Saturday, J.C. Caroline's dad drove 800 miles from their home in South Carolina to see his boy scamper for 157 yards on "Dad's Day." Purdue was the Illini's victim, 21-0. Fourteen of Illinois' points came in the fourth quarter, a frame that had been good to them all year, as in it they had outscored their opponents 66-6.

Against Michigan the next week the Illini did not score in the fourth quarter, but did in each of the other three, downing the Wolverines 19-3. Somebody made the mistake of bringing up the Rose Bowl after that scramble, and caught the half-kidding ire of the coach.

"Get out of here with that talk!" Eliot growled with a hint of a smile. Then he said seriously, "Before we get over-enthused, let us remember that our last two games are away from home against teams that beat us last year. There's plenty of time to talk roses after you've actually earned them." Of course, if the Illini would win the next two, Pasadena would be all theirs.

However, against the Wisconsin Badgers in Camp Randall Stadium, the Illini hit the wall. Down just 14-7 after three quarters, the last period betrayed them and the Badgers racked up 20 unanswered points to win going away 34-7.

"It was our best game, definitely," confirmed Wisconsin coach Ivy Williamson. Eliot, of course, couldn't say that about his club, but with a big game still awaiting them in Evanston he remained as upbeat as possible. Calling Wisconsin the best team the Illini had faced all year, he said, "It was just one of those days." Later the coach would state that his boys "just wore out physically and mentally."

They were celebrating in East Lansing, though. For Michigan State, the door to a Big 10 championship and Rose Bowl berth had just cracked open again. Now they and the Illini were atop the Big 10 standings, both having one loss in conference play. (Wisconsin was also tied for the lead, but ineligible for the Rose Bowl because they had gone the year before. They ended up in second place after a season-ending tie with Minnesota).

As it had been for Wisconsin and Purdue, if the Illini and Spartans ended deadlocked for the top spot, then the Tournament of Roses representative would be decided by a vote of conference athletic directors. Michigan State was now done with Big 10 play, but the Illini had one league game left. While the Spartans were to take on a comparatively weak Marquette squad, the Illini caught a bus to Evanston to duke it out with the winless, but dangerous, Wildcats. They had to win or they could forget a vote or any trip to Pasadena.

They won. The Fighting Illini did nothing to diminish their chances of being selected to represent the Big 10 conference out west after demolishing Northwestern 39-14. Their suffocating defense held the Cats to just 45 total yards in the first half, and they left no doubt from the opening kickoff that they were there to win.

Because of the margin of Illinois' loss to Wisconsin, the media had swung its support strongly in favor of Michigan State during the last week of the season. But when the Illini crushed Northwestern and the Spartans just squeaked by Marquette 21-15, the momentum was checked. The decision was not obvious to anybody, especially the athletic directors of the conference who had the only vote that counted.

Eliot, as one might expect, was noncommittal in word but convinced in his heart who should go. "I don't know," he said after his boys had waxed Northwestern. "This is a great team—one of my greatest. It's up to them (the athletic directors) to say who goes."

Line coach Burt Ingwerson lobbied cautiously in the media, stating, "I'm not saying whether this team should go to the bowl, but you can be certain these boys would give a good account of themselves."

Stan Wallace, one of the few Illini left from the Rose Bowl team two years prior said he'd like to go again. "It's lots of work and everything, but it's worth it." Mickey Bates simply said, "I like the smell of Roses."

Of course, in East Lansing coach Biggie Munn and his boys were saying similar things. The cases for both sides were compelling. As a matter of fact, if an Illini fan and a Spartan fan were making their (heated) arguments for their respective teams, it might have gone something like this:

"It is only fair that we go because we have never gone and you guys went just two years ago," the Spartan would begin his argument. "You have players on your squad who have been to Pasadena, we have none."

"It makes no difference," the Illini would counter. "The only Big 10 rule about eligibility states that a team cannot go twice in a row. That's not the case here."

"Yeah, but it is an unwritten code that the last to go stays home. It would only be right for you to concede that the boys from East Lansing should have a chance to go to Pasadena."

"So we're being punished for being consistently good over

the past few years? It's just because we have been there before that we should go."

"Oh, God. Here comes the speech," the Spartan would roll his eyes.

"Listen. We at Illinois have a history in this conference. We have been in it from its inception and we have been to Pasadena and represented the Big 10 well—not just by winning but by being a first-class bunch. This is your first year in the conference. You have no track record—no history here."

"I say there is no better way to welcome us to the conference than by voting for us."

"Just to be included in this conference should be good enough for you. Besides you guys have been on probation for rules violations up 'til now."

Offended, the Spartan would spit back: "'Up 'til now' is the key phrase! The faculty reps took us off when the season ended."

"How convenient."

"What are you implying?!"

"Me...implying?" a look of complete innocence would come across the Illini's face.

"And because of some violations a couple of years ago, our representation of the conference would be tainted?"

"You said it, I didn't," the Illini would shrug his shoulders.

"Well," the Spartan would continue, trying to ignore the slam. "The bottom line is we are the better team anyway."

"The better team!" the Illini's eyes would flash. "Are you nuts? Look at the stats. First of all, you had the easier schedule."

"How's that?"

"Well, you didn't have to play us."

"And you didn't have to play us either!"

"But you didn't have to play Wisconsin."

"Well, from a look at the score it doesn't appear you played Wisconsin either!"

"Alright let's look at common opponents," the Illini would press on.

"We beat Minnesota by a bigger score!" the Spartan would quickly assert.

"Oh yes, excuse me. You beat them by 21 and we beat them by 20."

"Hey, a point is a point."

"My point exactly," the Illini would say. "Now let's continue. You beat Ohio State 28-13, we beat them 41-20. You beat Michigan 14-6, we beat them 19-3. We wailed on Purdue 21-0 and they beat you 6-0—case closed and we're it! Oh, and may I add, what a job you did against that mighty Marquette team!"

"We had the best overall record, though," the Spartan would argue. "We were 8-1 and you were 7-1-1."

"Conference play is all that matters here."

"Then don't bring up the Marquette score."

These arguments made for a prolonged ping-pong match between the athletic directors, too. They first voted by wire Saturday night and the tally came out even at 5-5. They voted again and came up with the same thing. Finally, they decided to sleep on it and get together the next day in Chicago. Everybody made it accept Fritz Crisler of Michigan, whose plane was fogged in at a Detroit airport.

Upon sitting down together, they immediately took a vote (Crisler casting his ballot by phone) and it came out even again. After that, Doug Mills of Illinois and Ralph Young of Michigan State stopped voting, as it was obvious that they weren't going to change their choices. The remaining eight athletic directors would talk and cast votes, talk and cast votes, and the dice would keep coming up box-cars.

After the controversy the year before, they voted by secret ballot and so it was never really clear who voted for whom. Wisconsin was said to be leaning toward Illinois the last week of the season, as was Northwestern, and it was obvious who Purdue was going to vote for. There were bad feelings from the "Fruit Bowl" the year before in Iowa, but Michigan was known to be in the Illini's corner. Beyond that, it is all a guess. As the meeting wore on late into the evening, however, somebody finally cracked.

Some say that the Michigan legislature applied pressure on Crisler and the University of Michigan to change their vote to their fellow home state school. On the other hand, Mills told Lon Eubanks in 1976 that he, "Always felt that if Crisler had been at the meeting and had been able to talk to the other directors in person, it would have been different."

In any event, what became the final tally went 5-3 in favor of the Michigan State Spartans. The reason given was that the Spartans had not been there before and Illinois had.

Officials of the Sugar Bowl then seized the opportunity and invited Illinois to play in New Orleans on New Years Day, but the Big 10 hierarchy wouldn't budge from its policy of only one team being allowed to go to a bowl, and the Illini stayed home—their great, astounding season over.

Eliot met with his boys and gave them the bad news. He disagreed with the decision and was greatly disappointed, but he kept it out of the papers and called Biggie Munn, congratulated him and wished the Spartans well.

The year, of course, had been improbable but sensational. Sophomores Caroline and Bates created the greatest one-two punch ever in an Illini offensive backfield—just ask Bob Zuppke: "They are the most rugged, fast men we've ever had," said the old coach that year. "In this particular they are even better than my two best halfback combinations, Grange and McIlwain and Macomber and Pogue." It was big praise from the "Little Dutchman," but well deserved.

Caroline himself had shattered many an Illinois and Big 10 season rushing record. As a team the Illini led the Big 10 in scoring, first downs, rushing and total yards gained. They had shattered every low expectation that even their coach had had the previous November.

"You want to know what made this a good football team?" Illini guard Wally Vernasco held court the afternoon Illinois vanquished Northwestern. "I'll tell you what I think did it. This ballclub had no dissension. Everybody liked everybody else, everybody would do anything for anyone else. When the team went on the field, no one was pulling for them any more than the guys on the bench. And I mean everybody—every single football player on the team."

There was another factor, too. Echoing the refrain of the Illini coach, when he sat in his sun room the year before, contemplating the future of his football team, Jack Prowell wrote: "That scene came back into focus Saturday afternoon because if there was one thing which has distinguished the 1953 Illinois football champions, it was that of what Eliot spoke—the desire to play football. The Illini loved the game of football and they played like it."

Rather than sulk about a lack of talent, Eliot transfused his love for the game and his enthusiastic, never-say-die spirit into the hearts of his boys, and made them something that on paper no one thought they could be.

Reflecting on Eliot's magic during the 1953 season, Bert Bertine of the *Courier* scribed. "Sure Illinois had a great running attack and two of the finest ballcarriers in the nation in J.C. and Mickey. But beyond those two this team essentially was what was left from a squad that lost five of nine contests last year. There had to be more difference than the addition of two sophomore backs—and don't forget Illinois had lost a record-setting passer in Tom O'Connell. You can credit the rest to spirit, a quality that Ray Eliot rarely is unable to arouse in his athletes. We'd say most of the time the Illini players were playing to win because of Ray—because it would please him."

To some, 1953 was Eliot's finest accomplishment. Maybe it was and maybe it wasn't, but it certainly was the crowning achievement of the crest and zenith of his career. Since 1946, when the playing field evened after the war, Illinois and Michigan had won or shared seven out of a possible eight Big 10 championships—the Illini had three, Michigan four. In 1950 and 1951 the Illini were 16-2-1, and in the last four years from 1950 through 1953, their record was 27-8-2—best in the league. They had not had that successful a four-year run since 1926-29 and have not had one since. All of this was accomplished in what was then, indisputably, the toughest conference in America.

Even Michigan State's own Duffy Daugherty, soon to be promoted from assistant to head coach, was quoted by the *Chicago Sun-Times* late in January of 1954 saying, "There's no question about it, Ray did the best coaching job in the country last season for the Fighting Illini."

These accolades were far from Eliot's mind on Monday, the day after the athletic director's vote. After hearing the somber news, about 2,500 students still crowded the front of the Auditorium on the university campus in 40 degree temperatures to cheer their champions at a pep rally. President Lloyd Morey misread the mindset of the crowd slightly, though. "Our good friends in central Michigan are celebrating today, too," he said over the public address. "But we have been there twice before. This is their first trip." This is not really what the listeners wanted to hear and when he said, "We'll all be cheering for them on January 1st," boos and hisses were spewed back at him from some of the faithful. What Morey said was true enough, but the wounded   Illinoisians were not ready to hear it yet (The president, a fast learner, changed his tune for the athletic banquet held a few days later. As he leaned into the microphone, he called the Illini, "Members of the best football team in the Big 10—no matter what they say!")

Eliot, on the other hand, the sting still fresh in his heart, predictably got a big cheer when he said his "Cinderella team deserved more than it got." Of the vote he said no more, and used the rest of his speech to thank the fans. "We are here to pay tribute to you folks who have been with us all season," he said.

Afterwards, he went to his Huff Gym office, tied together a few loose ends from the season past and went home.

17

The Racket

*"We'll have the will to win,
And if we go down,
We'll go down fighting—hard and clean.
That's the Illinois way."*

—Ray Eliot

Seated across from Coach Eliot, in the spring of 1954, was a strapping farm boy from Iowa. Big and burly, he was one of the most sought-after defensive linemen in the country coming out of high school. As Eliot welcomed him and began to tell him what he could expect if he played football at Illinois, the boy inattentively looked around the coach's modest Huff Gym office.

"What will you give me?" the boy interrupted.

"What will I give you for what?" responded the startled coach.

"What will you give me for coming here and playing football?"

"Nothing more than anybody gets," came the response.

The Iowan looked incredulous. "I've got offers from people at other places for stuff—you know, money and things. What are you going to give me?"

"Son, I'll promise you one thing," Eliot stared down the prospect. "If you come to Illinois you'll get an education and have the privilege of playing for one of the greatest universities in the land. But beyond that, I don't have any handouts for you or anybody else."

"O.K. See ya' later." The boy flew off his seat, turned and went out the door, brushing past Assistant Coach Lou Agase, who was standing outside.

Eliot got up and walked toward Agase with a disgusted look on his face. He told him what had transpired in the few minutes the boy was in his office, and he shook his head in disbelief. "This is what we've come to," he said. "Where a high school boy walks into your office and brazenly demands money under the table."

Ray Eliot retired from coaching in 1959, still a young man at 54. He got out because of the pressures, rigors and unsavoriness of recruiting. He said almost to his dying day that, "If it were just coaching, working with kids, teaching them the game of football and the game of life, I'd still be doing it." Unfortunately, football coaching had become so much more.

It wasn't that he wasn't good at recruiting. Quite the contrary. "Eliot was a master recruiter," wrote Don White, Sports Editor of Moline's *Daily Dispatch*. Not only had Eliot developed a close and loyal relationship with high schools across the state of Illinois (most of his players were from Illinois), but he used his powers of persuasion to the maximum with young America. He truly believed Illinois was the best place for them.

Gary Brown, for example, who played for Eliot's last Illini eleven, had made up his mind to go to Northwestern, but wanted to hear what Illinois had to say. "I went down to Champaign that weekend to have a good time," he told White. "But after listening to Eliot, I was completely turned around. I never met a man who could get you fired up like he could. That's the thing that sold me. He made you really want to play ball at Illinois."

Em Lindbeck had a similar story with a little different twist. Lindbeck had made up his mind to go to either Wisconsin or Army—then he went to the Illinois high school all-state banquet in Champaign. "Thirty-three of the state's best players," he described the scene, "the Illinois band playing, Chief Illiniwek dancing around the room and Ray Eliot giving one of his best speeches. Darn few kids could turn that off."

To every parent whose son Eliot recruited he promised, "If you send your boy to Illinois, I know we'll give you back a boy as good as when he came to us—or better."

As good as he was at it, Eliot, like Bob Zuppke before him, detested recruiting. "Why I should have to go out and beg so-called blue-chip athletes to come to one of the greatest learning institutions in the world, I'll never know," he said more than once. "They should consider it a privilege to come here."

If he had his druthers, the Big 10 would return to the days when a boy came to school for an education and if he happened to play football, too, then he'd play football; when, even if an athlete did select a school for its football team, it would be because of the team's reputation or the coach's abilities, not because of inducements. In his perfect world there would be no recruiting or scholarships, and winning would only be secondarily important to the education offered by the school and the game. He was not for a complete de-emphasis of the sport, as some were, because striving to win had its educational merits and the entertainment value of the game was considerable, but the extremes it was exhibiting disheartened him.

"A college's first duty should be the education of its students," he'd say. "And this can be achieved only when scholastic standards are maintained at a high level. Lavish entertainment and fabulous financial aid should not be the way to attract athletes to school. We can't afford to hurt boys by giving them something for nothing." In other words, inducements obscure the real reason a potential student should choose a school and that is the school's ability to educate—a non-diluted education they should earn.

Player after Illini player can recite the words Eliot spoke to them when they first set foot on campus.

Eliot would point to the library and say, "That's where you study."

And he would point to Memorial Stadium and say, "That's where you play." And then he would add, "If you don't study, you don't play."

"Ray was one of the few 'big-time' coaches who had the proper attitude towards the game and the athletes participating," said one-time Louisiana Tech head coach and athletic director Joe Aillet. "He was also one of the few who had a genuine respect for the institution for which he worked."

Notre Dame's Reverend John J. Cavanaugh, C.S.C., former president of the University and in 1959 Director of The Notre Dame Foundation, recognized that Mr. Illini had life and sports in perspective. He wrote him shortly after his announced retirement from the game: "You have not only been an excellent coach. But you always seemed to realize that football is a part of education. You respected football 'material' as if it were human, personal, in many senses, sacred. Many young men will remem-

ber you long for the lessons and inspiration which you shared
with them, and you will look back upon the shaping of lives with
much more pride than upon the times you won and lost."

Much to Eliot's disappointment though, football had moved
on from being a school extra-curricular activity and a game, to
become a job and a money-making venture. More time was
being required of players by coaches, and graduation, which was
just about a given for athletes prior to the 1950s, was suddenly
less important. The pressure on coaches to win increased as big
money hopped into the driver's seat of the sport.

To Eliot, if scholarships were going to be given, as it was
obvious they would be when the discussion dragged on into the
late 1950s, then at least it should be done with a standardized
format and with priorities, namely high scholastic requirements,
intact. Unfortunately, with a mandate to win or else, coaches
were put in a position to argue that standards should be lessened
so that there would be a larger high school athletic crop to
harvest. "Either lower the standards or tell us we don't have to
win," they said. This saddened and troubled the Illini coach.

Though he despised chasing blue-chip athletes, it was
Eliot, ironically, who first put Illinois on the recruiting map.
Between 1910 and 1930, when recruiting was largely nonexist-
ent, Illinois was one of the great national football powers,
winning four national championships along with seven Western
Conference crowns. When other schools began to recruit heavily,
and Zuppke refused, the Illini's football fortunes plummeted.
(One former football power that acted was the University of
Chicago. Because football began to overshadow studies, and
recruiting and the desire to win were getting out of hand, that
institution abandoned its football program entirely after the 1939
season). But Zuppke's stand caused a terrible rub with the
Illinois alumni and athletic department. Surely they would be
certain their next head coach would be willing to sell the University to prospective athletes.

In Eliot they found someone whose approach was a little
different than his mentor's: he also considered recruiting an
evil—but a necessary one (Zup used to call Eliot after each game,
win or lose, and say, "A good game. I couldn't do what you are
doing."). Zuppke and Eliot knew that the alumni demanded a
winner and would only keep a coach that produced on the field.

Eliot loved to coach and relished his work with young America. Thus, he found himself in the old catch-22. If he was going to have the opportunity to do what he loved, then, like it or not, he had to find a way to get the players on the field to win his share—within the rules, of course, of the collegiate governing body.

"By the time I took over as head coach, more and more schools were working hard to recruit players, and it was pretty obvious to me that you couldn't be any better than the young men you had playing for you," he told Lon Eubanks. "So we set out to actively interest good players in coming to Illinois, and we spent many hours trying to line up jobs to help them pay their way through school. We tried to get the boy one job during the school year, which would pay for his room and board, and another one in the summer that would pay for his tuition, books and fees for the coming year. (There were no athletic scholarships at the time).

"The legislative scholarships helped us a lot. At that time each legislator was able to give out four to persons in his district, and I frequently would work closely with them to encourage them to provide one of those to a young man we wanted to play for us. But they still only provided tuition, and we still had to get them jobs to pay for some of their other college expenses."

The process was tiring. The season itself was a seven-day-a-week job, but recruiting made the off-season just as bad. It became so time-consuming that soon coaches would no longer be required to teach—their profession would be coaching alone.

"It was just too much, too consuming, Sunday through Sunday," he explained. "On the road all the time. It kept getting increasingly worse. And there are so many hidden frustrations involved."

And Eliot did not believe in handing the responsibility over to an assistant. "The young athlete always wants to meet the man he might some day play for," he explained. "The head coach must be involved in every recruiting situation, from watching the hundreds of high school films to locating jobs and arranging quarters."

It is not technically true that a head coach must immerse himself in the entire recruiting process. Many coaches today have staff members whose chief job is to recruit. But that was not Eliot. Not only did every kid want to meet the head man, but, according to Eliot, he had the right to. And he never felt that any aspect of getting a boy situated at his new school was beneath him—he wanted to be a part of their lives from day one. He also didn't favor any one over another, so if one boy had a right to his personal scrutiny, they all did. Many coaches are more than willing to live at arms length from their players, but Eliot couldn't.

His desire to be close to his boys created another irritation for the Fighting Illini head coach. He liked to treat them like human beings. Back in his Illinois College days, he'd take a group of kids to the movies or let a new student-athlete stay with Maggie and him until he got settled, or he'd have players over for a meal—normal, kind-hearted stuff. But the NCAA was reacting to cheating going on in the recruiting process by going so far as to take away the coach's ability to show everyday kindness to his boys. He couldn't be a friend anymore.

"Can you believe it?" he would exclaim. "If I want to have a boy in my house and offer him a Coke—I can't do it. If I want to give a boy a hot meal—I can't do it. Even if I am driving down the street and I see one of my boys with his car broken down along the side of the road and I want to stop and offer him a ride—according to the rules—I can't do it."

It was a vicious cycle. The cheating led to stricter rules and the stricter rules led to more cheating because the rules had evolved into something ridiculous (it has not been uncommon for schools to cheat unintentionally because of the complexity of the NCAA code). The further cheating, of course, led to the rules being wound tighter still.

Most cheating, of course, was not accidental, and that fact ate at Eliot constantly. "The thing that disturbed me most was that, even in those days, there were so many illegal things going on in recruiting," he said years after his retirement. "Of course, it was very difficult to prove, but I have no doubt that it became gradually worse. There is no question that the reason I retired from coaching was the rigors and demands of recruiting. That and the fact that I became increasingly disgusted with the recruiting methods used by many of the other schools. But when I was involved in recruiting, I worked hard at it. Recruiting is the name of the game, but it drove a lot of good men out of college coaching."

Eliot was an extremely trusting individual. The knowledge of cheating among his peers cut him like a sharp knife. It not only disgusted him, but pained him deeply.

"Ray's inability to believe fellow humans could be dishonest likely hurt him in the rugged recruiting wars," Bert Bertine once wrote of the broken promises and backstabbing that had become part of the recruiting racket. "If an athlete or his parents promised enrollment at Illinois, Ray believed them. With such ideals, Eliot was not cut out for the dirty infighting that recruiting seems to demand. At heart he was a Huff-Zuppke amateur, although he recognized their era had passed and did his best to adjust to the modern quasi-professional trend."

To cut back on the cheating, Eliot suggested a return from one-platoon football, where each player had to play on both sides of the ball, to free substitution. "There are only a limited number of high school players who can go both ways, offense and defense," he often pointed out. "These are the blue-chip athletes and they're at a premium. Schools realize they must have these blue-chip players so the competition begins for them. Now, if we were under the old substitution rule, there would be more available prospects for the colleges. It would mean boys who are specialists in high school wouldn't get lost in the shuffle and would have a place in college ball. This would greatly equalize schools throughout the country as well as in the individual conferences. It would mean teams like Illinois wouldn't get outstaffed so often."

It was obvious that Eliot felt Illinois was put at a constant disadvantage in the 1950s by the unscrupulous practices of some other schools. He wasn't the only one who thought that way. "You know even better than I that you could win every year if you were to buy your athletes," wrote Ora D. Dillavou, Assistant Director of the Illinois Department of Financial Institutions in Springfield, to Eliot in 1959. "I hope that the University of Illinois will never put athletics above integrity and studies."

Still, though his solution made practical sense, it was too generous with the heart of man and miscalculated its greed. First, football squads were growing. In the 1940s, a typical Illini roster had between thirty and forty players. In 1959 that number had grown to over sixty. Today, though the NCAA has cut back slightly on available scholarships to try to improve equity, many squads have over 100 boys. So when free substitution returned, the numbers needed to fill out a roster grew at the same time. Then teams needed more blue-chippers than ever, and competition for those athletes remained intense.

In addition, most teams do not approach their seasons with equality or fairness in mind. Coaches, either because they are under the gun to win or just to stroke their own egos, try, as in poker, to hoard as many blue-chips to themselves as possible. When money is the single aim, and education and sportsmanship are not, then people will do whatever it takes to win—illegal as it may be—because winning means money. The lesson passed down to our youth then, is that "all's fair—as long as you win!"

Although he wanted to win as much as anybody, Eliot did not view losing as a waste of time. Frank Wodziak, who played for Eliot in the early 1950s, said he learned from Eliot that "to lose occasionally is also of value." Indeed, everyone in life will lose at one time or another—so one must learn to win and he also must learn how to lose. To Eliot, education, once again, was the issue.

Was there ever a boy who played for Eliot that was given some kind of illegal stipends? Possibly. One would have to be naive to say "absolutely not" about any program. Regardless of what the NCAA may rule, a coach cannot control outsiders (whether they be alumni or others with financial interests in the success of the team) determined to gain by cheating. But Eliot himself was "Simon Pure," as Lou Agase liked to call him.

"Through his policies," said Rex Smith, "most that played for the U of I did not come with the idea to 'get rich' from college football. They came because they thought they could get a good education, have fun playing football and receive reasonable financial help through school."

Academia appreciated Eliot's standards and priorities as well. "I can truthfully say," stated University of Illinois Professor L. Ingle, "that (Ray) never once asked for any special consideration for a single one of his football boys, which I had in my Zoology classes, and I had quite a few."

Friend and alumnus J.I. Dilsaver said: "I admired him for placing development of character ahead of winning football games. I know it was always his purpose and ambition to mold them into men first and into football players second. Winning of football games is too often forced out of proportion to the real purpose of the game. He, as most of us, liked to win, but not at all costs."

It was because he followed the rules as strictly as he did that his boys threatened to strike in 1943. It was just before the famous "fifth-quarter" game at Ohio State.

"When we played different teams we would talk with their players," says Eddie Bray. "We found out that they were getting unbelievable things to play for their schools—cars, money—the whole bit. We were getting nothing—not even any spending money on road trips. These other players would laugh at us because we weren't getting anything. We thought fair is fair. So we decided we weren't going to play. It was after breakfast on the day of the game, about 11 o'clock, and Ray came up and said, 'What are you going to do Ed? How are you going to get home (if you strike)?' I said, 'I've got a thumb.' Then Doug Mills, the Athletic Director, came in and talked to us for about a half hour and he couldn't stir us. So we decided to negotiate. They picked me and George Bujan and we had a private meeting with Doug Mills. He asked us what we wanted and we told him we just wanted a little spending money. I mean, I told him that if I wanted to buy a magazine I couldn't buy one. If I wanted a candy bar I couldn't even afford that. Well, we went out and played at Ohio State. After the game I got on the train to go home and there was Doug Mills with a box of candy for us."

Eliot would have loved to give the boys anything he could, but it was against the rules and he was not going to stain his name or his university's name for a few dollars or a few hundred dollars. Even the rules that were petty had to be followed.

Sadly, Eliot's retirement did not keep him from the reality of recruiting inconsistencies. Several years after he got out, his own school embroiled itself in the stew that became known as the "slush fund scandal."

Eliot was an Assistant Athletic Director in December of 1966 when Mel Brewer (the same man who inspired the upset over vaunted Michigan in 1939) presented University of Illinois President Dr. David Dodds Henry with a book that detailed illegal payments of about $20,000 to Illini football and basketball players. The money came from what was called a "special need fund" and head football coach Pete Elliot claimed it was not used to bribe players to come to Champaign, but was used to help them with necessary things that they could not afford. For example, some was spent to send several kids home at Christmas, and some was used for travel expenses so a poor boy could go home for the funeral of a family member.

Rumors circulated that Brewer's motivation to call the athletic department to the carpet was his belief that the Athletic Director position was going to be his when Mills retired. Instead, Mills was set to give that position to Pete Elliot, at which time Billy Taylor, Pete's number one assistant, would become head coach.

Considering that Dr. Henry brought the violations voluntarily to the attention of Big 10 administrators, that the proven violations were relatively minor, and that Illinois was a first-time offender, the Big 10 administration seemed ruthless in its punishment. Not only did eight athletes get booted from the basketball and football squads, and the NCAA put Illinois on probation for two years with sanctions that prohibited participation in postseason bowls and television games, but the Big 10 gave an ultimatum to the school regarding Pete Elliot, head basketball coach Harry Combes, and assistant basketball coach Howie Braun. Either they quit, were fired, or Illinois would be suspended indefinitely from the Big 10 Conference.

Athletic Directors voted 8-1 for the mandate, with only Michigan holding out for less severe sanctions. Illinois appealed and lost again 8-1. Finally, Dr. Henry was granted a hearing before the faculty representatives, but the decision remained unchanged. Illinois was given three days to comply or be suspended. Rather than put "Illinois in an impossible position," they said in a joint statement, Elliot, Combes, and Braun resigned.

With a few exceptions within its ranks, Illinois had never been a "win at all costs" university, as some schools seemed to be. Even through some trying times it only had two football coaches in the 47 years before Eliot's retirement: Zuppke and Eliot—a record of stability unmatched in major college football. The University felt it consistently put its values and principles first.

So one theory of why the crackdown was so brutal was that Doug Mills had become quite self-righteous about Illinois' squeaky clean image. The decision of the Athletic Directors, then, was a backlash because of Mills' smugness—they took a delight in hanging Illinois.

Be that as it may, Illini fans were not the only ones who felt the punishment went well beyond what seemed reasonable. David Condon of the *Chicago Tribune* wrote that Illinois had been brought before "two separate kangaroo courts," and in an editorial the *Tribune* ripped the Big 10. Other newspapers across the Midwest followed suit in protest, but the gavel had fallen.

When Eliot had retired seven years earlier, he had had his eye on the Athletic Director position himself. When Doug Mills stepped down, he wanted to step up. By 1966 at the age of 61, though, he was deemed too old by the University administration, thus, Pete Elliot was to be the man. Now that Elliot was out of the equation and the University's ship was crashing on the rocks, Eliot wanted the helm more than ever. He had a ground swell of support, too, made up of friends, associates and former players.

"Ray, with his love for Illinois, figured he was the only guy left whom they couldn't claim did anything wrong or illegal (he was officially cleared of any guilt by Big 10 Commissioner Bill Reed), and he assumed that he was going to get the job," says long-time friend and colleague Larry Stewart. "He felt that he could pull things together and get things going in the right direction again quicker than anyone. He wanted the position very badly."

The powers that be, however, after inviting Eliot to interview, gave the position to 43-year-old Gene Vance. They said they wanted someone who could serve at least 10 years. Eliot would need special permission to go beyond the automatic retirement age of 67.

"To say Ray was crestfallen was putting it lightly," says Stewart as he described Eliot when he got the news. "He was shattered."

Speaking out of the shock and hurt of the moment, for the first time in his Illini life, Eliot told Stewart that he was going to leave the University. He felt he had poured his life into the school and now, when it needed him most, he felt it turned its back on him. Sensing the struggle in his friend's heart, Stewart had Eliot and Vance meet him at the offices of WDWS Radio in Champaign.

"They both happened to get to the station at the same time—it was about 5:30 at night," relates Stewart. "I took them over into the owner's office and I said that this school is in deep trouble and you two have got to be their salvation. And you are not leaving this room until you make your peace with yourselves. I closed the door and I locked it and I wouldn't let them out for about 45 minutes. Ray stayed (at Illinois) because Gene needed him badly. Ray knew the ins and outs and Gene was a compromise candidate. It was a very difficult five years for Gene, and Ray was a great help to him."

At the same time, Stewart was trying to convince Eliot that he had done plenty for the University and he could slow down now. "I'd say 'Ray, you've paid your dues,'" says Stewart. "I said, 'I know your love for the school overshadows everything but, listen, so you're in the secondary position. Big deal. At least you're your own man.' And he finally, I think, accepted it."

After the initial blow, Eliot righted himself and announced with his typical graciousness of spirit: "I am delighted to be of service to our president, to Gene Vance and to the University of Illinois anyway I can. I am a loyal Illini through and through and we have a wonderful leader in Gene Vance, and I am certain his leadership will put us in the same respected position we have held in the athletic world all these years."

Turning to the recent scandal he said, "I want to say without hesitation that we have one of the finest athletic associations in America, with remarkable talent and wonderful people. If we have made some mistakes, as is quite obvious at this point, we can only let bygones be bygones, pick ourselves up by the bootstraps and pull together."

He was sailing straight now, but all of the circumstances surrounding the "slush fund scandal" forever rested like a bullet near his heart.

"It was almost like a personal thing with him," says close friend Fritzi Frary. "Like he had to then go out and prove things were so much better at Illinois than people thought they were. It was like he had a mission."

Ironically, in just five years the athletic director's position came open again and, at 66 years old, Eliot wanted it. Like before, he was passed off as too old.

Upon his retirement from the coaching ranks, 50 of Eliot's boys had gone on to become college coaches and myriads were coaching on the high school level after they graduated from Illinois. Mike Kasap was one of them. During the summer before the 1968 football season, Eliot ran his annual football clinic in Champaign and Kasap, as always, came down for it.

Before the clinic began, though, Eliot pulled Kasap aside. "I have to give a welcoming address to these coaches," he said. "Mike, what do you think about this: This damn football is going to where it shouldn't go. It's all money. They are not taking care of the kids. They are not making them go to school. (The kids are) not getting an education. All of these kids that are coming to school and playing for five years don't have three years of college, and if they have three years of college it doesn't mean a damn thing. What do you think is gonna happen if I give a talk about getting back to the old principles? I'm afraid these guys will shout me down or boo me."

Kasap told Eliot that if he felt that strongly about it, he should let her rip. "The hell with 'em," said Kasap.

So Eliot got up in front of 300 to 400 coaches and preached his gospel like he never had before. He spoke of education, graduation, big money ruining the game, winning being important only to a point, boys learning good citizenship, boys not letting their notoriety supersede their common sense and boys becoming life-long contributors to society. He preached it with all his heart. It was one of the only times that witnesses can remember Eliot did not receive a standing ovation.

The conversation at the coaches tables the rest of the week? "What does that old guy know," they said. "Doesn't he know that that's not the way football is played anymore?"

He knew. In 1977, when his grandson wanted to go into coaching, he advised him to coach on the high school level.

"That's where it's still fun," he said. "That's where it's still a game."

18

Tribute to Desire

Dear Mike,

Since the day you were born, like any proud father, I've nursed ambitions that some day you would develop into a fine football player and go to the University of Illinois.

It is for this reason that I am especially saddened that Ray Eliot is stepping out of the coaching profession after this season.

Mike, you could search the world over and never uncover a man I would rather have you play for than Ray Eliot.

Sure, you may find me a little disgruntled on Sundays after Illinois has lost a tough one. By the next week, though, I've forgotten all about the game. But I'll never forget Ray Eliot.

As I watch him work with the Illinois football players, molding them into men first and into football players second, it makes me realize how often the role of the winning coach is forced out of proportion.

I'd like to have you play on a winning team, Mike, but not at all costs. I want you to come out of your football experience a better man.

If Ray Eliot were your coach I would have no worries.

Ray's retiring after next week's game, Mike, so you won't have the opportunity of playing under him. I can only hope that Illinois, when it decides on a successor, will pattern him after the nation's greatest coach in my book, Ray Eliot.

—Your Daddy,
Bill Schrader (Champaign
News-Gazette Sport Editor, in the
News-Gazette, November 15, 1959)

On October 24, 1953, Major General B.E. Gates hosted "Ray Eliot Night" in the officer's club at Chanute Air Force Base in Rantoul. The turnout of dignitaries and 600 townspeople exceeded anyone's expectations, and they packed all of the rooms in the club.

"We're here tonight to pay tribute to a great guy who also happens to be a good coach," said General Gates to the crowd.

"He and his puny little boys may cause us to have ulcers, but they win their share. But a man doesn't need friends when he's winning." And, turning to Eliot he said, "We're here to say we're behind you—even when you lose."

Those sentiments, no doubt genuine, may be easy to express when one's team is in the middle of a conference championship campaign. But the teeth of those words would be tested for the remainder of Eliot's coaching career.

Just one year later the Illini would be in the throes of Eliot's worst season ever (1-8). After that the Illini had records of 5-3-1, 2-5-2, 4-5 and 4-5 leading up to Eliot's final autumn of 1959. By and large, because of Eliot's priorities, such as the betterment of his boys and the educational value of the game, he continued to enjoy the support of the alumni, administration and students. He was an extremely popular man, who had become the dean of Big 10 coaches and, though some thought his principles were outdated, received a sage's respect when addressing issues involving college athletics.

Still, there were factions that applied the heat. Once, for example, he had been given a brand new car by the Champaign-Urbana community following a successful year—the next season it was egged by a few irate fans after a loss.

Of course, like any coach, he had his days of being derided and booed from the stands. But after a 31-12 loss to Wisconsin in 1958, he was hung in effigy. But, amazingly, the student who did it came to Eliot and apologized.

"At first I thought the boy was coming to finish off the job," joked Eliot, "but soon I realized I was talking to the   true personification of the Fighting Illini spirit. He is a fine boy and he has apologized. Nobody forced him to come; he just wanted to."

Every now and then, derogatory banners could be seen dotting Memorial Stadium. But his players never let those gesticulations remain for long. As a matter of fact, three years in a row they knocked off a team ranked number one in   the country—to the knowledge of this writer, an unmatched feat in the annals of American college football.

The second in that streak was in 1956, when a 1-3 Fighting Illini squad took on the unbeaten Michigan State Spartans. The week before, the machine from East Lansing had dispatched Notre Dame without hardly breaking a sweat 47-14.

At different places in the stadium, signs came out demanding Eliot's scalp, but the Illini did the only head-hunting that day. After trailing 13-0 at halftime, they ravaged the Spartans, beating them 20-13. Abe Woodson, the soon-to-be pro star, scored all three touchdowns for the Illini.

Michigan State head coach Duffy Daugherty left Champaign suspicious. "Any coach who took a team into Illinois after Ray had lost a couple of games in a row had to be especially wary," he said once. "We were sure there would be those 'Good-bye Ray' signs around the place, which we suspected he had placed himself."

Later in the evening another sign appeared that Eliot surely did not place, this time on Eliot's front lawn. It read: "Brother Ray is Here to Stay!"

Indeed, every time it seemed Eliot and Illinois had become like a wobbly pass about to fall incomplete, they would come up with a catch that would capture the imagination and attention of the entire country. Some called them upsets, but he insisted he "didn't know if there really is such a thing as an upset." That may be why he got so many.

In 1956 it was Michigan State, but the year before it was Michigan. The Wolverines also rolled into Illinois top-ranked, and the Illini, led by the great future Pro Football Hall of Famer Bobby Mitchell (10 rushes, 173 yards, one touchdown), smacked them 25-6.

Minnesota was number one in the nation in 1957, too, when Eliot had a dream—literally. "Coach Eliot came to practice a couple days before we ended our preparation," former quarterback and Los Angeles Dodger catcher Tom Haller related the story once. "He told us he had a dream that night and woke up at 4AM."

Eliot told the team that the vision showed him how to contain Minnesota roll-out quarterback Bobby Cox, and win the game. The Illini blew the Gophers out 34-13. Ray Nitschke, the Illini and Green Bay Packer legend, led a stubborn Illini defense in shutting down the Gopher signal-caller and his offense that had scored 108 points in its first three games. Ernie McMillan, an All-Star pro linebacker for St. Louis, was also a part of that Illini eleven.

"After that we kept telling him to have more dreams," Haller laughed.

That year they beat another highly touted and nationally ranked Michigan team 20-19. If that weren't enough, Michigan State was again ranked in 1958 when Illinois iced them 16-0. Bill Brown, whose younger brother Jim was also an Illini fullback, ran for 130 yards in 22 carries in that one before going on to a stellar career with the Minnesota Vikings.

It is not to say that, aside from these glorious upsets, the Illini were doormats. Actually, they were competitive in just about every game they played. In the worst span of those years, 1956-58, when they were 10-15-2 as a team, the Illini lost by an average of only 10.5 points per game. Any of those seasons could just as easily have been winning ones as losing.

Of all the losses during that time, though, one stood out well above the rest, and it took place far removed from any football gridiron. On July 13, 1958, just four days after his third grandchild was born, Ray Eliot received the news that his mother, Annie Nusspickle, 78 years old, had died. She was found face down on her Manhattan apartment floor with a bottle of aspirin in one hand and an empty glass nearby. She had felt chest pains that warm summer morning and went to the medicine cabinet to get something to ease the discomfort. Annie didn't know she was having a heart attack. She had just gotten a glass of water to wash the aspirin down when she collapsed. She lay dead for three or four days until she was found.

On July 16, Annie's only child put her to rest next to her husband Adolph in St. Michael's Cemetery in Queens, reuniting them after 47 years. As Mr. Illini stood with Maggie by the fresh grave, and the sympathetic breeze trickled over the green grass of God's acre, his tears seeped deep into his own fractured heart. Tucked away in his cherished belongings are found the words of this prayer penned by William Livingston:

> "Cold is the hand that smoothed my hair,
> And vanished the wondrous joy
> That came when, spite of my manhood's years,
> She would call me still her boy.
> But still she loves me, her child and thine,
> As once at her gentle knee;
> And, true to her faith, my heart remains
> Unchanged in its love for thee."

God had taken His "most precious gift to man," back to Himself.

Eight months later, in March of 1959, Ray Eliot shocked the college football world by resigning as head football coach of the University of Illinois, effective after the 1959 grid season.

"It is always difficult to decide that one will leave the firing line of the fierce competition which is Big 10 football," he said in a statement. "But the choice was made in the offseason when unhurried reflection on the future is possible without the heat of battle or influence of a winning or losing season."

Eliot, unlike so many in the coaching ranks, went out on his own terms.

"A guy has to quit sometime and I think I have done it without pressure," he answered the queries of the media. "I wouldn't have liked the situation about coaches some schools get into. Here at Illinois we hope we're a little more dignified in the way we do things.

"Actually, the last few years I took a long look at myself and said 'How far do you want to go in coaching' and 'How do you end.' I said to myself, 'If an administrative position comes up, I'll take it.'"

The administrative position that was made available to him was an assistant athletic director to Doug Mills. Those duties he would assume after the autumn campaign.

Eliot's last season, 1959, had been a bucket filled with promise, but before a game was ever played it became a bucket filled with holes. First, All-American candidate Rich Kreitling decided in July that he was going to turn pro.

"We've been hurt terribly by the loss," said Eliot. "He was the nation's top receiver last year in spring drills, and we worked on some new twists in our offense, thinking that he would be with us. Considerable practice time has been lost because of his departure." Some called Kreitling "fifty percent of the offense" in 1958.

In addition, Eliot's top two right halfback candidates were declared ineligible, and Johnny Easterbrook, his number one quarterback, got hurt.

Just before the season began, Joe Buscemi sent a letter to Eliot. "You must realize," he wrote, "that every Illini who has ever played for you will be blocking, tackling and carrying the ball every time your boys do this fall." The personal note from Buscemi and the hundreds of others he received as he embarked on his final campaign warmed his heart. Surely he would not have minded, though, if he could have taken that particular letter literally. He could have used one of his old ends or right halfs or centers...

The Illini had not played a Big 10 opener since 1919 and were reluctant to schedule another. But Indiana wanted a 1959-60 first game series with the Illini and offered, as an incentive, the inaugural game of their new 47,000 seat stadium the first year. Mills and Eliot agreed on those terms, but, come September, the stadium wasn't ready yet. Of course, with the large amount of money being spent on the new digs, the minimum was used to keep up the old. So instead of playing in a brand-new facility in front of 40,000-plus, the Illini faced the Hoosiers on a bare and hardened gridiron in front of only 20,000 fans.

Meanwhile, because of the personnel setbacks, the coaching staff had to scramble to put a team together before opening day against a school they had not played since their undefeated season of 1951. Back then the Illini whipped Indiana 21-0, but now, eight years later, the Hoosiers almost turned the tables completely, clubbing the Illini 20-0. The Illini fumbled ten times and lost five, showing a tendency toward the dropsies that prompted Bert Ingwerson to quip later in the season, "I know one thing. All our boys are going to go to heaven. The way they give things away they can't miss."

The Indiana debacle did not leave Illinois fans brimming with confidence when Army came marching into Champaign the next week, ranked fourth nationally and having won ten games in a row. They had shoved the football down the throat of Boston College in their first game 44-8. But the Illini showed up with courage in their hearts, and Eliot with a plan up his sleeve.

Army employed what was coined "the lonesome end" in their offensive scheme. This was basically a wide-out that generally lined up opposite the strength of the offensive formation. As normal as wide-outs are today they were relatively uncommon in the 1950s. Army used the set-up often, seeking to lull a team into forgetting about him and then utilizing him when the opponent least expected.

Defensively, Eliot doubled and tripled teamed that end all day and never let him get on track. Offensively, Eliot designed a slight variation to his normal attack in what would become known as the "un-lonesome end." Eliot also employed a wide-out, but then sent a man in motion in the direction of that end. Thus he would flood one side of the field with multiple receivers and then roll out his quarterback in the same direction. If the Cadets covered the receivers, quarterback Mel Meyers would run. If they converged on him he would throw to the man left open.

It sounds quite simple, but Illinois had two first-quarter touchdowns before Army's blackboards found an answer. By then the Fighting Illini defense had brutally established itself. Army picked up only seven yards on the ground in the first half and added only 25 more in the second. What success they had was through the air, and they scored in the second and the fourth quarters to match the Illini's 14. But it was not enough. In the third, Bill Brown had bullied over from the one, capping a tough, 13-play, 45-yard drive, and Illinois once again shook college football at its foundations by whipping Army 20-14. The Illini's Doug Wallace picked off a Cadet pass with thirty seconds remaining to seal the win.

Asked what the turning point of the game was, Army head coach Dale Hall responded, "When we first walked onto the field."

To Eliot it was another confirmation of the principles that he lived his life by. "The thing I reveled in," he said, "was the way the kids hung in there against what appeared to be insurmountable odds. It was a great tribute to desire."

After the Army masterpiece, Michigan State coach Duffy Daugherty called and sang "Illinois Loyalty" over the phone to a laughing Eliot. The *Florida Times-Union* in Jacksonville, Florida scribed: "It's hard to remember the last time a season went by without Illinois springing at least one big upset on some unsuspecting foe...(Eliot) is a master psychologist."

Eliot's swan song was just getting tuned up.

The next week the Illini headed to Columbus, Ohio, to take on Woody Hayes and the Buckeyes of Ohio State. Illinois needed a win to remain in the Big 10 race, but on Friday afternoon, while his boys were going through their final workout at Ohio Stadium, Eliot found time to remember an old acquaintance.

"Where," he asked newspapermen, "is the nice policeman who always guards our dressing room door?"

He was inquiring about 86-year-old campus officer Bill North. Told that the policeman's health would probably keep him from the game on Saturday, Eliot said: "I want to send him a card and tell him I missed him. Who has his address?"

An Ohio newspaper related the story and added this edi-torial comment: "Ray Eliot of Illinois—coach and gentleman."

Journalists in Ohio thought highly of Eliot. After reflecting on the long rivalry between Illinois and Ohio State, for instance, sportswriter Johnny Jones penned, "If I were a cheerleader tomorrow before the game and when he was warming up his team, I would shout a, 'Yea, Eliot! Good-bye and good luck.' It is such sentimental things that carry on the grace, the discipline and the fellowship of sports." They admired his demeanor, his principles and the way his kids played football.

Surely their admiration grew the next day as the Illini shut out the Buckeyes 9-0. The boys from Champaign racked up 369 total yards to 160 for Ohio, but the Illinoisians still had to rely on a field goal and a miracle to win.

Long before Franco Harris pulled down the "Immaculate Reception" to beat the Oakland Raiders in the 1970s, Illinois had one of its own. In the first quarter the Illini faced a third and 12 on their own 27 yard-line, when Meyers dropped straight back to pass and looked for halfback Johnny Counts deep. Pressure was coming hard up the middle from the Buckeye defensive line. Meyers shook off one tackler and then, as three other Bucks were bearing down on him, saw end Jerry Patrick open momentarily. He let the pigskin fly. Patrick, now sandwiched between two defenders, went up but the ball was batted. As it was heading earthward, Counts, galloping ten yards behind any Ohio de-fender, swept it out of the air and scampered the last 43 yards for the touchdown. The extra point was missed, but the field goal was added in the fourth period.

It was only the third time in their long rivalry that Illinois had shut the Buckeyes out, and it was the first time in Hayes' eight years as the head man that Ohio State had lost twice in a row. The week before, Ohio had been beaten by the USC Trojans in Los Angeles. After that game Hayes had an altercation with some reporters, and two sportswriters claimed Hayes threw punches at them. The Buckeye coach's story was that he asked the reporters to leave and when they were slow in complying he, "shoved them along." During the week he had been ripped by some Ohio media members, including Tom Keys, Sports Editor of the *Columbus Citizen*, who claimed that he saw Hayes hit one of his own players several years before.

Some reporters wrote of animosity between Eliot and Hayes. That was probably too strong a description. They were both passionate men, but in their approaches they were polar opposites. Eliot could not abide the many antics, on and off the field, that Hayes provided. But, in the end, they knew that each wanted the same thing—the betterment of young America.

Hayes invited Eliot to speak at certain banquets he was involved with in Ohio, and Hayes himself broke a long-standing self-imposed rule and tradition when he left his team the night before a game to honor Eliot.

In 1973, then-Illinois Governor Dan Walker proclaimed November 3rd "Ray Eliot Day" in the state of Illinois. That day the Illini were to take on Ohio State, but Friday night a banquet was held to honor Eliot, and Hayes accepted an invitation to speak. That night Hayes called Eliot "One of the truly great men to have come out of your university (Illinois)—a great man, a great coach and a superlative adversary."

In turn, Eliot wrote to Hayes shortly after the Buckeye mentor had been fired for punching a Clemson player during the 1978 Gator Bowl. As quoted by Paul Hornung in his book, *Woody Hayes: A Reflection*, Eliot wrote: "I just want you to know that I hold you in high regard as a gentleman and sportsman because of the many wonderful things that you have done for the coaching profession and for the boys that have played under you in your years of coaching. They have always been great sportsmen, and that reflects only the great techniques of their coach."

Because of their apparent differences, though, a number of reporters were alarmed that the two coaches did not shake hands after the 1959 game. But there was nothing to it, as both Eliot and Hayes said they had talked before the game and decided a handshake was unnecessary that day. Hayes even said he would have come across and greeted Eliot anyway, but one of his boys suffered a concussion on the final play of the game and he felt his place was with him. In fact, with the Ohio State faculty in a state of upheaval over the events of the previous week, the Ohio State coach was every bit the kindhearted gentleman as he spoke with the media afterward.

Observed Bert Bertine of the *Champaign-Urbana Evening Courier:* "A controversial type like Hayes usually has to win to keep his job since he's bound to split fans into two factions: admirers and the unenchanted. As long as he wins the latter group is quiet. When he loses they are heard."

By contrast, it was a tribute to the respect Eliot commanded even in the towns of his so-called gridiron enemies, that as the Ohio newsmen stood at the dressing room door waiting for the time to run out on the clock, they said almost as one, "It's nice for Ray."

The Illini kept it "nice for Ray" at their homecoming the following week, downing Minnesota 14-6. But, just when people began giving them some respect in the conference and nationally, they went back to Ohio—this time Cleveland—to play in front of a paltry 15,045 fans and lose to their unbeaten nonconference foe, Penn State, 20-9.

They came back into the league but missed a last-second field goal by four inches and settled for a 7-7 tie with Purdue, and were upset by Michigan 20-15 after leading 9-0 after the first quarter. The toughest two teams in the conference, Wisconsin and Northwestern, loomed ahead, and the Illini were considered dead in the water.

As exciting as his career had been, and as heartstopping the games, Eliot had never been a part of a team that won a game on the final play. "I've been trying all my life to end a game with a touchdown on the last play so (the other team) couldn't come back at you," he smiled. "And it took a little bit of doing."

Indeed it did. The stage was set for his dream to come true as a capacity crowd in Wisconsin's Camp Randall Stadium and millions in a T.V. audience watched the Illini and Badgers battle down to the wire on November 14th.

The Badgers came into the game at 4-1, a full game-and-a-half ahead of the Illini. They wanted to chuck the final nails into Illinois' coffin, and needed a win to keep pace with Northwestern, who had an identical record. Michigan State was still in the mix also, at 3-2.

With 5:05 remaining until the final gun, and the Badgers leading 6-2, the Illini took over on their own 17 yard line after a Wisconsin quick kick, and Eliot's dream sequence was set in motion. The boys from Madison dug in, hoping to keep Eliot's bunch bottled up in their own end. As they entered the huddle, though, Illini linemen Joe Rutgens and John Gremer demanded, "Let's get going. We have just enough time to score!"

Quarterback Mel Meyers settled in under center. In the second half, the Illini had found the middle of the Badger defense somewhat vulnerable, and it is there that Meyers decided to attack. "I didn't think there was a team in the country that could move the ball against us in the middle," declared Wisconsin halfback and Champaign native Stu Clark later. But move it they did.

Meyers handed to fullback Bill Brown, who blew through a big whole in the line, and gained 21 yards on the first play of the drive. Johnny Counts went off right tackle for four, then Brown barrelled through the middle for another seven and a first down. Gary Kolb got the call next and went off tackle for 10, followed by another Brown gallop of 19 yards to the Wisconsin 22.

There was but 2:45 left when Brown picked up another three yards and Counts blasted for four. But it looked like the dream clouds had shattered when, on the next play, Kolb got hammered by a Badger linebacker and committed Illinois' sixth fumble of the day. They dodged the lethal bullet, though, when Jerry Patrick beat the Badgers to the ball and recovered for the Illini at the 15. It was now third and three. Money-man Brown again got the call, and came up with another Illini first down at the 11 with 1:28 showing on the clock. Counts then gained a yard. Next, Meyers gambled in an attempt to cross up the defense and passed to Kolb over the middle. The halfback squeezed the ball, got hit at the four, and stumbled to the one with only 28 seconds left. On first down, Brown tried for the goal line, but was stopped cold with 22 ticks remaining.

Illinois signaled its last timeout and Meyers called two plays in the huddle. The first was a quarterback sneak and the second was, what else, Brown up the middle. Meyers set the offense down and, off a quick count, burrowed behind his center. Pumping his legs, he drove right to the doorstep but at the last was repelled. "Actually I was in," he would say later. But the officials, as if God had predestined every circumstance to give the Illini head man a win on the very last play, said he was not.

Illinois sprung to its feet and lined up quickly, the clock running past seven seconds. Brown, leaned into his three-point stance and set his sights on the Badger defense and the goal line beyond. Meyers barked the signals, then turned and handed to his fullback, whose driving legs propelled him into the Badger forward wall. He slammed into the grip of the charging defense but lowered his shoulder and plowed into the endzone. The Illini had their victory, and Eliot his dream come true.

"The funny thing, Ray," famed broadcaster Mel Allen told Eliot later when he came in to offer his congratulations, "was that the camera was on you as that touchdown was scored, and you just stood there with arms folded and seemed impassive."

Eliot gave out a big, happy belly-laugh. "Maybe I was in a state of shock. We had failed so often before I guess I couldn't believe it finally happened."

In stark contrast to Eliot's "pinch me to see if I'm dreaming" response, the several thousand Illinois loyalists cascaded out of the stands and ripped down a goalpost in celebration. "It came down easy," said one.

Illini fans may have assisted that goalpost to the ground, but it was the Wisconsin crowd that gave the Illini a big assist on the final drive.

"Early in the game," said Meyers in an electrified Illini locker room afterward, "I told the official no one could hear the signals because of the crowd. So he said whenever the crowd got that noisy he would call time out and quiet them down."

Three times in the final drive, with Badger players running over to the student section trying to shut them up, officials stopped the clock to turn the volume down on the paying customers. As it turned out, the seconds that were saved were the Illini's own—and were crucial.

A celebration was waiting when the Illini arrived in Champaign. In the midst of the hub-bub, Illinois' great captain and All-American linebacker Bill Burrell, a man who would take home the Silver Football as the Most Valuable Player in the Big 10 and finish fourth in the Heisman Trophy balloting, was asked about Eliot's upcoming grand finale at home against Ara Parseghian's sleek Northwestern Wildcats. "We'll get him that one too," he promised.

Realistically the Illini had little or no chance to go to the Rose Bowl. Even if they won and Wisconsin lost at Minnesota, the Illini would be 4-2-1, and Michigan State, who was done with league play, 4-2. As the system was—ties counting a half game won and a half game lost—the tie dropped the Illini percentage points behind and only an unusual vote by conference athletic directors could get them in. But there was something else at stake here—the game would be the last for Mr. Illini. On the other hand, Northwestern had, what seemed to be, the ultimate incentive—only a win would give them a chance for their first conference championship in 33 years and their first Rose Bowl berth. Adding spice to the contest was that the series between the two football schools stood tied at 24-24-4.

"Just as nervous as I was before my first game back in 1942," Eliot responded to questions about butterflies on the same night the Illini cheerleaders brought over a cake and serenaded the first couple of Illinois football on their front doorstep. "Maggie tells me I'm eating every meal. But don't ask me what—all I can think about is Saturday's game."

A beautiful, sunny, 55-degree day bathed the 65,697 fans that came to say good-bye to Ray Eliot on November 21st. Gleaning from Captain Burrell's confidence, the seniors awarded the game ball to their coach *before the game*. They actually had it painted already with Illinois at the top—all they had left was to fill in the score.

Eliot skipped any pep talk, saying that "if the boys don't know how important this game is, then nothing I can tell them will help." Actually, he didn't want to be in a position of asking the team to win one for him. But, just to be sure, Athletic Director Doug Mills gave the team "one of the most emotional and inspiring talks I have ever heard," said Burrell later.

With Bill Brown rushing for 164 yards and two touchdowns, and Johnny Counts scooting for 109 yards and one score, the Illini gave their beloved mentor a 28-0 pasting of the Wildcats. By so doing, they dashed any hopes Northwestern had of going to the Rose Bowl, (Wisconsin went after posting an 11-7 comeback victory over Minnesota), and sent Eliot out on top.

Afterward Parseghian declared that, Rose Bowl or no Rose Bowl, Eliot's Illini were "the best team in the conference. I don't know how anyone beat them." Michigan State coach Duffy Daugherty agreed with the Wildcat coach, but Minnesota's Murray Warmath went further when he said, "The Illini were the best team in the country by season's end." The UPI and AP voters were not quite as generous and Illinois ended up 12th and 13th respectively, but their defense did finish first in the Big 10. No one could deny that no team had improved more from the start of the season than the Illini. And Eliot was name the Chicago Midwest Writers' Coach of the Year.

In the flush of victory Eliot had only one disappointment—that the team took as long as it did to jell. "I would have liked to take this team to the Rose Bowl," he said, "and these kids deserved to go."

There were rumors whirling that some alumni and students were going to start a petition to draft him back to coach again in 1960. That might have tempted some men because this was a young team with great potential, but Eliot would not go back on his word. "I will not coach next season," he laid the kibosh to it. "I made my decision long ago."

Yet then, for a moment, as he watched the buzz of celebration all around him, he waxed nostalgic and became just a little misty-eyed when he said, "These are the things I'll really miss. The wonderful people...the coaches, the sportswriters, the fans. And the kids, those tremendous, unpredictable, wonderful kids. They're the ones I'll miss the most."

How had an incentive-laden Northwestern bruiser succumbed to, what seemed on paper, a lesser band of Fighting Illini? How was it that Illinois not only beat this Wildcat eleven, but annihilated them? Why is it that the Illini played with more desperate, life-and-death emotion than a team that had a chance to share a title they hadn't won since 1936?

"Illinois proved against Northwestern that it is more important to play for a great man than for a conference championship," said Eliot friend Dean Frary. That was all that need be said.

Two days later at the annual football banquet, Eliot was presented with hundreds of letters from admirers all around the country, bound in a pigskin cover. But no tribute was more satisfying to Mr. Illini than the one eloquently and emotionally delivered by Stan Dotson of Tuscola, the Illini's senior manager. "A lot of senior managers look forward to managing a team that goes to the Rose Bowl," he said simply. "But going to the Rose Bowl is nothing compared to being manager for Coach Ray."

19

Final Drive:
Master of the Two-Minute Offense

"What would you do," asked a friend, "if the doctor told
you that you shouldn't continue at this pace?"
"I'd fire the SOB of a doctor," replied Ray Eliot.

The athletic director confidently strode to the lectern and
briefly looked over a room filled with media members, University alumni and officials.

"To me, the way I look at it, the biggest thing we need is a
change up and down the pike in our attitude," he started in. "All
we have to do is make ourselves loved and respected by the high
school coaches, the I-Men out there and the great alumni around
the country. We need to get back that Illini family feeling. This
University shouldn't take a back seat to any. We just have to put
a smile on our face and go out and earn their respect—speaking
and being free with people."

And that's just what Athletic Director Ray Eliot did. Indeed, on May 11, 1979, two weeks after Cecil Coleman had been
fired for what Illinois Chancellor William Gerberding called
"some morale and legal problems and a noncompetitive record,"
Eliot was asked to step in as interim director and accepted
without hesitation. It was ironic that a man who had been passed
over for the post twice because he was too old now had it—albeit
temporarily—at the age of 74.

"I know it sounds corny," he said as he finished his first
appearance as A.D., "but I love this University. I have stayed
close to the athletic program. This is a challenge I welcome."

He added wryly, "This is going to really cut into my golf
schedule though."

Eliot did love Illinois and he had, as he said, remained within the heartbeat and heartbreak of its athletic body. From the time he got out of coaching until 1973, he served first as an assistant athletic director and then as associate athletic director. During that time he was always on call to help at every turn. In 1963, for example, the Illini Hockey Club was in trouble for lack of interest and finances. They came to the man who brought the sport to the University in the first place, and he stepped in as coach and revitalized it.

At their first game they drew a standing-room-only crowd of over 1,600 to the University Rink, and crushed Notre Dame, the first team they had faced and lost to 22 years before, 9-1.

Then in 1970, with the results on the gridiron worse than ever, officials made noise about firing Jim Valek as head coach midway through the season. They approached Eliot asking if he would be willing to fill in until the end of the season when a search could be conducted for a new head coach. Eliot said he would, but Illinois players said that if the officials fired Valek at midseason, they would walk too. The Athletic Department backed off, but Eliot had to smile at the display of loyalty by Valek's boys.

Eliot "retired" in 1973. But that word does not describe his transition accurately.

"When you've been active in sports all your life and in front of people and always doing things, it's hard to go to the rocking chair," he said more than once. "I don't want to go to the rocking chair." And he didn't. At the retirement age of 67, he continued on as an Honorary Associate Athletic Director at the handsome salary of one dollar per year. "I think I can pick up enough (money) on the side playing gin rummy," he joked.

At his banquet on the eve of "Ray Eliot Day" in November 1973, many former players and well-wishers feted him with memories and compliments. When Eliot arose he couldn't resist the irony. "Here's a guy standing before you whose virtues have been extolled all night long," he teased, "and all I get is one buck a year."

Waxing serious he said, "I'm proud to look at these men here tonight and see how far they've come. I have pride...And each night I kneel down and thank God that I've been a small part of this great picture." By all accounts, it was an awesome night that had to be seen to be believed.

As Honorary Associate Athletic Director, he continued his torrid speaking pace and acted as a goodwill ambassador for the University.

Later, his office was moved out of the Assembly Hall, where the athletic offices are located, into a trailer adjacent to it. Some thought that was disrespectful, but he never complained, calling it his "little house on the prairie." In 1976 he received the University of Illinois Distinguished Service Medallion (the highest honor bestowed by the University Board of Trustees) for his outstanding contributions to the University.

Needless to say, on May 11, 1979 he was moved back into the Assembly Hall to assume the directorship of the department he had loved and served faithfully for over 50 years.

"Ray enjoys the esteem and affection of this community, and of Illini supporters around the nation," said Chancellor Gerberding upon the appointment. "He is the ideal person to provide leadership during these next few critical months."

Unfortunately the reputation that the Illinois athletic department had gained with the public was one of chaos, and its performance, on and off the field, abysmal. The confidence of the alumni was at an all-time low, and to some Eliot was doing the department "one more favor."

Eliot was asked to comment on the past problems in the department. Mr. Illini was not interested in looking backward—only forward. He demurred. Someone else asked what the job would specifically entail. "I haven't given it any thought," he smiled. "We'll take things as they come."

Eliot's job was made even more difficult when Associate Athletic Director Lynn Snyder moved on to another position in Missouri at the same time Coleman was fired. But then, Eliot had spent a life living against the odds. As a UPI story pointed out, "Normally, someone in that (interim) position might view the job as purely administrative or transitional in nature. Not Ray Eliot."

The first thing Eliot did was replace the 1970's orange football jerseys with the traditional blue.

"I didn't like the orange," he told reporters. "For a while, everybody was running around in orange sport coats. I thought they looked like a bunch of goll-darned pumpkins."

More than how the sport coats looked, though, was the deviation from tradition and continuity they represented.

"You have to have that line that holds you to the greatness of your past," he would say. "Michigan, Notre Dame and others don't change. The uniforms are a reminder of where they've come from. Even prospective high school athletes look for tradition in universities."

Next he met with the different coaches and assistants within the department. "Ray had a keen interest in the whole department—both the men's side and the women's side," says Dike Eddleman, the retired Executive Director of the Fighting Illini Scholarship Fund. No stone was left unturned in his desire to unify and restore a positive attitude from top to bottom.

Then he traveled: from Pontiac to Peoria, from Springfield to Streator, from Lincoln to LaSalle, from Moline to Metropolis, from Carbondale to Kankakee, from Chicago to St. Louis. He barnstormed from one end of the state to the other, preaching the Illini gospel, rallying the alumni and restoring faith to the faithless. He spoke to Illini groups, met with high school coaches, went to golf outings, wined and dined and gave himself to interview after interview with the media.

"Anyone less respected and beloved would have been jeered on such a mission, accused of misleading the public," wrote the *News Gazette*'s Loren Tate. "But Ray was something special..."

Eliot told Arnold Irish of the St. Louis *Post-Dispatch* in an interview that, "We lost the confidence of a lot of high school coaches around the state, and rightly so. We lost the confidence of a lot of I-Men, too, and a lot of alumni. We were at a low ebb and our athletic department fell into a negative attitude, but we're thinking positive and aggressive now. We're wiping away our dark image and replacing it with a bright one.

"We're putting smiles on our faces and shaking hands," he continued. "We know we've lost friends, but we intend to get them back and make new ones as well. We're not trying to place blame or name names, we're trying to correct mistakes. We're forgetting the (recent) past and remembering the great Illini tradition. Red Grange, the Galloping Ghost, and the Whiz Kids."

He said again and again, "Good heavens! There is no question we can turn things around. And I'm not talking through my hat. I mean that sincerely. Gee whiz, if Michigan can do it and Ohio State can do it, we can do it too. There is no reason why we can't. But the only way we're going to do it is to get a positive attitude and get this god danged defeatist attitude out of this University and athletics!"

Said Tom Porter who was Eliot's assistant during his directorship, "We were under a huge responsibility, but (Eliot) was a tireless worker. I really respected him because he never knew what time it was."

There were those who were concerned about the unadulterated pace of this 74-year-old man. Longtime friend Fritzi Frary was one. "I told him, 'Ray you don't need to work this hard. Nobody works this hard.' But he felt he had a short period of time and he had to make it count. This is the opportunity he had been waiting for, and now that it was here he wasn't going to let anything stand in the way of him doing an excellent job. And he won so many people over at that time."

Said Chancellor Gerberding later, "he had the vigor of a man in his 50s."

And Ed Sherman of the *Daily Illini* described a typical scene when interviewing Eliot: "He would bounce around his office, tease his secretary, and make you feel at home in a place of business. One felt welcome. I could only fantasize that I would have half that energy when I hit 74."

As for Eliot himself, he predictably insisted that, "you're as young as you feel, and I don't feel 74. It's all in the mind. We've been busy and we're going to be busier until we get this thing to a place where, when the new man takes over, he'll have something to come into that is really fine. There is no slow time here. I think we've got some fine coaches here, some great facilities, some fine players on the campus. Now the whole thing is to mold the whole thing together and go some place with this thing."

Along the way, Eliot was invited to the Illinois General Assembly in Springfield to be congratulated on his appointment. Mr. Illini turned it into another one of his tent revivals with another stirring call to action. The Assembly's resolution then was quite appropriate as it read in part: "If (Eliot's) pride and spirit is passed down to the athletes, the University of Illinois will no longer have to settle for the silent sound of defeat, but can savor in the thunderous sound of victory."

Not a few media members suggested the idea of keeping Eliot on permanently. Head football coach Gary Moeller was all for it. "I wouldn't mind seeing Ray in the A.D. position for a couple of years or so," he said. "He's already brought a lot of people together, and there isn't anybody who is known and loved by more people than Ray. Certainly no one who can make our alumni, I-Men, and the public pull in the same direction."

Strangely, Eliot was excluded from all meetings that involved discussion of a permanent athletic director. In a column at the time, after 43-year-old Californian Neale Stoner had been chosen but before an official announcement, Loren Tate related this conversation he had with Eliot: "Ray, what do you think of the new director?" asked Tate.

"What can I say?" came the response, "I've never met the man. But I'm sure he'll be fine because the board spent a lot of hard work and time selecting him."

"You mean you weren't a part of the search?"

"I was never asked to sit in on any of the meetings, nor did I meet any of the candidates except Bob Hitch, who happened to be here for the Missouri game. I don't even know who the other candidates were. I had no input."

"But Stoner was here for the Missouri game too. Didn't you see him then?"

"No, as I said, I've never laid eyes on the man."

"You mean you haven't even talked to him by phone?"

"No."

Tate quoted Jim Grabowski, the former Illini great, who was shocked at the oversight. "I presumed Ray was at all the meetings," he said. "I can't understand why they wouldn't want Ray's input. When you consider the job Ray has done in keeping the department going this summer, it's hard to understand why they wouldn't seek his counsel—or at least take him into their confidence."

On September 27th, Eliot and Stoner met for the first time at the official announcement of Stoner's accepting the athletic directorship. Stoner took over November 1st.

Eliot made one strong practical suggestion to the new A.D. on his way out. He recommended that Illinois honor the remainder of Gary Moeller's contract. Moeller was under fire from Illini fans and alumni for three subpar seasons, but Eliot felt the young coach was about to turn the corner with his team.

More importantly, Eliot expected the University to be loyal to a coach who had just completed the third year of a five-year contract. In his view, if they weren't going to give him the five years they never should have signed him for five years. Most agree that it takes that long to turn a program around when you're working from the bottom up. He hated to see Illinois become another revolving door for coaches, as so many institutions had. He always felt that the 47-year reign of he and Zuppke said as much about the institution as it did the coaches themselves.

"I probably didn't hold my job this long because of any great record," he humbly overstated the point to reporters in 1959, "rather because of the great University, great alumni and trustees."

Now between 1960 and 1980, the Illini, if Moeller were fired, would hire their fifth head coach. He didn't like the fact that written contracts were becoming worthless. Whose word was good anymore? Where had loyalty gone? A commitment was a commitment.

Besides, Eliot saw Moeller as an upright, sincere man with his priorities in order; the type of guy worth being loyal to.

Neale Stoner and the Athletic Board did not agree. Gary Moeller was fired, and in came another Californian named Mike White.

Ed Sherman asked Eliot what he was going to do now that Stoner had taken over and he was no longer athletic director. "I'll just fade out of the picture," came the response.

Mr. Illini served almost six months as athletic director. A little more than three months after he stepped aside, he was gone forever.

20

Sketches

"The foundation honors men who honor the game. You have to demonstrate good citizenship, love of community, love of country. It's a question of what you give back to the game. Citizenship is very important. If we're just going to pick all of the All-Americans every year, there's no sense to having a National (College) Football Hall of Fame."

—James L. McDowell
Former Executive Director
National College Football Hall of Fame
as quoted in Big Ten Football.

They drove to Kenora, Ontario, about 350 miles north of Duluth, Minnesota, then traveled by seaplane to Barney's Ball Lake Lodge, which was inaccessible by any other means. When landed, the four fishermen proceeded to their cabin and were introduced to the man who would be their guide for the next five days. Ray Eliot wasted no time in pulling him aside.

"Listen," he said in a hushed tone. "We have a wager on who will catch the most each day on this trip. I want you to help me by telling me how to fish this lake."

The guide paused, took off his cap and shook his head thoughtfully, scratching the back of his neck.

"If you help me win, I'll share the winnings with you," Eliot pressed his sale.

"I've been a fishing guide for 40 years," the man finally spoke. "And I have never been able to get anyone to follow my advice to the letter. But if you do, I'll guarantee you'll win."

"It's a deal," whispered Eliot excitedly.

According to the October 1954 issue of *Hunting and Fishing Magazine*, his companions, Harry Combes, University of Illinois basketball coach; Chuck Flynn, the University's publicity director; and Dr. William Johnston, the football team's dentist, came armed with a lot of fancy equipment and lures. Eliot came with just two artificials, a weedless spoon and spinner.

While his three buddies tossed in their bait their way, Eliot followed the advice of the guide by carefully trolling along the bottom of the lake. On the first day he landed 27 fish before his cronies even got a strike. He won the first four days, tied the last and kept his word by sharing his take with the fishing guide. Of course, his three friends never heard the end of it the entire trip back to Champaign.

Eliot looked for ways to have fun and relax away from the pressures of the gridiron, and one of his favorites was fishing. Hunting, he said, was "too much like real work."

He liked the outdoors and actually found employment at a ranch in Wyoming for part of the summer in his years at Illinois College. He overconfidently called himself "Two Gun." He used to tell the story of the time he was riding his horse (he named the horse "Butch") along a lonely stretch of Wyoming road, when a family from the East happened by. A little girl pointed at Eliot and exclaimed, "Look, a real cowboy!"

Eliot heard her and rose high in his saddle, putting on an air of cowboy arrogance, while tipping his hat to his little fan. But the girl might have realized she was pointing at a fellow Easterner when, in the next moment, "Butch" was spooked and took off on a torrid pace, setting Eliot's elbows flapping and his hat to flying off, completely out of control. "Two Gun" never saw that family again.

While Eliot was coach, he and Maggie would spend about a month during the summer at the New Jersey shore, where Ray's mother used to take him when he was a boy. Early in their marriage Ray took advantage of these trips to earn his masters degree, which he received in 1936 from Columbia University. This was Maggie's chance to visit family with Jane and, while he was head man at Illinois, was Ray's chance to recharge his batteries for the coming football campaign.

"For the first few weeks of the trip Ray would not see anyone," says cousin Julia "Totsie" Drury. "He would lay by the pool and read or just relax until he felt revitalized, and then the last week or so we would all visit, play cards and he would talk football with Maggie's family. Maggie's parents just loved Ray. He would sit at the kitchen table and sketch plays for his father-in-law on the table cloth. They were fun, fun times."

Golf is a game he picked up after his retirement from coaching. He used to scoff at the sport, but when he had to replace those long hours he spent coaching, golf came in handy. Eliot jumped with both feet into everything he did, and golf was no exception. He took a lot of lessons and it soon replaced fishing as his first recreational love.

Interestingly, even in his avenues of diversion the character that made him such a great man and powerful force in the world of sport would rise to the surface.

"I remember one time playing golf with him," Denny Frary, the son of longtime Eliot friends Dean and Fritzi Frary, tells the story. "We were going to play nine holes and we were on the second tee. Well, Ray hit a duck-hook right into a robin and—boom—feathers of the robin went flying all over. He felt so bad that he had killed this robin that he wouldn't even go get his ball—I had to get it for him. He wasn't the same for the rest of the round. He just wanted to get out of there because it hurt him so bad. When we brought it up later he didn't want to talk about it either. It was an accident, but it completely ruined his day."

Ray Eliot was a tender-hearted man. Causing pain to anyone or anything was impossible for him and his compassion made him feel other people's struggles as his own. The robin was one example, but the fate of Jimmy Wynn drives home the point.

Wynn was one of the great athletes at Illinois College in the 1930s, and played both football and baseball for Eliot there. By 1957, though, Wynn was entangled in a personal crisis.

"The Eliots hosted open houses after all (Illini) home games," says Charles Bellatti who spent his boyhood in Jacksonville while Eliot was coach at Illinois College (Later Bellatti was the Sports Information Director at the University of Illinois). "I used to wait and get the statistics after the games and then I would bring them to his home. One evening I went out there and Margaret came to the door. She said that Ray must have forgotten to tell me, but that he wasn't going to be there that evening. I was, of course, surprised. She said that a friend of Jim Wynn's called. Jim had a drinking problem and this friend called and said that Jim was just in terrible shape. He was inebriated all the time and he needed help. No one had had any success with him. So Ray had gotten a University plane chartered, and flew down there to talk to Jim to try to straighten him out. Ray took time right in the middle of the Big 10 season to do that for Jim.

"I remember, too, that he was not successful in straightening Jim out, and how heartbroken he was. Jim died shortly thereafter. This is one time when the inspirational kind of guy and the caring kind of guy Ray was didn't work. And it really, really hurt him."

Eliot was used to inspiring and helping others chart big paths for their lives. To see someone hurting was painful enough, but when he tried to help and the end result was apparent failure, it agonized and confused him.

"He was always shocked and dismayed when he saw players fail to live up to their capabilities because of indifference or laziness," wrote Bert Bertine. "He'd give such boys countless opportunities to make the grade. Some did eventually; those who didn't were a complete enigma to a man whose own athletic career was limited by poor eyesight."

Life was so uncomplicated to Mr. Illini—so black and white. If one had a problem, one needed to face it courageously and overcome it. Eliot had conquered life that way, and so had thousands he encouraged, so he assumed everyone could.

"For many, many years I smoked cigarettes," he said as an example. "I smoked a lot of them. One day I just put one out like that and threw the pack away and that was the end of it. It did take a little courage to get the job done."

Unfortunately, the formula that worked for him did not work for everybody, and he never learned that you can lead a horse to water but you cannot make him drink. The problems of this world had simple answers to Eliot and he was impatient with the complexities of life. He couldn't come to grips, for instance, with what was happening to his young America in the 1960s.

"I don't think he understood, nor did he care to understand, what was happening," says Denny Frary. "He thought America's youth was going to hell in a handbasket."

Indeed, he hated long hair on men, beards and beads. He had no time for the attitude of the counter-culture, flower-child generation and he had no patience for beatniks. "Drop out, tune in and turn on," was to him the ambivalent battle cry of uncaring, non-involved, irresponsible do-nothings.

"In all of my coaching days I have never been associated with beatniks," he said in a speech once. "And it was not beatniks that went to the moon and back. It was the type of Americans who have the same spirit you see on college football fields—the real American spirit."

But then he couldn't comprehend the women's movement either. Equal pay for an equal job was just common sense to him, but he didn't get what all of the fuss was about.

"I don't understand women," he would say sincerely. "Here I have spent all of my life holding them up on a pedestal and now they want to come down to my level." Far from patronizing, there was not a woman alive who didn't feel like she was on a pedestal around him—he treated them like gold.

He never lost his faith in youth or the human race, however. Even those with whom he disagreed he treated with the highest dignity. One of his grandsons had hair past his shoulders at one point, but you never would have known it by the way his grandfather spoke of and treated him (the worst thing he ever asked was whether or not his grandson was posing for holy pictures). Eliot still believed in young America, and young America still leant an ear.

"Even as the cynics and the salesmen took over the game," Loren Tate once wrote, "and young people grew up with a different view of human values, they still listened to Mr. Illini."

Dave Nightingale of the old *Chicago Daily News* wrote in 1965, "There are very few speakers who can stand before a 'knowing' generation of teenagers and use such terms as 'self-denial' and 'self-discipline' and 'loyalty' and 'competitive spirit' and 'building the whole human being' and have them hanging on every word. But Eliot does it without sounding trite or corny."

It is not to imply that because he disdained the counter-culture, he was stuck on the reigning social order and elitism that sometimes prevails in America. Just the opposite. Money, for example, meant nothing to this man, who grew up on the poorer side of the tracks. He never demanded royalties on the record album made of his speeches, and he refused to do a television show while he was coaching that would have meant a handsome revenue because he said it would take him away from his boys. He gave and he gave and he gave. Money and investments were not a part of his thinking, and his trust for others bordered on naive. Co-signing once on a loan for a former player's widow, he paid the balance in full without hesitation when she defaulted. Maybe his attitude would have been viewed as foolish had it not been so heartfelt.

Finally, in 1968 he was mugged in Los Angeles, and the assailants came away with about $200 cash. Afterwards his friends sat him down and almost forced him to be more cautious with his finances. Maggie always said, "If Ray dies with a nickel in his pocket, I'll tape it to his tombstone." You won't find a nickel anywhere near his grave and indeed, though he left Maggie secure financially, he still died spent—not a nickel remained in his heart.

Once he was in a cab making his way across the campus of Miami of Ohio. He peered out the corner of the window and spotted Don Himes, the son of a friend. Don was college aged and going through a difficult time and Eliot stopped his driver, leapt out of the cab, greeted the boy and invited him to have dinner.

Don had worked as a manager on the Illinois baseball squad when he was an underclassman, and Eliot took the opportunity to introduce him to the Miami coaches. It so happened that they had lost their senior manager and so called Don in for an interview and he was taken on board immediately. There wasn't anything Eliot wouldn't do for a friend.

"My first year playing for Ray was when I was 24 years old," said former Illinois College baseball player Mike Zupsich. "He had me batting cleanup and some of the other players were jealous about this first-year player batting in the cleanup position, and they started talking about me to each other. When the team was all together, Ray asked them if anyone was hitting better than I was. They admitted nobody was and he said, 'Case closed.' We never had a problem after that."

Zupsich continued: "He took care of you, Nuss did. I remember I broke my leg one year and I was in great pain. Nuss asked what he could do and I asked him if he would get me some spirits to kill the pain. He went all around town and finally found a tavern and brought me some. I even remember exactly what he got me, it was Seagram's Eight Crown. My leg felt better."

Stories like these are too numerous to count. Stated one newspaper column: "He is a man who will take time from a busy schedule to thank a high school boy for an article on him in the school paper."

"(Ray) always seemed to have the time to see how an injured player was or to say hello to a person who, at that time, didn't seem important," said Ethan Blackaby who played for Eliot at the twilight of his coaching career.

He could make any player, "Feel as if he was the most important person on the field that day," said Don Smith.

Wrote Robert L. Burnes of the *St. Louis Globe-Democrat:* "He has a million friends and when he meets you, you always get the impression that you are his number one favorite."

Actually, Eliot's benevolence became somewhat of an irritant to some when, after his retirement from coaching in 1959, he went to work in the broadcast booth. He first went to work on the radio for WDWS in Champaign with Larry Stewart, who would become his 20-year play-by-play partner. He also slid in alongside Bill Flemming in the ABC Television booth as a color commentator.

His problem, as perceived by some listeners, was that he refused to criticize anyone on the field—coaches or players. As a result, some thought his analysis lacked punch.

"I would tell him, 'Ray, you've got to criticize,'" says Stewart. "I told him that if someone blows a play you've got to say he's blown the play. Or if a coach blows a call you've got to point it out. But he insisted he could not and his reason was simply that he had been down there. He had been in those players' and coaches' shoes. He knew what it was like and he refused to get down on them. For 20 years as an analyst he taught me what I know about the game, but he would not criticize."

A good heart literally was the issue when, shortly before he died, unbeknownst to even his closest friends, he began to test an experimental heart medicine as a favor to science. He had had an irregular heartbeat and his specialist asked if he would try the new drug. He agreed, but had to come off some months later when he experienced adverse side affects.

Eliot's kindness extended to his worst and most two-faced critics, too. During a season when the Illini were struggling, a number of fans had gathered on a Friday night before a game at a hotel bar. There was a man in attendance who was continually inciting the crowd and the piano player to join him in renditions of "Good-bye Eliot, I hate to see you go." He derided the head coach and made it very plain whose fault he thought it was that the Illini were not winning as often as he thought they should. The next day Illinois won, though, and this same man was over at Eliot's open house slapping the coach on the back, eating his food and telling him what a fine coach he was.

"I went up to Ray," says Fritzi Frary. "I told him what the guy was doing the night before. I couldn't believe that he could let him in and not be upset about the fact that he was there. Ray just looked at me and said that he knew all about his kind and not to worry about it. He went on as if nothing was wrong."

When the Eliots opened their home it was, as Maggie said, "to every out of town alumnus, old grad, well-wisher, friend...and critic."

Maggie, of course, had to deal with the naysayers as much as Ray did, maybe more. From game to game, win or lose, she sat in the stands with happy fans or boo-birds, depending on the score. She was always with Jane, the Eliots' only child, in the front row of the east balcony at the 50 yard line.

One time, several rows behind them, a group of men began bellyaching about the Illini head coach, denouncing and booing him without mercy. Finally, Maggie had had enough and she turned around in her seat.

"I don't care if you belittle the coach," she, firmly yet diplomatically said, wrapping her arm around Jane. "But don't you put down this little girl's father." The men sat stunned and shut their mouths. They and the Eliots became fast friends later.

Often Eliot was very interested in his wife's adventures in the stands and sometimes before she could ask him about the game, he asked, "Well, what happened in the stands today, dear?"

"There's always plenty to tell him," Maggie told a *Los Angeles Times* reporter in 1951. "Ray usually gets a kick out of second-guessing, but I don't always relay it to him unless I'm curious myself. For instance, if Illinois punts on fourth down when my stadium neighbors (and I) think the team should have run, I'm apt to repeat the conversation. Ray's on to this. 'Is it the fans or Mrs. Eliot that wants to know?' he'll challenge.

"In one game Ray varied his constant sideline pacing by sitting down through most of the game. The fans around me were perplexed. 'Eliot's sitting this one out,' they puzzled. 'Must be a new signal he's worked up for the team.' When I told Ray this he roared with laughter. 'You tell 'em I sat down because my feet hurt!' he said. He's threatened to outfit Jane, our 18-year-old daughter, with a football helmet to dim her acute hearing. After one game, she needled Ray with, 'Hey Dad! I heard something good about you for a change!' 'Well, what'd the fans say?' Ray asked eagerly. Jane grinned. 'This man behind us said, "Eliot looks real sharp today. He's changed his necktie!"'"

Through all of the bustle of public life, Eliot remained a deeply devoted husband and father. He loved Maggie, and as the two grew older and she, suffering from severe arthritis, became physically incapable of getting around independently, he waited on her hand and foot.

Of course, to the outsider their relationship sometimes seemed like a two-man comedy routine. He would tease her and she would say, "Keep still, Eliot!" But when the lights went out at night, she was grateful to have a husband so loyal and loving. "He's a great guy," she said often. And Ray never regretted that day in Boston, many years before, when she had captured his heart.

Once one of Ray's former players asked Maggie what it was like to be a coach's wife. "Why do you want to know?" she pried. As she got him to admit that he was thinking about becoming a coach himself, she said, "Come on in, the water's fine."

Maggie developed a close tie with many of the boys that played for her husband. In 1950, for instance, when the Illini just missed going to the Rose Bowl on the last day of the season, Johnny Karras sent her a bouquet of roses with a note that said, "Next year we'll have the real thing." And, of course, they did.

Eliot was not a religious man, if religion is defined by how many times one goes to church—he did not attend on a regular basis. He did, however, have a sincere faith. He prayed before bed, his mother's *Bible* and prayer book on his nightstand. And his guiding principles were certainly Biblical. "Do you know how I define sportsmanship?" he once asked. "It is very easy. Doing unto others as you would have them do unto you." One reason he was not in the habit of going to church on Sundays, of course, was that he was a coach, and for years he sat at the altar of Sunday morning film sessions.

Coaching is a grueling occupation, and it took him from many things he preferred, including his family. "I don't see him for the four months of the season, except at breakfast," Maggie said. That's why she always had mixed emotions about the Rose Bowl trips. "Well honestly," she'd say, "I'd be much happier back in Champaign spending a quiet Christmas with my husband and daughter Jane." Off-seasons meant recruiting trips, speaking engagements all over the country, spring practice and coaching clinics in the summer.

Jane tends to put all of this in a positive light. "I had opportunities that so many my age did not have," she says. "I had a chance to travel many different places and meet so many different people. I wouldn't trade any of it for the world."

As one might guess, Ray and Maggie filled opposite roles as parents. Maggie was stern and somewhat demanding, but, while Ray was strict, his approach was more positive and kind.

"Once there was a fire in an apartment building across the street from us and I was told by Daddy not to cross the street to look at it," says Jane. "Well, I went across anyway and he became very upset. He took me into my bedroom, got down on his knees in front of me and said, 'You know what I have to do now don't you?' I said, 'Yes, you have to spank me.' And he looked into my eyes and bowed his head. He couldn't do it."

Another time Jane was given strict instructions by her mother not to walk home alone from kindergarten because there was a very busy street that she would have to cross. When school ended she came out and didn't want to wait for anybody, so she walked home alone.

"Mom hit the roof," she says. "She was very angry with me. But as Daddy took me aside, he smiled and said, 'I knew you could do it!'"

Eliot was a very encouraging father, but sly as well. "He never pushed me for straight A's," Jane remembers. "I went to University High in Champaign and that was kind of an experimental high school with new and higher level courses. He told me that he would rather have someone who got A's and B's and was a well-rounded, well-liked person than a straight-A student who was not. Still, to egg me on to higher grades he would always say that he would compare his grades to mine any day, implying that his were better. I should have called his bluff, because I saw his grades later, and mine were better."

When it came time for Jane to choose a college, Illinois seemed like a lock to outsiders. But Ray and Maggie were open-minded, wanting what would be best for their daughter. "We talked over a number of possibilities," Jane says. "But after thinking it over, I came to the conclusion that if Illinois was good enough for my father it was good enough for me."

Jane eventually married in 1955, moved to Park Ridge, Illinois and gave her parents five grandchildren. Ray and Maggie were wonderfully active, yet hands-off grandparents. They never interfered in the children's upbringing, but were always available at a moment's notice.

When the grandkids were young, they used to ride with their Gram and Grampa Ray to New Jersey, to vacation along the beach. During Ray's coaching days the trips East may have been to rest and recoup, but now it was to be with family. Gram liked the ocean, Grampa Ray liked the pool, and the kids liked them both. On one of the trips, Ray told the story to the grandkids of how he went prematurely bald. His baldness was caused, he said, by driving under a viaduct and not ducking quick enough. "The bridge shaved my hair right off," he said. Of course, he was almost sorry he told the tale because the kids ducked at each viaduct for years and demanded that he do the same.

At Christmas he and Maggie would visit, shouting "Ho, ho, ho" as they came up the walk. He did the Christmas shopping with Jane and his eldest granddaughter and complained about how they wore him out. But it was he who was always saying, "Double up your speed every chance you get (He was always punctual, never late)."

Eliot was energetic and his energy was contagious. "He brightened up a room whenever he walked in," says Fritzi Frary. He enjoyed himself, life and other people. It was not that he basked in attention (to get him to even accept a Christmas gift was a difficult chore), but he enjoyed making other people feel good about themselves.

"I remember a day in Chicago Heights," recollected Loren Tate, "when Eliot walked in among a circle of former Illini— Bernie Krueger, Sam Zatkoff, Vern Seliger, the late Julie Rykovich and all those mid-forties stars from northern Indiana—and fevers shot straight up as he pointed a finger at each and recalled their accomplishments.

"'Hi Julie, how's the boy?' he boomed. 'There was a day against Wisconsin when this man, Julie Rykovich, was a whirling dervish, the greatest football player in America. Julie Rykovich wouldn't let us lose that day. He put us in the Rose Bowl.'

"And as Ray spoke on, building that beautiful story of success against the odds, tears welled in the eyes of these big, broad-shouldered former athletes who owed so much to him."

Said former Illini Ruck Steger, "People who thought Ray was just a rah-rah missed the point. He always felt good, and he always made you feel good."

After one game, which Illinois lost, the Eliots hosted their traditional open house. Eliot was so jolly, upbeat and happy that radio announcer Harry Wismer marveled, "I wonder what this guy is like when he wins!"

Iowa sports columnist Gus Schrader said, "Ray was an engaging guy, one you couldn't help liking. He was friendly as a puppy and seemed to like everyone he met."

Indeed, the press and media loved Ray Eliot, too. Fred Russell of the *Nashville Banner* spoke for many when he called Eliot, "One of the most approachable, quotable men in sports."

Eliot's favorite song (except for *Illinois Loyalty* of course) was "The Wiffenpoof Song," and at parties he eventually got everybody singing with him. "The Wiffenpoof Song," made famous by Bing Crosby, became so synonymous with Eliot that some wanted it played at his funeral. But Maggie would not allow it because she didn't think she could handle it emotionally.

It was, however, played for him 19 years prior, the night he received his most cherished honor: The Amos Alonzo Stagg Award. A national award bestowed by the American Football Coaches Association, he was especially proud of it because it was presented "to perpetuate the example and influence" of Stagg, a man he deeply admired. The award was presented each year to "the individual, group or institution whose services have been outstanding in the advancement of the best interests of football." His mentor, Bob Zuppke, had won it in 1948. Of course, Eliot didn't accept it without a fight.

At the A.F.C.A.'s annual meeting, Paul Stagg, the son of

Amos, tapped Eliot on the shoulder. "Ray, members of the A.F.C.A. have chosen you to receive 1961's Amos Stagg award."

"You've got the wrong guy," came the immediate response. "I can name you a dozen who are more entitled to the award."

"Yeah, I know," said Stagg. "Meanwhile you've got a spot at the speakers' table."

That night, in front of 600 coaches and associates, Paul Stagg was called to the lectern. David Condon, in his "In the Wake of the News" column in the *Chicago Tribune*, summed up what he said: "My father, Amos Alonzo Stagg, was the first winner of the coaches' award. He still cherishes it and it still is on his mantel...This season the committee has chosen a gentleman with high ethical standards...who has fostered high principles...chosen to perpetuate the example and influence of Amos Alonzo Stagg in American life and sport...Ray Eliot, former head coach at the University of Illinois."

This award touched Eliot deeply because it had come from his peers, and he had been on the selection committee before and knew the great pains they go through to pick a worthy recipient. "This award overwhelms me," said Eliot that night.

Eliot was elected to the Helms Athletic Foundation Hall of Fame for coaches and was up for entrance into the National College Football Hall of Fame in the early 1960s. He was on the selection committee, though, and, according to Margaret Selin his former secretary, he came up one vote short because he refused to vote for himself.

"I said 'why didn't you vote for yourself?'" she relates today. "He said that it just wouldn't have been right. Most others would have done it, but that's just the kind of man he was." Stunningly, he has not been voted in to this day.

There are coaches with better won-loss records than Ray Eliot, but his was not bad either. Over 23 years as a head coach, including his five-year stint with Illinois College, he compiled a 106-81-12 record. In 18 years at Illinois he knocked off seven number-one teams, many other highly ranked clubs, and he retired as the seventh-winningest active coach in the country. Eliot won two resounding Rose Bowl championships, three Big 10 titles (at the time he retired he was the only Big 10 coach who had qualified three teams for the Rose Bowl) and, if the powers that be handed out bowl game invitations then like they do today, he'd have been coaching in at least 13 of them.

Besides receiving the Stagg award, Eliot served as a trustee and president of the American Football Coaches Association, received honorary lifelong membership in that organization in 1965, served a distinguished term on the Football Rules Committee, was on the committee that drew up the Association's Code of Ethics, was the Illinois State Chairman of the National College Football Hall of Fame and a board member of the American Association of Health, Physical Education and Recreation.

As a coach he won countless coach of the week, coach of the month and coach of the year honors, was asked to coach the *Chicago Tribune* College All-star Game, and coached many other senior all-star tilts. His abilities were not hidden from his peers.

"Eliot was probably the greatest motivator—for a single game—that we've ever had in football," said Lou Holtz, present head coach at Notre Dame.

"He was resourceful, creative and unpredictable," stated arch rival and former Michigan mentor Bernie Oosterbaan.

Eliot was "one of the great coaches and inspirational leaders in football," Rip Engle, the highly successful coach at Penn State, said plainly.

And Bud Wilkinson the former Oklahoma coach and athletic director said that under Eliot, the Illini played "technically brilliant football."

"It's difficult to give Ray all the plaudits he deserves," Bobby Mitchell, the former Illini and now Pro Football Hall of Fame running back, was quoted as saying on Ray Eliot Day in 1973. "I would have run through a wall for Ray Eliot before I even had run for a first down for Illinois. I've been fortunate to be associated with Paul Brown, Vince Lombardi and George Allen—all wonderful men who recognize motivation. But of all the inspiration I received as an athlete, none has touched me more deeply than those Saturdays when my coach here stood before his athletes and got us ready for the grid wars. And the Lombardis, Browns and Allens just didn't measure up to him."

In addition to his fabled coaching career, Eliot became an Assistant Athletic Director at the University of Illinois, was named Chairman of the North/South Shrine game in 1976 and filled in like a ball of fire as the interim Athletic Director at Illinois in 1979.

"When the mark of greatness is given to those who served the University of Illinois and intercollegiate athletics during his lifetime," Chuck Flynn was quoted, "the name of Ray Eliot will stand at the top."

As Flynn did, former University of Illinois Chancellor John Cribbett realized that Eliot's influence went way beyond the borders of his home state: "He had become a legend in his own time," he said.

"Over the years, no one in intercollegiate athletics has contributed more, directly or indirectly, to the game of football," said Bud Wilkinson.

He spoke all over the country and, indeed, his influence was limitless and the scope of his effect knew no bounds. He was one of the greatest representatives that college football has ever known.

An *Atlanta Journal and Constitution* sports columnist once said that "the smartest move the NCAA could make would be to buy about 30 minutes of national television time and put Ray Eliot in front of the camera."

His proudest legacy of all, though, beyond wins and losses, x's and o's, speeches and awards, remains his boys. He taught them, he worked with them, he disciplined them, he inspired them and he befriended them. In a word: he loved them—and they loved him, too.

"Even the fellows who didn't get to play liked Ray," marveled Bill Burrell.

"The total of youths who arrived here as 'dead end kids' and left as solid citizens due to Ray's guidance is imposing," penned Bert Bertine. "Not all of them made good college football players but the great majority attained mental maturity."

His help and guidance did not end with a boy's playing days either. "It's been almost 30 years," said former Eliot player, Don Gnidovic, echoing what every one of the coach's boys knew, to a reporter in the late 1970s, "but I honestly believe that if I picked up the phone right now and asked him for help, he would drop what he was doing and do what he could for me."

He may not be in the Hall of Fame yet, but he will never die in the halls of his boys' hearts.

"Ray taught all of his boys a game plan—a plan for the game of life," says former Illini Bill Butkovich.

Captain Herb Neatherly, an Illinois grad in 1952 said once that, "He instilled in me self-confidence. There have been times, such as the Suez, Lebanon, and many others that one could easily have doubts in my business of being a fighter pilot. But because of Ray, I never had these doubts. His faith, integrity and guidance taught me much more than how to play football."

"Even though I am not coaching, I put his teachings to a good use," said Don Stevens. "In dealing with the delinquent children that I have been working with I have found that there is always a solution as to how to handle each one if you are only patient."

"I consider myself very fortunate," added Bill Franks, "to have been a part of the 'Fighting Illini' and to be led by such a great molder of character, teacher of fair play and competitive spirit which has carried me over numerous rough roads in life."

Said Chuck Studley: "No man has had a bigger impact on my personal and professional development. To no man do I owe a greater debt of gratitude."

"He was the second most important man in my life, next to my father," says Alex Agase. "If he had not been our coach, I would have never graduated from college because I would have gone home."

"(Ray) did not give to me, or to anyone else, anything that can be measured in physical size, or dollars and cents, but a gift that is far greater, as it can be neither stolen, spent or lost," said Ray Ward, who played for Eliot his first two years as head coach at Illinois. "He gave to us a part of himself, by building in us the character and confidence that no job is too big if you give it all you have with 'reckless abandonment.'"

Stated Paul Furimsky to Eliot upon his retirement from coaching in 1959: "When a man with the problems I know you must have, takes the time to help an insignificant fellow like me, this shows greatness. Greatness, yes, but typically Ray Eliot...I always did say that Ray Eliot was not only a man, but a way of life."

In 1955 Pop Warner held a national huddle-prayer contest. Fifteen-hundred prayers were sent in from high school and college coaches from coast to coast. The winning entry was penned by the head football coach at the University of Illinois, and President of the American Coaches Association, Ray Eliot.

He was so surprised to win that he had to clip its lines out of the newspaper because he had lost his copy. Straight from the heart, it says:

> "As we gather here today,
> We take a moment, Lord, to pray
> That you will guide us in our play,
> And show us how to go Thy way.
> Make us honest, fair and true
> In this game and all we do."

21

His Own: A Word to Us

From Ray Eliot's Speeches

"I think I know what makes young Americans tick. I am not reading from a book. I am taking it right out of the pages of my life—observing young America, working with them, getting the job done, if I can.

"But first let me tell you about yourself for a moment. We have heard so many times that cliche that 'the times have changed.' It is time to no longer hide behind these cliches. The human being is the same, sir. You can go back and in the history of time immemorial you'll find that back then people had two eyes, two ears, a nose and the rest like you do.

"In leadership or otherwise you have got to have the courage to make decisions or forget it. You have got to have the courage to withstand people who, as soon as you make a decision, say, 'It wasn't right.' You must realize what has to be done and go and do it. You've got to be able to face yourself in the mirror and say, 'What kind of person am I?' Have you got the courage to do that? Or are you just one of those people that go along with everything everyone else says. If you are, then forget anything in leadership, forget about success and forget about getting anywhere in the game of life. Who is going to choose you for anything if you are milque-toast?

"You can fail, sure, but don't lay there, pick yourself up and come on again. The real failure is the guy who has failed and can't get up. Hell, we all fail, but it is that tinted soul who will not try anything who is the real failure in life. How would you like to be in the cockpit with that guy? No way. I like the guys who believe they can fly that job, even if maybe they can't.

"Have you ever heard of a guy named Lincoln? Abraham, that is? You've heard of him haven't you? I have a bust of

Lincoln on my desk and when the going gets rough for me he looks at me with a twinkle in his eye and he tells me something. You know what he tells me? He says, 'Ray, remember now, I ran for public office 27 times. Twenty-seven times I tried to be something. And I failed 25 times!' Can you imagine if he had quit after failing five times? How many of you would fail five times and say, 'I'm licked, I can't go on, how can I do it?' Or can you fail 10 times and still persevere? How many of you can fail 25 times and still, with your head up and a smile on your face, go out to conquer!

"It's that moment when we let doubt creep into our hearts; that one moment we give up, when success might have been right around the corner; that one moment we had fear that we were going to make the wrong decision. 'Why did you put me in this situation?' you say. 'I'm scared.' Sure, we're all scared! That one moment that you stood around with 43 other guys in an American city and watched two little people beat the hell out of a 76-year-old man because you didn't want to get involved. You didn't want to get involved? You had better get involved or forget anywhere you want to go in this game of life.

"Think positive. I don't mean you go around like an arrogant guy saying, 'I defy the world!' You do it nice and quietly within yourself, with a nice quiet confidence that exudes what you are going to do.

"Yeah, all too often, you know, we think we're great guys, geez. Football's a great leveler, but holy cow, any one of you fellas or any of us that can think that we're great and we're the only thing in the world...why sure I think you should have that warm confidence in your heart, a belief that you're a fine man, sure. But forget this thinking we're great, because when that sets in, self-satisfaction sets in, sir, there's only one way we can go and that's down! We can't go up. How can we go up if we believe we're the best now?

"And don't take credit for doing the things that everyone does everyday in the week. I got off the plane in Tokyo not so long ago. Thirty-six hours across the Pacific Ocean. Thirty-six hours across water all the time! Well, when I got off at the airport there I thought here I am, boy Eliot what a guy you are! You're terrific! Why, you're a pioneer! You crossed the Pacific Ocean in a plane! And then right when I was slapping myself on the back you know, I all of a sudden came abruptly to the thought, 'Gee, every day there's people doing that. So what I'm doing is not so great. Everyday they're doing it. Right at this moment there are hundreds of kids, people going across that Pacific Ocean in planes.' And then you know my hand really stopped short when I was praising myself there, when I all of a sudden thought that not so long ago a guy went across the Atlantic Ocean in a crate...a guy named Lindbergh.

"We must be awfully cognizant of individual differences among young athletes. I hope that everybody is very much sold on the idea that each human being is different in his body and in his mind. He is individually different, and there sometimes comes the crux of coaching, when we coach en masse instead of individually. We want to be organized as a team but, by the same token, we are a group of individuals and if there is too much militarism, that may strain feelings too much.

"We feel at our place we get a pretty decent job done off the football field as well as on it by bringing the boy into the office and talking to him about things that are not going just right. We try to pep him up. It is amazing what you can do if you will just think that way. All too often we say, 'Gee, that guy should be doing this and that and so forth.' Well, just keep in mind that he is different. We believe in teaching him individually.

"We also try to teach him the 'why' of the thing as well as the 'how' of the thing. I think a boy, if he knows why he should do something, he'll try harder because he understands what is happening out there. I think, in the hurry of teaching a boy something, we say to him, 'Do it this way, do it that way, do it this way, do it that way,' and we don't say to the boy, 'This is why we are doing it this way,' because of the situation that is going to arise in a given football game or a given practice session. Consequently his learning and his effort are less.

"I hope we keep in mind that a boy is a human being. Don't try and fool them. Be fair in everything you do. Once he has lost his feeling of respect for you and he thinks you might be unfair, you have lost great ground.

"We try to make sure in our daily practice session that every man does the same amount of work. Hear me—every man does the same amount of work! One day out there I heard a halfback say, 'Those linemen ought to pay to get into the game.' So we put him down in the line for a workout. He was only down there a few minutes and he said, 'I want to go back with the other folks.' And then one day I heard a lineman say the same thing about the backs, that they were soft, so I put him back there running with the boys for a while and that was the end of that. I think if we can sell the boys all the time that everyone is doing the same amount of work, that one is not doing any more simply because he is not an All- American, then I think we all go out on the football field feeling good, feeling that what we are about to do is sincere and every man is a part of it.

"I like to think that on our football field we have a type of discipline that is awfully fair, democratic and fine. I like to think that every football coach I have is respected highly by every man we have, because of the fact that we have been honest and fair with every boy.

"Concentration is one factor that we have got to have from the athletes to get the job done. And so we have got to watch to make things interesting and we try to keep our breakdown drills quick and terse, 15 minutes of this and 10 minutes of that and five minutes of that and maybe as long as a half hour on this, going from one drill to another, to keep the boy's interest at a high pitch. When monotony sets in learning goes out.

"A laugh once in awhile won't hurt either, if it is well placed, something that will bring into this job of practicing a little bit of interest and a little bit of life, because if the athlete has that, he will have so much more.

"Praise and criticize. You see in football we tend to do one thing well, and that is we criticize the boys severely. We are saying, 'No don't do it that way; do it this way. No, no, no, no!' Constantly we are criticizing. Be sure then, sir, that when a man does a thing well, you praise him. First of all they are learning, and praise teaches as much as criticism does. Second, it is a relief to the boy to hear praise and he'll think, 'Well, this fellow is human after all.'

"I will say one thing about training rules in passing: if you set one, you'd better be ready to enforce it, because once you don't enforce it you have lost everything.

"Give me the boy who can think, has the will to win and the spirit to accomplish his aim. More games are won by good thinking and more are lost by bad thinking than the abundance of, or lack of, power.

"In this game sir, we have to accept every challenge and we have to have men on that football field of challenge, men of desire, men who will sacrifice, not just men with bodies, because bodies don't win this game.

"In the game of football, as in the game of life, it isn't just the brains and muscle but the moral fiber that counts. I know people laugh at this kind of philosophy, but I've seen too many young men emerge to take it lightly.

"Emphasize the physical, and if you can tell me that for one moment these bodies went down the field as robots, I'll go with you. I believe everything we do needs direction from within us. Gentlemen, insofar as I know, with exception of the reflex action— that could be described as sitting on a hot stove and jumping quickly without thinking—everything we do in this life we will it to be done. Everything we do we will it to be done! The bodies don't just walk around as bones and muscles by themselves; they must be energized by something, impelled by an inner force. There must be guidance; there must be some place from which they are told, 'This is the way it is done.' And when those eleven guys run down the field to get that Illinois back with the ball, they will themselves as they go to get the job done. And the tougher the thing is the more courage and will they've got to have sir!

"When it comes right down to it everything we do is based on our attitude. We may know our French or the square root of something, and we may have a fine body, but it is the inner man that is most important. You may have the ability to write a book or compose a symphony, but without perseverance and dedication, it won't happen. And I don't know what to call it because I'm not that kind of a guy—it's common sense I guess—it's this sir, it's this: it's the proper state of mind. The proper state of your mind. And by the proper state of mind, I perhaps mean defined: that dynamic something that comes into your very hearts and souls that says, I can, I will, I must; that regardless of odds, regardless of odds, regardless of what the odds may be I will get the job done! Tempered only if you will by the phrase, 'In a sportsmanlike way.' There is no savor, to the victory that is ill-gotten. And we can only enjoy that we won in a sportsmanlike way. That is living by the rules as they are given to you that come out of a book that you have. And not only the rule book that you carry in football—but another book...another book...called the *Bible*.

"You who lack the heart, you who have the spirit gone from you, you who have lost hope, you who have no confidence—you are dead sir, you are done!

"As a leader, I think, of young America I aim to go into the inner man and put something up and down his spine. Can you do something about someone's will or courage? Of course you can! And don't let anybody in the world tell you that you can't—if you work at it, if you'll coach off of the field a little bit slowly and carefully. You are working with a man's mind, and in working with that man's mind, you want to be careful, because you as a coach can help him attain great things.

"I'd hate like the devil to have to tell you how many fellas whom I've poured courage down their throats. I'd hate like the devil to have to line up before you the men that I put a strong thing up and down a guy's spine. I wouldn't know what to do, fellas, if I didn't have to do something about this courage business. I just don't tell a fella to get down off the squad just because he lacks it. I've got to do something about it. And we do something about it, by teaching him, talking with him and giving him some beliefs. Putting something in his spine that should be there. Teaching him to be a man and not a coward. Teaching him not to duck his head—keep it up.

"So when you say it can't be done, I say it can be if you'll work at it. But if you are the kind of a man who works for two hours on the football field with the boy and then says, 'Good-night, good-bye, I'll see you tomorrow,' I don't think that is coaching. I think that off the football field so many things can be accomplished.

"Now, in college, I cannot, like some fellas do, trade a boy to somebody else and get a new one. I have got to work with him and get out of him every bit that he has in him, not just physically gentlemen, but I have got to get the job done from within his heart, within his mind and it takes a little bit of doing. And I hope that we can temper the courage of these young chaps so they can go out in this game of life, where courage is sorely needed, and have them live a big life, courageously.

"Why do I love athletic sports? Why? First because the impact of football as a rallying point for the university is clear. You have all of these young people coming in from cities and hamlets, and the one thing that pulls them together each September is their university football team. Ties are established through football, for the players and the young fans, that are everlasting. It is a marvelous game, primitive yet sophisticated. It's identified with America.

"Mostly though, through athletics I have the instrument in athletic sports to bring someone to big heights as a human being. If you are smart, you will use these programs to build human qualities of leadership and courage to great heights. Oh, you laugh at me. Oh baby, I wish I could tell you a million stories.

"Now look, I'm out of it right now, but I loved every moment of being a football coach. I believe in the coaching profession. You are great guys. You are the greatest men in America with the greatest opportunity. You have before you, in the palms of your hand sir, the future, believe it or not, of these fine boys.

"All too often the alumni only look at the scoreboard, but forget them and go on with the great job you have and never flinch and never go down, because of this great thing in your hands. Now, you love this game and I'm telling you never to flinch no matter how rough it comes your way. And if they start from the stands criticizing one of your boys, defend yourself and defend those kids with your life, because you're in this great game where you do so many great things for young America!

"What a beautiful sight! What a beautiful people young America is! Yes sir, young America hasn't changed—only its leadership has. It's still what the young Americans have inside that counts. Don't you realize what the American boy and girl has assumed? Everything challenging them since time immemorial has been hurled at them, from everywhere in the world, and they have always emerged triumphant. And they will again if only you'll lead them...yes reflect...if only you'll lead them."